D1048356

MUSIC · SOCIETY · EDUCATION

MUSIC · SOCIETY · EDUCATION

A radical examination of the
prophetic function of music in
Western, Eastern and African
cultures with its impact on society
and its use in education.

by

Christopher Small

John Calder
LONDON

First published in Great Britain 1977
by John Calder (Publishers) Ltd
18 Brewer Street, London W1R 4AS

Second revised edition October 1980
Second impression 1984
© Christopher Small 1980

ALL RIGHTS RESERVED

ISBN 0 7145 3614 8 paperback

No part of this publication may be reproduced, stored in a retrieval system, or transmitted in any form by any means, electronic, mechanical photo-copying, recording or otherwise, except brief extracts for the purpose of review, without the prior written permission of the copyright owner and the publisher.

Any paperback edition of this book whether published simultaneously with, or subsequent to, the casebound edition is sold subject to the condition that it shall not, by way of trade, be lent, resold, hired out, or otherwise disposed of, without the publisher's consent, in any form of binding or cover other than that in which it is published.

Photoset in Photon Times by
Specialised Offset Services Limited, Liverpool
Printed and bound in Great Britain by
Redwood Burn Limited, Trowbridge, Wiltshire

CONTENTS

In memory of my mother and father

'The imagination, therefore, is much more than the imaginary. It embraces the entire existence of man. For we do not only respond with feeling or admiration, but participate, through the symbols offered by a work of the imagination, in a potential society which lies beyond our grasp.'

JEAN DUVIGNAUD
The Sociology of Art

INTRODUCTION

It is generally acknowledged that the musical tradition of post-Renaissance Europe and her offshoots is one of the most brilliant and astonishing cultural phenomena of human history. In its range and power it is perhaps to be matched by only one other intellectual achievement — the science of post-Renaissance Europe. It is understandable, therefore, if those of us who are its heirs (which includes not only the Americas and many late and present colonies of Europe but also by now a large portion of the non-western world as well) are inclined to find in the European musical tradition the norm and ideal for all musical experience, just as they find in the attitudes of western science the paradigm for the acquisition of all knowledge, and to view all other musical cultures as at best exotic and odd. It is in fact precisely this inbuilt certainty of the superiority of European culture to all others that has given Europeans, and latterly their American heirs, the confidence to undertake the cultural colonization of the world and the imposition of European values and habits of thought on the whole human race.

We should not, however, allow the brilliance of the western musical tradition to blind us to its limitations and even areas of downright impoverishment. We may be reluctant to think of our musical life, with its great symphony orchestras, its Bach, its Beethoven, its mighty concert halls and opera houses, as in any way impoverished, and yet we must admit that we have nothing to compare with the rhythmic sophistication of Indian, or what we are inclined to dismiss as 'primitive' African music, that our ears are deaf to the subtleties of pitch inflection of Indian raga or Byzantine church music, that the cultivation of bel canto as the ideal of the singing voice has shut us off from all but a very small part of the human voice's sound possibilities or expressive potential, such as are part of the everyday resources of a Balkan folk singer or an Eskimo, and that the smooth mellifluous sound of the romantic symphony orchestra drowns out the fascinating buzzes and distortions cultivated alike by African and medieval European musicians.

It is only comparatively recently that Europeans have developed sufficient interest in these and other musical cultures to hear in them anything more than quaintness or cacophony; we were in the position of the fish in Albert Einstein's metaphor, not aware of the water because it knows nothing of any other medium. Today, partly through our increasing knowledge of other musical cultures, we have the opportunity to become aware of our own tradition as a medium surrounding and supporting us and shaping our perceptions and attitudes as the needs of hydrodynamics shape the fish's body; this book is in part an attempt to examine the western musical tradition through this experience as well as in itself, to see it through the mirror of these other musics as it were from the outside, and in so doing to learn something of the inner unspoken nature of western culture as a whole. We shall try to look beneath the surface of the music, beneath the 'message', if any, which the composer consciously intended (and even the fact that a message is intended may be in itself significant), to its basic technical means, its assumptions, which we usually accept unawares, on such matters as the nature of sound, the manner of listening, the passing of time, as well as its social situation and relations, to see what lies hidden there.

For it is in the arts of our, or indeed of any, culture, that we see not only a metaphor for, but also a way of transcending, its otherwise unspoken and unexamined assumptions. Art can reveal to us new modes of perception and feeling which jolt us out of our habitual ways; it can make us aware of possibilities of alternative societies whose existence is not yet. Many writers and critics have undertaken, in the visual and plastic arts and in literature, to make plain the social implications of their chosen arts; it is to me perpetually surprising that so few writers have made any comparable attempt in music, whose criticism and appreciation exists for the most part in a social vacuum. Perhaps it is the lack of explicit subject matter in music that frightens people off. I make the attempt here with much trepidation, but feel it imperative, not merely for the sake of constructing yet another aesthetic of music (though even to do this in a way that takes note of the musical experience of other cultures would be a worth-while project) but because of what I believe to be the importance and urgency from the social and especially the educational point of view of what I have learnt from my explorations. In following these explorations in this book the reader will notice that I occasionally return to the same point more than once; I must ask the reader to regard these repetitions not as signs of simple garrulousness but rather as nodal points in that network structure which my argument resembles more than it resembles a straight logic-line. The explorer (to introduce a metaphor which will become familiar) in a strange territory may cross and re-cross the same point many times, but will come towards it from a different direction each time as he traverses the terrain, and, if he is lucky, will each time obtain a new point of view. And if I appear to leave the subject and introduce irrelevancies I must ask the reader to trust me eventually to make relationships plain.

I shall begin my investigation with an exposition of what I see as the principal characteristics of western classical music, and of the conventions, both social and technical, of that music. I shall try to show how both western classical music and western science speak of very deep-rooted states of mind in Europeans, states of mind which have brought us to our present uncomfortable, if not downright dangerous condition in our relations with one another and with nature. I shall suggest that education, or rather schooling, as at present conceived in our society has worked to perpetuate those states of mind by which we see nature as a mere object for use, products as all-important regardless of the process by which they are obtained, and knowledge as an abstraction, existing 'out there', independent of the experience of the knower, the three notions being linked by an intricate web of cause and effect. In holding up some other musical cultures to the reader's attention I shall try to show that different aesthetics of music are possible that can stand as metaphors for quite different world views, for different systems of relationships within society and nature from our own. I shall describe the various attempts, in the music of our century, to frame a critique of our present society and its world view, while a brief survey of music in the United States will show that that country possesses a culture which is not only more remote from Europe than we imagine but has also long contained within it the vision of a potential society which is perhaps stronger and more radical than anything in European culture. And finally, I shall attempt to show how the new vision of art revealed can serve as a model for a new vision of education, and possibly of society.

I have based my investigations upon two postulates: first, that art is more than the production of beautiful, or even expressive, objects (including sound-objects such as symphonies and concertos) for others to contemplate and admire, but is essentially a *process*, by which we explore our inner and outer environments and learn to live in them. The artist, whether he is Beethoven struggling to bring a symphony into being, Michelangelo wresting his forms from the marble, the devoted gardener laying out his garden or the child making his highly formalized portraits of the important people and things in his life, is exploring his environment, and his responses to it, no less than is a scientist in his laboratory; he is ordering his perceptions and making a model of reality, both present and potential. If he is a sufficiently gifted artist his art will help others do the same. Art is thus, notwithstanding its devaluation in post-Renaissance society, as vital an activity as science, and in fact reaches into areas of activity that science cannot touch. The second postulate is that the nature of these means of exploration, of science and of art, their techniques and attitudes, are a sure pointer to the nature and the preoccupations of the society that gave them birth. We shall find that our culture is presently undergoing a transformation as profound as that which took place in the fifteenth and sixteenth centuries which we call the Renaissance, and that this transformation, like the Renaissance, is taking place not just on the level of conscious opinions and concepts but, more importantly, on that of perception and the often unconscious habits of thought on which we base our everyday speech and action. And since it is perception and the subconscious that are the concern of art it is the methods of art rather than of science which can provide a model and a guide for the new conceptual universe towards which we are moving.

It is a grave but common error to think of the aims of art and of science as identical, or complementary, or even much in tune with each other. Art and science, it is true, are both means of exploration, but the intention, the method and the kind of reality they explore are very different. This is not simply the Cartesian split between matter and mind (we must indeed start from the assumption that they are identical); it is rather that the aim of art is to enable us to live in the world, while that of science is to enable us to master it. It is for this reason that I insist on the supreme importance of the art-process and the relative unimportance of the art-object; the essential tool of art is the unrepeatable experience. With science it is the finished product that counts, the theory, the hypothesis, the objectified knowledge; we obtain .it by whatever means we can, and the tool is the repeatable experiment. Art is knowledge as experience, the structuring and ordering of feeling and perception, while science is abstract knowledge divorced as completely as possible from experience, a body of facts and concepts existing outside of and independently of the knower. Both are valid human activities, but since the Renaissance we have allowed the attitudes and values of science to predominate over those of art, to the detriment of the quality of our experience.

Our schools, for example, concern themselves almost exclusively with abstract knowledge, which pupils are expected to absorb immediately and regurgitate on demand. The pupils may or may not wish, or be able, to absorb the knowledge, but the one lesson that all do learn is that they can be consumers, not producers, of knowledge, and that the only knowledge that has validity is that which comes to them through the school system. They are taught much about the world, but their experience of it, apart from the hermetic world of classroom and playground, is seriously impaired. And so, too, of our culture as a whole. We know more about the world, and experience it less, than perhaps any previous generation in history; so, too, musicology has made available to us more knowledge about music than ever before, and yet our experience of it is greatly diluted by being mediated through the knowledge of experts. We become afraid of the encounter with new musical experience, where knowledge and expertise are no guide and only the subjective experience honestly felt can serve, and retreat into the safe past, where we know what to expect and connoisseurship is paramount.

This book will suggest that artistic activity, properly understood, can provide not only a way out of this impasse in musical appreciation, in itself an unimportant matter, but also an approach to the restructuring of education and even perhaps of our society. Simply because the artist sets his own goals and works with his whole self — reason, intuition, the most ruthless self-criticism and realistic assessment of a situation, freely, without external compulsion and with love — art is a model for what work could be were it freely and lovingly undertaken rather than, as it is for most today, forced, monotonous and boring. The spectacular changes which western art has undergone in our century are metaphors for changes that are still only latent in our culture. They show, however, that there are in fact forces within the matrix of society that are favourable to these changes, which could bring about our liberation from the scientistic and technocratic domination of our lives, from the pointless and repetitious labour that passes for work for most people, and, for our children, from the scars inflicted by our present schools, well-intentioned though they may be, on all those, successful and unsuccessful alike, who pass through them.

1   *The Perfect Cadence and the Concert Hall*

It is often said, but cannot be too often reiterated, that every human being is conditioned, to a degree impossible to fathom, by the assumptions of the culture in which he lives. The late Harry Partch called it bewitchment, and in a ringing phrase added, 'Like the Mindanao Deep in the Pacific, the bewitchment is deep and mysterious'.[1] This deep and mysterious bewitchment pervades every aspect of our lives; the very structure of our language imposes modes of thought and perception upon us, our customs, mores and folkways seem to us God-given and inviolable, our science and technology seem final and uniquely valid answers to questions that are posed to us by nature. Our way of educating our young seems based on secure and obvious principles concerning the nature of knowledge and of the learning process, while our arts reflect culturally determined ways of perceiving and feeling, and in turn impose those ways back upon us; indeed, our arts can be seen from one point of view as metaphors for the attitudes and assumptions of our culture.

Here, for example, are a few sentences from Paul Henry Lang's monumental *Music in Western Civilization,*[2] by common consent one of the great histories of western music in the English language. I have italicized some phrases which contain, by implication, major assumptions about the nature of music and of musical values; these are tacitly assumed to be of universal validity, but we shall see that they are in fact unique to post-Renaissance western music. He is discussing the early classical symphonists:

> But orchestral "effect" and tone colour, however varied and rich, were never an end in themselves, for the classical style *subordinated all details to the one central idea* of organic growth, in which *mere effects* had no place unless they were *in definite and logical relationship to the whole.* This does not mean that the classical symphony did not abound in ingenious orchestral effects, but the latter are invariably *motivated by the musical material* and *not by the technical possibilities of the instruments* ... Orchestration and

tone colour serve to solidify and set off the *architectonic construction*.

This conditioning, of course, is not necessarily to be deplored, but is to be thought of rather as a means by which we reduce the 'buzzing, blooming confusion' of external and internal stimuli to manageable order, and in more tranquil times men may live their lives well, quite unaware that other possible ways exist of organizing their experience. But although we cannot escape the conditioning which our culture imposes upon us we do not need to remain bewitched by it; the fish can learn to be aware of the water in which he swims. Indeed, in such times of profound and turbulent change as we seem to be entering at such uncomfortable speed, the need to do so becomes imperative and urgent.

Of all the arts, music, probably because of its almost complete lack of explicit verbal or representational content, most clearly reveals the basic assumptions of a culture; let us begin, then, by examining a phenomenon which is familiar to most music lovers: the great western post-Renaissance tradition, which lasted roughly from 1600 to 1910. This is the period of nearly all the well-known 'greats' of the concert and operatic repertory, and it is sometimes known, from its outstanding technical feature, as the period of tonal functional harmony. So close are we to this music that for many music lovers it occupies the whole field of their musical perception, and becomes the unique embodiment of what they think of as the eternal verities of the art. But, as Harry Partch observed, 'Music ... has only two ingredients that might be called God-given – the capacity of a body to vibrate and produce sound and the mechanism of the human ear that registers it ... All else in the art of music, which may be studied and analysed, was created by man or is implicit in human acts and is therefore subject to fiercest scrutiny.'[3] In other words, certain assumptions of our 'classical' music tradition, which we think of as basic and universal elements of all music, are very far indeed from being so. Further, we need to disabuse ourselves of the delusion that western music is the supreme achievement of mankind in the realm of sound, and that other cultures represent merely stages in an evolution towards that achievement. Other cultures make other assumptions and are interested in other aspects of organized sound; they are neither inferior nor superior, only different, and comparative value judgements between ourselves and them are at best irrelevant, at worst tending to reinforce our dangerous delusion of European cultural superiority. Curt Sachs, in his attempt to summarize the wisdom of a lifetime of experience in world music, *The Wellsprings of Music,* says, 'We cannot escape the culture we ourselves have made. But seeing and weighing the difference between the two musical worlds might help us to realize that our gain is our loss, our growth is our wane. It might help us to understand that we have not progressed but merely changed. And, when seen from the cultural point of view, we have not always changed for the better.'[4]

We should remember too that this tradition is geographically restricted to the peoples of the European subcontinent (and today its offspring and outposts) and that, even in terms of European history, it occupies only a very small portion of time, a mere three hundred years or so. Its assumptions are those of post-Renaissance humanism and individualism, and it has the characteristic virtues and limitations of that viewpoint. If we compare it with the music of the rest of Europe's history, not to mention that of the rest of mankind, it begins to look like something of an historical freak. This is not to deny the greatness of its achievements, but merely to point out that it has characteristics that are not shared by any of the world's other musical cultures, and that many of these characteristics are not necessarily more sophisticated or 'advanced' than those of other cultures − including that of our medieval ancestors. The notion of 'progress' may have some meaning in regard to science, which is concerned with the accumulation of abstract and objective knowledge divorced from personality, but is impossible to sustain in the arts, based as they are on experience, which is unique to the individual and must be renewed with each succeeding generation.

The music of the tonal-harmonic tradition over its three centuries or so of life is of course of an incredible richness and diversity. Nevertheless, there are certain characteristics which unite Monteverdi and Wagner, Beethoven and Delibes, Caccini and Reger, certain themes that can be traced throughout its history, and it is these that I shall now consider.

One could trace the origins of the tradition back beyond 1600, of course, perhaps at least as far as the work of Guillaume Dufay, whose motet *Ave Regina Coelorum* of 1474 contains, as Wilfrid Mellers points out,[5] a beautiful early example of the minor third being used in contrast to the major third for dramatic, personal, expressive effect. Through the work of such masters as Dufay and Ockeghem, and of the great sixteenth-century contrapuntists, Palestrina, Byrd, Victoria and Lassus, we see the change in

European consciousness that we call the Renaissance having its
effect in music, with the personal, humanistic viewpoint substituted
for the theocratic, universalistic viewpoint of the Middle Ages,
expressed in technical terms by a greater interest in chords and their
effects in juxtaposition, and specifically in the perfect cadence and
the suspended dissonance, rather than in polyphony and the
independent life of the individual voice. Thomas Mann makes one
of the characters in his *Doctor Faustus,* the Jewish scholar
Breisacher, turn the conventional view of these masters, as pure,
abstract and infinitely lofty, on its head:

> This, then, was the decline, namely the deterioration of the great
> and only true art of counterpoint, the cool and sacred play of
> numbers, which, thank God, had nothing to do with prostitution of
> feeling, or blasphemous dynamic ... The softening, the effeminizing
> and falsification, the new interpretation put on the old and genuine
> polyphony understood as a combined sounding of various voices
> into the harmonic-chordal, had already begun in the sixteenth
> century, and people like Palestrina, the two Gabrielis and our good
> Orlandi di Lasso ... had already played their shameful part in it.
> These gentlemen brought us the conception of the vocal polyphonic
> art, 'humanly' at first, oh yes, and seemed to us therefore the
> greatest masters of this style. But that was simply because for the
> most part they delighted in a purely chordal texture of phrase, and
> their way of treating the polyphonic style had been musically
> weakened by their regard for the harmonic factor, for the relation
> of consonance and dissonance.[6]

Mann's narrator, a gentle, conservative academic, is shocked by
such talk, and we are left wondering how tongue-in-cheek Mann
was, but that passage does make clear the nature of the continuity
between the work of the Renaissance masters and their successors
after 1600. Nonetheless, something did change around that date,
even though remnants of the older medieval tradition lingered even
until the time of J.S. Bach. One might say that chords, and
suspended dissonances, assembled in Renaissance music, started to
move in the Baroque. As Richard Crocker says, 'Around 1600
several major shifts in emphasis coincided to give musical style a
new shape. The main shift was a long-range one; long in the
making, its effects are still operative today. It involved the
recognition of harmonic triads as the basic units of musical
composition. The significance of this shift is hard for us to grasp,
simply because it took place; triads now seem obvious entities to us

today because they became so around 1600, whereas they had not been so before.'[7] It was at this time, too, that the shift of interest from the movement of individual voices, which almost incidentally made harmonic combinations, as in medieval polyphony, to progressions of triads, which governed voice movements and hence all melodic shapes, became so complete that a quantitative change became a qualitative one. At this point was born the technique of tonal functional harmony, the formalized movement of chords in succession which became an expressive means in its own right and was to be the dominant technique of western music for three centuries. I shall have more to say about tonal harmony later; here we need only note that tonality, the logical arrangement of chords around a key centre, became a major force in European music from around that date. With harmony, too, goes the concept of music as a drama of the individual soul, adumbrated in the work of the Renaissance masters, and brought to first maturity, conveniently in 1600, with the performance of the first real opera, Peri's *L'Euridice,* by a group of Florentine litterati and amateurs of music who believed themselves to be reviving the performance style of ancient Greek drama.

Such a definite date does not attach itself so easily to the end of the tonal-harmonic tradition, and the choice of 1910 iş only arbitrary; indeed, certain aspects of the tradition survive today. But 1910 was Mahler's last complete year of life, and the year of Stravinsky's *Firebird*; by then Debussy had written *La Mer,* Schoenberg his *Second String Quartet* and *Erwartung,* Webern the *Five Movements for String Quartet* and Ives *The Unanswered Question.* True, much of the work of Strauss, Sibelius, Vaughan Williams and others still lay in the future; these represent the afterglow of the tradition, as beautiful perhaps and as moving as the afterglow of any glorious day. The real work of exploration had moved elsewhere. Debussy, Schoenberg, Stravinsky and Webern in Europe, and Ives in America, were looking beyond the tonal-harmonic tradition, beyond the individualist-expressive function of music, and were beginning to explore a new landscape whose laws were not those of the logical daylit world of tonal harmony. In 1910, too, jazz, that most forceful of the many musical styles which emerged in the Americas from the enforced contact between African and European musics, was beginning its challenge to many orthodox western ways of making and listening to music.

Europe in the centuries before the Renaissance was an oral,

mainly non-literate communal culture, not so very different in style from the rest of the world. It was around the middle of the fifteenth century that our culture began to reveal those new attitudes and concepts, ways of feeling, seeing and hearing, that were to cut Europe off from the rest of mankind and make her culture, including her music, unique. The changes are a familiar matter of history: the growth of humanism and individualism, the questioning of the theocentric world, and the desacralization of nature which gave rise to the scientific worldview, the 'invention' of man as a private individual — the last possibly associated with the contemporary development of printing and the rise of the printed book. These changes became visible in painting as far back as Giotto in the thirteenth century, long before they became audible in music. The medieval painter had seen his subject matter as it were under the eyes of God, who sees everything, to whom all events are simultaneous, and he gave expression to a communal, rather than a personal, consciousness. Thus we might have a painting of a city in which all its features are depicted in a way which would be impossible for an individual standing in a single spot to see, but which might be said to represent God's view, as well as the whole community's experience, of the city. As long as painters took such an attitude perspective did not develop, not because painters were not capable of it but because it was of no use or interest to them as a technique. Similarly, we might see the representation of the life of a saint, in which his birth, several miracles, his martyrdom and his apotheosis are all contained within the single visual field. This can be taken as representing not only the combined vision of all who knew the saint, the communal experience, but also the divine, timeless, god's-eye-view of his life, in which all events are, not foreordained, but simply simultaneous. (The painter was so little concerned with the individual experience that the picture was usually unsigned.) The post-Renaissance artist, on the other hand, saw his subject as if through the eye of a single spectator, in a particular spot at a particular instant. Perspective, the placing of all the elements of a picture in logical relation to one another and to a 'vanishing point', assumes that we look through the eyes of man rather than of God, the individual rather than the community, while the instantaneousness of the painter's vision speaks of a concept of time very different from the medieval. Man the individual, living in time, has displaced God, living in eternity, from the centre of the universe.

Sir Donald Tovey, writing in the nineteen-twenties, spoke more truly even than perhaps he knew when he called tonal harmony the musical analogue of perspective. Like perspective, tonal harmony is a logical affair, and expresses through its successions of tension and relaxation the experience of the single individual. Henri Pousseur has said, 'Tonal harmony is in fact the type of musical language in which the most transparent logic reigns, in which logic is truly made flesh, and becomes, as proof of the absolute transcendence of individual reason, the object of unique and irreplaceable pleasure'.[8] Certainly quite untalented people, once they have grasped the nature of the logical relationships of triads within a key, can write perfectly correct (if uninspired) harmonic sequences, just as equally untalented people, once they have grasped the sets of logical relationships which surround the vanishing point, can make perfectly correct perspective drawings.

Logic, and logical relations, are in fact key concepts of western art. The work of art is logically explicable and ultimately knowable; nothing in the relationships which it contains can be left unclear or resistant to analysis. Every element relates logically to every other and to the main structure of the work. The listener to the music can 'hear his way' through the sounds, and understand the processes at work, even if he cannot put a name to them. And, as Pousseur says, it is tonal harmony which is at the heart of the logical processes of the music.

We need to be clear what we mean by 'tonal harmony'. It can be defined as the linking together of triads in succession in relation to a key centre, in such a way as to make a sequence which is meaningful and expressive to the accustomed ear; nearly everyone in western culture has become accustomed since infancy to comprehend these tonal sequences (if this seems like a circular definition, it is because comprehension of these harmonic sequences is essentially a learnt process). Harmony concerns itself with the relationships *between* triads rather than with the triads themselves, which acquire real meaning only when linked together in succession.

The triad, the raw material of tonal harmony, is a group of three tones sounded together: a first tone, the tone a major or minor third above it, and the tone a perfect fifth above it (for example C, E, G or C, E flat, G). We all know the sound of the triad, even if we cannot put a name to it; it is the sound that has dominated western music from Monteverdi to Debussy and even later. It is in itself a logical sound-structure (we disregard here the distortions introduced by tempered tunings), consisting of tones whose frequencies stand in a simple arithmetical ratio to one another. We recognize the sound of the triad at no matter what pitch level it occurs and no matter how the three tones are laid out (they can occur in any octave and be duplicated, or 'doubled' in any octave, but as long as all the tones are (for example) C's, E's and G's the combination is known as the triad of, or based on, C) because it is the *relationships* between the pitches, rather than the pitches themselves, that define the triad. This is an important concept, but we take it for granted as we transpose melodies and chord sequences from one octave to another and from one key to another. The groups of sounds are clearly *not* the same after such transpositions, yet we treat them as if they were. We can do this only because the music of the tonal-harmonic tradition is interested, not in the sounds themselves, but in the relationships between them.

Triads are arranged in sequences in such a way as to make meaningful relationships between them. When we sound the first two triads of Ex 1, for example, the way of thinking that has developed over three centuries or more leads us to expect the third, making the relationship between the second and the third that we call the perfect, or five-one, cadence, the strongest and most fundamental harmonic relationship, out of which all the complexities of tonal harmony have grown. It was historically the first harmonic relationship to emerge as an entity, and can be heard in the works of the great sixteenth-century contrapuntists, usually at the end of a musical sentence.

Ex 1.

If we delay the arrival of the penultimate triad by inserting others into the sequence before it, we feel an even stronger 'homing' impulse in the five-one cadence (Ex 2):

Ex 2

The historical development of the art of harmony, and of those large-scale dramatic forms such as symphony, concerto and opera which are based on it, may be seen from one point of view as the longer and longer delaying of the final perfect cadence. Similarly, the addition of a dissonant tone, as long as it can be shown finally to relate logically to the basic harmonic sequence, can also strengthen the 'homing' impulse of the cadence. In Ex 3 we have two such dissonances: the F added to the chord of V is explicable as a 'passing note', moving smoothly and stepwise between the two harmony notes G and E. This tone was later to be incorporated by a process of elliptical condensation, analogous to the processes which occur in verbal languages, into the triad of V itself, making the mildly dissonant chord we know as the dominant seventh. This process of condensation has been an important factor in the development of dissonant chords. The second dissonant tone C in the preceding chord increases the forward impulse on to the chord of V; its logic will be explained later.

Ex 3

From this point of view, the historical development of harmony and of the large-scale harmonic forms can be seen as the introduction of ever more and sharper dissonances in order to increase the tension and forward drive towards resolution of the sequence. In practice both the delaying of the resolution and the increase in dissonant tension occurred simultaneously and were used by composers in various ways through the tonal-harmonic era. The climax of the dual process can be seen in a work such as Wagner's *Tristan und Isolde,* where the quite strong dissonance established in the opening bars of the *Prelude* is not resolved until the final bars of the *Liebestod,* three enormous acts and nearly five hours later.

We need not look for anything in the physics of sound to explain the feeling of expectation and satisfaction, tension and relaxation, which we obtain from the association of triads in this way. It is a purely linguistic convention, a syntax, and is no more and no less arbitrary than any other syntax (which, if Chomsky and others are right, may not be arbitrary at all). The expectation and even frustration created by sounding, say, the first bar of Ex 3 without the final tonic triad is of the same kind as that created by saying 'The cat sat on the ...'. In both cases we have a feeling of residual tension, of incomplete meaning (though of course both poets and composers have used the fact that once we know how the sequence should end we can supply the missing elements ourselves, and indeed may even gain pleasure from doing so). This is a purely learnt response; people from other musical cultures, even musicians, who are unfamiliar with the syntax of this music, on hearing the most ravishing (to our ears) harmonic progressions of Schubert, remain as unmoved as a monolingual Englishman hearing Homer read in ancient Greek.

The development of tonal harmony had an important consequence for the rhythmic dimension of European music: a restriction of that freedom of accent and measure which we find in non-harmonic music. A dissonance attracts to itself an accent, whether or not we intend it so. One of the earliest resources of harmony, used extensively by the sixteenth-century masters to create tension, was that of the 'suspended dissonance', the increasing of dissonant tension by holding over a tone from one triad into the following, with which it is not compatable. This transient dissonance, which may last no more than a single beat before it moves on to the consonant tone (or resolves), has a highly emotive effect, and is an important means of building tension and expectation. We see a mild example in Ex 3, where the C of the second triad is held over into the third, creating a dissonance against the D of that triad before moving smoothly down to the B of the penultimate triad. We note how this dissonance gives the third triad an accent that the corresponding triad in Ex 2 does not have. The regular succession of such suspensions early imposed a regular alternation of weak and strong beats. As Wilfrid Mellers says, 'The harmonic revolution is inseparable from the rhythmic revolution ... Similarly, the concept of the suspended dissonance — the sigh of sorrow, the cry of pain — is inconceivable except in reference to a strong and a weak beat on which the dissonance is prepared and resolved.'[9] So arose the regular alternation of strong and weak beats which has characterized our music over three centuries and more; even today the popular conception of rhythm means corporal rhythm, the rhythm of the dance.

The rhythmic impoverishment that this has produced is illustrated neatly in a story told by Curt Sachs of a fine Albanian folk musician who was taken, as his first taste of western concert music, to hear Beethoven's *Ninth Symphony*. After much persuasion he gave his opinion of the work, which was, 'Fine – but very very plain.' Sachs comments, 'The Albanian was neither arrogant nor incompetent. He just had a different standard. The unified, oversimplified rhythm could not possibly satisfy his eastern ears – exactly as to an illiterate African, the crotchets and quavers of western music would appear dull ... He was presented with 'divisive' rhythms, where quite mechanically a stress preceded every two or three unstressed units of equal duration as ONE-two-three – an impoverishment of European music owed to the growing impact of chordal harmony.'[10]

The technique of the suspended dissonance was the principal agent in the increasing complexity of harmonic textures from the sixteenth to the early twentieth century. Major works such as *Tristan und Isolde*, or Schoenberg's *Verklaerte Nacht*, have long sections which are kept in motion by overlapping chains of suspensions, one being prepared in one voice while another is resolved in another, so that the tension never fully relaxes and we are continually drawn forward in time.

The logical nature of tonal harmony is such that the harmonically attuned ear will accept practically any dissonance provided that it can finally be shown to relate logically to the harmonic structure of the whole; indeed, the ear may not even notice the dissonances. (The music of Mozart teems with very sharp dissonances, cunningly and unobtrusively placed so that although the mind does not consciously register them they probably contribute to its poignant emotional quality.) We know that however far afield the composer may take us into dissonance and remote tonal areas we shall eventually emerge on to the final cadence in the home key. He may tease us a little, even engage in paradox. When we hear Oscar Wilde's quip that 'Work is the curse of the drinking classes', we have a moment of thinking that he has it the wrong way around, and then we comprehend the unexpected logic of it. In the same way the composer may upset our expectation, lead us in unexpected harmonic directions; we enjoy the surprise so long as we can finally be made to understand its logic. Schubert was perhaps of all the great masters *the* master of harmonic paradox; I hear, for example, in the three or four false endings he gives to the lovely tune at the end of the slow movement of his Fifth Symphony that kind of lazy, gently sensuous teasing that lovers engage in one to the other.

That the logic of tonal harmony can indeed be an 'object of unique pleasure' is something that J.S. Bach understood very well;

despite his reputation as a contrapuntist he is first and foremost an exploiter of harmonic device. In the C major prelude of the First Book of the *Welltempered Clavier,* harmonic relations form virtually the only material. Bach chose to break the chords into arpeggio patterns in order to enliven the texture, but we can play the chords in unbroken form and still obtain pleasure from the pure harmonic sequence. It is important to note that our pleasure comes not from the qualities of the individual sounds, or even the individual chords, but from the relations between them, from the way one chord succeeds another in relation to the key centre. The individual chords are in fact commonplace and lacking in meaning or interest; their meaning comes from their association in a particular order. Tovey observes that the listless organist in Sullivan's song must have found, not a lost *chord*, but a lost *progression,* which threw an essentially commonplace chord into a new and unexpected light. In the same way too, a group of commonplace words can come together to become what to me is one of the most magical utterances in the English language:

> Be not afeard; the isle is full of noises,
> Sounds, and sweet airs, that give delight and hurt not.

Of course, just as in spoken language, the law of diminishing returns can set in, and surprising and beautiful harmonic sequences can become cliché. Debussy noted this, saying, 'Régnier spoke to me of the debasement through usage of certain words in the French language. I thought that this also applied to certain chords that have become vulgarized in the same way.'[11] Indeed, the history of tonal-harmonic music can be seen from one point of view as the constant struggle to keep ahead of cliché; once one starts to ride the tiger of harmonic surprise it is very difficult to dismount. Later Romantic composers would build ever more complex and dissonant chordal structures on the basis of multiple suspensions, and then reveal the logic behind the paradoxical relationships of the tones; their purposes tended to be less those of wit than of heightened emotional expression, and the often frantic need to surprise. One sometimes hears in the music, notes or even whole phrases which seem to have travelled so far from the dominant logic of the key — in Strauss, for example, in Reger or the early Schoenberg — as to have lost touch with it altogether, and sometimes the piece finds its way back to the final cadence in the home key only, one feels, by the skin of its teeth; but all the same they never lost touch with the key completely for the entire duration of a piece. It was Schoenberg who, in 1909, understood where the situation had led, and, in the last movement of his *Second String Quartet,* took the crucial step; in this movement, the absence of a key signature means, for the first time in European music, not the key of C major but the absence of a key and of the logical relationships which define it. By the end of the movement, the key of F sharp, the ostensible key of the work, has been re-established, but Schoenberg had glimpsed a new, keyless sound world, untrammelled by the demands of harmonic logic, and, in the sequence of works that followed, learnt to move in this world with increasing freedom and confidence. The problems that the new situation posed, and the methods he adopted to deal with them, will be discussed later. Here I suggest only that it is, at least in part, the logical inexplicability of the harmony, rather than any inherently high level of dissonance (that of much of Strauss, for example, is almost as high but the harmony remains logically explicable) which makes Schoenberg's 'atonal' works so difficult for the traditionally-trained listener.

The extent to which this art is one of relationships in the abstract rather than of sounds themselves is attested by the fact that the triadic sequences of Examples 1 to 3 contain no reference whatever to the concrete sound, that is, to the instruments upon which the sounds are supposed to be heard; nor is this important. Their meaning is the same whether they are sung by a choir, or played on a piano, a harmonium, a symphony orchestra, saxophone quartet or synthesizer. It is the pitch relationships and their occurrence in time (that is, rhythm) that are the basic material; it is these that are first conceived by the composer, to be clothed only later in instrumental sounds. Those readers who have worked their way through books of harmony exercises may remember having covered pages with these highly abstract designs, often without the slightest reference to what they might mean in terms of actual — that is, instrumental or vocal — sound. This is not the pedagogical aberration it might seem to be — it merely expresses the real priorities of the post-Renaissance musical tradition, in which the concrete sounds are merely the bearers of the composer's message. Of course, in order to compose, one needs to gain mastery also of the concrete sounds — texture, chordal layout, instrumentation — but these remain essentially decorative elements. The basic material lies in the melodic and harmonic structures, and these can be studied in the abstract. It is interesting, too, that harmony, the logical element par excellence, is the one most systematically taught and most bound by rules. In teaching melody writing, instrumentation, rhythm, the teacher may give advice and criticism, but there are 'rules' only for harmony.

A piano transcription of an orchestral work of the classical tradition (or indeed an orchestral transcription of a piece for piano) will reveal the extent to which pitch relations are the primary material of the music; it remains in all essential respects the same piece after transcription. The loss of the exquisite colours of Mozart's orchestra or the bold and vigorous colours of Beethoven's does not destroy the work's essential identity, though it may diminish it somewhat as an experience, like a black and white reproduction of an oil painting. It was in fact in the form of piano arrangements, usually for the companionable combination of four hands on one keyboard (more companionable perhaps, and therefore truer to the inner nature of musical experience, than gramophone records), that most music lovers out of earshot of an orchestra gained their acquaintance with the orchestral works of the day before the advent of records and radio. (The significance of the keyboard, which places complex textures under the control of a single individual, bears consideration in the light of post-Renaissance individualism; it is the essential tool of post-Renaissance music.) Again, Schumann was able to write an extended analytical review of Berlioz' *Symphonie Fantastique* from a study of Liszt's piano transcription – a tribute no doubt to Liszt's genius as arranger but one also to the primacy of pitch and rhythmic structures in the construction of the work. It is to these structures that Lang refers in the quotation at the beginning of this chapter as the truc 'musical material' of a classical work, to which tone colours – 'mere effects' – are subordinated. As with colour in the paintings of the post-Renaissance era, the actual instrumental sound has no *structural* function, although it may serve to draw attention to certain structural features – as indeed may colour in a painting.

If the basic material of post-Renaissance music is pitches and the logical relations between them, it is to be expected that this music will show a drastic limitation of the materials suitable for use in music. These are reduced to no more, and frequently fewer, than twelve tones within each octave, arranged in one of only two possible ways, the major and the minor modes — and even these interpenetrate almost inseparably. Consequently, the only instruments that were admitted into the ensemble of European music were those capable of producing sounds of clear, definite pitch and possessing a precise harmonic structure. In this respect post-Renaissance music differs from nearly all other musics, which love to use noise – sounds, that is, of no precise pitch or definite harmonic structure – as well as those pitches which lie between our twelve divisions of the octave, and which our music considers to be 'out of tune'. Even medieval European music made much use of non-harmonic sounds – not only percussion such as bells, drums, rattles, tambourines and triangles but also pitched instruments which produce sounds with a high proportion of non-harmonic noise – the crumhorn, racket, bagpipe, shawm and sackbut – which to the post-Renaissance ear sound harsh, even primitive. It was probable also that medieval voice production used much more non-harmonic sound, and was thus harsher, rougher and more nasal than the post-Renaissance tradition would allow – not, it must be emphasized, because they did not know how to produce 'smooth' sounds, but because they liked 'rough' sounds.

Post-Renaissance musicians could not tolerate these acoustically illogical and unclear sounds, sounds which were not susceptible to total control. The instrumentarium of this tradition therefore came to exclude all percussion instruments; it was not until late in the seventeenth century that the first percussion instruments were readmitted, the timpani, which could be tuned to a pitch; but even then because the pitch was not clear and unambiguous their notes were always doubled carefully with cellos, basses or bassoons in order to make the pitches clear. (It is against this background that the originality of Haydn's use of timpani, all on their own, in his *103rd Symphony* must be appreciated.) It was in Haydn's time that other percussion instruments began to be introduced, or reintroduced, at first only as splashes of local or exotic colour; like so many technical developments of the period their use stemmed from the dramatic and emotional requirements of opera (we shall see later how dramatic criteria dominated post-Renaissance music). The late eighteenth century was fascinated by things oriental, especially Turkish. The Turks, having recently ceased to be a military menace to Europe, could now be viewed with no more than a slight frisson as picturesque (Mozart's *Entführung aus dem Serail* was only one of many such exotic dramas of the time), and the first unpitched percussion to be used in European art music was the so-called 'Turkish' percussion – bass drum, triangle and cymbals, usually all sounded together. They can be heard clearly in the overture to *Entführung*, as well as in the second and fourth movements of Haydn's *100th Symphony*.

Over the nineteenth and early twentieth centuries the full range of percussion as we know it today (more or less) was gradually domesticated into the accepted ensemble. Nonetheless, it still had no more than a decorative function, to salt and pepper the sounds and give power and emphasis to climaxes, always as more or less dispensible splashes of sound, never integral to the basic conception of the piece, which remained as firmly grounded as ever in the play of abstract pitch relations. As long as this remained so, the function of percussion, indeed of tone colour in general, could never be more than the provision of colour and excitement. When a work was reduced to a single tone colour, as in a piano arrangement, its basic identity remained intact. This is true even of such forward-looking masterpieces as Stravinsky's *Le Sacre du Printemps,* of which the composer was able to make a perfectly valid two-piano transcription (if indeed it did not, knowing as we do Stravinsky's method of working, start life at the keyboard). He and Debussy played it through together some time before its sensational Paris première and Debussy later wrote to him, 'You have enlarged the boundaries of the possible in the world of sound. It haunts me like a beautiful nightmare, and I try in vain to recapture the terrific impression'[12] — proof enough that the transcription contained all the material necessary for an understanding of its significance.

The central position of opera in post-Renaissance music, and its role as generator of most of its technical experimentation, emphasizes the essentially dramatic nature of this music. Not only opera, but all the large harmonic forms — symphony, concerto, sonata and tone poem alike — are in essence psychodramas, the spiritual voyage of an individual. In its origins opera was as much ritual as was medieval religious drama, though the ritual was no longer Christian but humanistic (the almost total absence of biblical subjects in early opera is striking). The physical structure of the opera house even today preserves something of the outer form of the ritual, though its inner spirit has long since vanished. In the early days of opera the whole community would attend, hierarchically separated into tiers according to social position, with the highest and greatest, who had probably paid for the presentation and whose wealth and power the spectacle was intended to celebrate, in the best seats, nearest the stage, and the lowest in the hot and stuffy top tier, to which they were admitted by a separate entrance, a practice which survives today in older theatres. The opera house was a model of seventeenth-century society, hierarchically and rigidly stratified, it is true, but still a community, while the Greek and Roman myths which provided almost all the subject matter of the dramas were the humanist equivalent of the medieval morality plays, with the mercy of God transmuted into the clemency of kings, the apotheosis of Orpheus paralleling that of Christ. Like the morality plays, indeed like all living ritual, the opera was at one and the same time entertainment and the re-enactment of the cohesive myths of the culture, which people attended primarily because they enjoyed it. As Umberto Eco observes, 'Scenic and musical action contribute to the formation of a complex melodramatic unity, which by virtue of its ordering tendencies carries the public into participation and acceptance. In its beginnings this "one-way" form represented an authentic mode of influence; within the dramatic structure the morality of the spectator could be involved in the treatment of momentous questions.'[13] What appears to modern audiences as the 'stiffness' or 'formalism' of seventeenth or early eighteenth century opera is in fact a function of its ritualistic nature; such formalism is a feature of ritual drama the world over, as are devices such as heavy stylized makeup, masks and stereotyped gesture, all of which tend to obliterate the individuality of the actor and assimilate him into the character. The actor *becomes* the god, hero or demon he is representing, and in so doing obscures his own character and appearance. In later secularized and non-ritual drama the actor superimposes the character he is representing on to his own personality so that we remain aware of him as well as of the character (this duality reached its apogee perhaps in the Hollywood films of the thirties and forties, where the personality − or 'star quality' − of a Bette Davis, a Garbo or a Gable frequently overwhelmed the characters they were ostensibly representing). The actor simulates the emotions and the reactions of the character while remaining essentially outside them; were he not able to do this he would be torn to shreds by the emotional demands of the long run of a play, even were it a farce. Ritual drama, on the other hand, like ritual music, is not something to be endlessly repeated in this way before successive virtually indistinguishable audiences; it belongs to an occasion, a time and a place, and the actor submits wholly to the experiences of the character. It could be that the custom in the opera house of performing operas 'in repertory', with a different work presented each night, is a remote echo of the time when opera was a communal ritual. In any case, little remains today of opera as a social force. Noble attempts, like those of Tippett and Berg, to revive its ancient function are doomed to triviality by the essential frivolity of the audience.

Umberto Eco continues, 'For today's audiences a major part of this impact is lost. The public which leaves after the ritual of an opera performance does not discuss the human problems underlying it, but instead is occupied in pronouncing judgement on the vocal power of the baritone, the graciousness of the soprano, or the imagination of the stage director. Unaware, they reduce to a comedy of forms what was once a great theatre of ideas and passions; they participate in a liturgy without faith, with its desecrated altar and its atheistic audience watching from the empty sockets of the boxes. Separated from its dramatic roots, the enjoyment of an aria tends to become archaeological scavengery or a pretext for sentimental escapism.'[13]

The musical performer of the post-Renaissance tradition is required to be even more versatile in simulation than the actor; it may be that in the course of a single two-hour concert he is called upon to behave musically *as if* he felt in succession the sorrows of Tchaikowsky, the sublime arrogance of Beethoven and the sober ecstasy of Brahms. He stands apart from each of these characters he is impersonating, using the great and fatal gift of western man: to act without reacting, to remain uninvolved.

Even composers behave in this 'as if' fashion. We read, for example, that the time when Tchaikowsky was composing the *Pathétique Symphony* was the happiest and most satisfactory of his life. He wrote to his publisher after completing the work: 'I give you my word of honour that never in my life have I been so contented, so proud, so happy in the knowledge that I have written a good piece.' It is a surprising mood in which to find the composer of a work that is generally held to contain nothing but the blackest despair, but only if we forget that a man in the extremity of disintegration such as Tchaikowsky portrays would be in no state to undertake the demanding task of writing a symphony at all. Conversely, we find that the time when Beethoven was writing the sunny and ebullient *Second Symphony* was the time when, the incurability of his deafness having been confirmed, he was contemplating suicide, as evidenced by the famous *Heilegenstadt Testament*. Beethoven and Tchaikowsky were of course by no means alone in their ability to stand aside from their creations; indeed, it is usually assumed that without this distancing no art would be possible. Wordsworth's definition of poetry as 'emotion recollected in tranquillity' could have been coined only by a European; other cultures have other views on the nature and function of art. It was part of Gustav Mahler's genius to recognize this 'acting' quality in western music. As a great actor reveals and communicates a character through selective emphasis and exaggeration, so Mahler through deliberate exaggeration of the gestures of western music reveals its true character. It is this that caused contemporary critics to decry the 'tastelessness' of his music; they felt, rightly, that some of the most fundamental qualities of western music were being subverted.

A similar distancing to that between the artist and his art can be seen between the art work and him who receives it, as well as between the world of the art work and that of everyday life. The post-Renaissance painting is placed in a frame, whose function is clearly to define its limits, precisely and unambiguously; it sometimes appears to the innocent visitor walking around an art gallery that almost as much care has gone into the making of the frame as has gone into some of the pictures themselves. Similarly, the rich decoration surrounding the proscenium arch in a theatre emphasizes its function in keeping the drama at a safe distance, while the rise and fall of the usually sumptuous curtain serves to mark precisely the limits of the drama in time. Such care, such decoration, is a measure of the importance placed, albeit unconsciously, on the function of the frame in distancing us from the art work. Music, too, is placed in a frame; as with the drama, it is in fact in a double frame, a spatial and a temporal. The spatial frame is obvious enough; we place the sounds in a building or other space built or set aside for the purpose and carefully insulated to keep the sounds of everyday life from entering — and also perhaps to keep the sounds from escaping into the world — while the performers are placed on a platform, apart from the audience. The separation of the world of the music from that of everyday life is emphasized by the small rituals of the concert hall and opera house — the purchase of tickets, the reserving of seats, the conventions of dress and behaviour for both performers and audience — which go to give the concert or opera performance the feeling of a special occasion, a time set aside from the rest of one's life. The temporal frame is less obvious, perhaps because it is more taken for granted. The period of time that is to be occupied by the music is very clearly defined. We know to within a few minutes how long the performance will last before it starts; the management often obligingly post a notice in the foyer announcing the exact time it will end. Once the audience is seated and quiet, the conductor raises his baton, the pianist brings his hands to the keyboard, and the musical work begins its fore-ordained course, which nothing but a natural disaster or a musicians' strike will prevent from running until the final chord. The first sound, often a loud chord, always a positive gesture of some kind, marks the beginning of the course, while the end is usually indicated even more forcefully, with a fortissimo perfect cadence or even a series of cadential chords. We are left in no possible doubt of the temporal extent of the musical work, no doubt of *when* is the music and when not. The care taken to delineate clearly the boundary of the art work is not a chance phenomenon, but a sign of the special, isolated position of art in post-Renaissance Europe.

Again, just as the elements in a painting are placed very carefully in relation to the surrounding frame, so the events in a musical work are placed in the temporal sequence with great care in relation to the beginning and the end. The large-scale planning of events in time that we call form is an element of great importance in this music. It is as if we do not like to be lost in time. Each work of music represents a linear progression in time from the clear-cut beginning to the inevitable end, and the listener familiar with the style always knows where he is in relation to the beginning and the end, even if he is hearing a work for the first time. It could be that the formal devices of this music — not only sonatas, ritornelli, rondos and suchlike, but all the devices of sectional organization from opera to ragtime — are devices for making the articulation in time clear; tonal-harmonic music could indeed be defined as the conscious articulation of time by sound. Contrast the prompt, often too prompt, surge of applause which greets the ending of a classical concerto with the brief, embarrassed silence and scatter of handclaps that acts as prelude to the applause at an avant-garde première. Many of the more traditionally-minded among the audience will dislike an avant-garde work simply because 'You don't know where you are in it.'

In both painting and music of the post-Renaissance period one can detect among the elements that comprise the art work a hierarchical order of importance. Some areas of a painting are fully 'present' and realized, and are meant to occupy the full attention of the spectator, while other areas are meant just to be glanced over, to direct attention to the more fully present elements. These lesser elements are nonetheless not unimportant, and are not there merely to fill in the space on the canvas; on the contrary, they are vital to the composition of the picture and to the ordering of the visual field. Similarly, in a work of music there are sections which are, as it were, background — transition sections, for example, often consisting of conventional scale or chord sequences which, if abstracted from the design of the work, would be virtually meaningless, or at best boring cliché, but which serve in the context of the piece to direct attention forward or backward in time to the more fully present sections (normally the latter areas are called 'subjects' or 'themes'). These elements have an important structural function, and their relative lack of intrinsic interest does not indicate a lack of inspiration or technique on the part of the composer; on the contrary, it places them firmly in the background of the work and allows the thematic matter to emerge more fully by contrast, much as does the largely undifferentiated sky in, say, a Canaletto landscape. An analysis of a classical sonata movement in terms of background, middleground and foreground, and in terms of those sections which are fully present, those which direct attention forward to coming events (introductions and transition sections, for example, and generally the concluding parts of development sections) and those which direct it back to past events (developments in their various forms) can prove more fruitful than conventional dissection into first and second subjects, expositions, developments and recapitulations, and will reveal a dynamic process taking place in time rather than a static paper symmetry.

But even in the high classical period of the late eighteenth and early nineteenth centuries, in the music of Haydn, Mozart and Beethoven, we see an opposite tendency at work, a tendency of which the first movement of Beethoven's *Fifth Symphony* is often quoted as a classic example: the tendency to incorporate those 'spacing-out' elements more and more into the fabric of the music, by seeking to derive every event from a minimal amount of given thematic material. A parallel process was under way in painting, as can be seen in Constable's glowing East Anglian skies, every bit as meticulously painted as every other part of the paintings, and as rewarding for the eye. The effect in both arts was to reduce the differentiation between foreground and background, leading to a breakup of the hierarchical aesthetic that had given rise in the first place to the 'classical' style in painting and music. As long as any remnant of tonal harmony remained in music, as in the later works of Brahms and the early works of Schoenberg, as long as some vestige of linear perspective remained in painting, as in Cézanne and the Post-Impressionists, the distinction retained some force, but with Cubism, in which the object is seen from every point of view simultaneously, and Schoenbergian atonality, in which all elements of a work are thematic and of equal importance, the

polarity of foreground and background was finally abandoned in
both painting and music. Picasso's *Les Demoiselles d'Avignon* has
in fact been called the visual analogue of Schoenberg's *Second
String Quartet.*[14] It is certain that the brevity of the works of
Schoenberg's 'free atonal' period — *Erwartung,* for example, the
Five Orchestral Pieces and the *Six Little Piano Pieces* — is in part a
consequence of this lack of background, or spacing-out, material.

But analogies between the visual arts and music, though
interesting and frequently illuminating, should not be pushed too
far. A painting is a solid object which can be found in a particular
place, and whose material existence is indubitable, but what
actually constitutes a musical work in our culture is less certain.
The score is merely a set of coded instructions to the players, and
cannot be said to be the work itself (although the fact that we call it
'the music' suggests that we think it to be of vital importance),
while any performance, by common consent, by however eminent a
performer, can encompass only part of the essence of the work.
The work itself seems to exist only as an idea in the mind of the
composer, the performer (who realizes it to the best of his ability
but remains painfully aware of the gap between his concept and the
actual sounds which he produces) and the listener (who looks in a
performance for those sounds which will accord as closely as
possible to his idea of the work); it is an abstraction which perhaps
can never be perfectly realized in concrete sounds.

This abstract quality of post-Renaissance music is linked with
another characteristic — its self-containedness. We have already
noted that the music is set within a frame, apart from the listener's
everyday life; we observe also that it is listened to for its own sake,
by audiences who, in the words of Curt Sachs, are 'wholly devoted
to its artful elaboration'.[15] The music of this tradition is essentially
without function. It is true that music is used on occasion in the
great rituals of state and church — a royal wedding, the interment of
an elder statesman or the enthronement of an archbishop — as well
as the smaller rituals of private men — a wedding, a graduation, a
funeral — but its association is a loose one. It adorns, but is not an
essential part of, the ceremony, which can take place perfectly well
without it. A couple do not feel any less married if no-one plays
the *Wedding March* — and conversely, the *Wedding March* can be
played when no-one is getting married (is it coincidence that both
the famous wedding marches used in western Europe derive from
the make-believe world of the theatre?). There is no feeling that a
particular music belongs exclusively to a certain time, season or

setting; masses, coronation anthems and requiems are commonly presented indiscriminately for our appreciation in concert halls without any feeling of inappropriateness. The development of records and radio have enhanced this tendency, making all music universally available at all times and in all places (one wonders whether a culture which was much concerned, as many are, with the fitness of a particular music to a specific time or place would have developed recording techniques at all). The listener's experience of the music is essentially private; the structure and seating arrangement of a concert hall or opera house does not facilitate communal interaction any more than does that of a conventional classroom. Both suggest a type of experience which radiates out from the performer on the platform to each individual listener. The music is concerned, not with the assertion of community through ritual but with the communication of a personal idea from composer via performer to each individual listener. It celebrates the autonomy and the essential solitariness of the individual in post-Renaissance European society.

The listener himself is not involved in any way in the creative process; his task is merely to contemplate the finished product of the artist's efforts, to respond to it inwardly, without any outward show or physical reaction (even to move one's foot in time to the music is to invite condemnation as an ignoramus or a boor). The work is offered to him complete and entire, like the product of a manufacturing process, and, as with the product of any other manufacturing process, the only choice he has is to accept or reject it; his separateness from both composer (whom it is unlikely that he will have even seen) and performer makes it impossible for him to play any part in the process of making an art work. He is, however, free to be uninterested in the whole of this art of music and never set foot in a concert hall or opera house – a course which is in fact taken by the majority of the population.

The idea of the composer as separate from both performer on the one hand and audience on the other is associated with a second idea which we think of as natural but which is in fact unique to post-Renaissance music: the idea of the composer as hero, as a man who has experienced an area of psychic reality, often at great cost to himself, and wants us to know about it, the music being a kind of communiqué from Out There – in fact the whole idea of music as expression or communication of the experience or personality of one individual. This message, not surprisingly in view of our culture's central concern with power and overcoming, tends to take the form of a struggle, a drama; accordingly the criteria by which we judge a piece of music are essentially dramatic – does it move us, astonish us, excite us, make us weep? The central technique through which this dramatic aim is achieved, what Pousseur calls 'the true terrain on which the drama of music unfolds',[16] is tonal harmony, with its power of creating tension and relaxation, sudden changes of mood and atmosphere, comic, ironic, or tragic paradox, while the composer himself is thought of as one who, in his struggle with, and hopefully triumph over, his fate (Beethoven of course is the supreme exemplar) has something to tell us through his art. The music is the medium for his message, and one may even say that it has no reason to exist apart from the message. The sounds, the natural raw material of the art, are thought of as mere recalcritrant matter, to be put in order by the force of will and intelligence. Leonard Bernstein has pointed out how Beethoven's sketchbooks have the look of a bloody battlefield on which the composer fought to bring his materials under control.[17]

A musician from another culture might be astonished to find that such a struggle, even admitting it to be necessary at all, should have taken place, not in sounds, but on paper. Many cultures, it is true, have developed ways of notating their music, but these notations have functioned mostly as mnemonics, *after* the creative fact, to help the musician remember what he did; only in western music has the written score become the medium through which the act of composition takes place, and this long *before* the actual sounds are heard, as the composer wrestles with the problems of composition in the silence and isolation of his study.

This way of working has its advantages, allowing the composer to think out and develop at leisure harmonic and formal structures of great length and complexity (though, as we shall see in the next chapter, some musical cultures manage to build extensive and elaborate compositions without recourse to notation at all), and, as Cornelius Cardew says, it enables people to 'say things that are beyond their own understanding. A twelve-year-old can read Kant aloud; a gifted child can play late Beethoven'.[17] It does, however, have the effect of placing both performer and listener at a distance from the real business of art – the act of creation. They receive the product, but have no involvement with the process, of creation, which is complete before any performer even approaches the work. The adventure is over and the explorer safely home before anyone learns anything of the journey; performer and listener must content themselves with a recounting of it rather than the direct experience.

Further, the notation system tends to set limits on what a composer can imagine or a performer play. As one might expect, it reflects the priorities of its musical culture; in our culture it is well adapted to the elaboration of harmony on the diatonic tempered scale (the more the music departs from the diatonic scale the more complex it is to notate and read, though not necessarily to play), to the simple and regular patterns of note lengths which are divided in multiples of two, and to the deployment of large ensembles of instruments and voices. The notorious rhythmic difficulties of music such as that of the Darmstadt School of composers after the second world war, and of Charles Ives before the first, are due to complexities not in the *music* (much African music features rhythmic patterns that make it sound almost childishly simple, but since nobody is called upon to write them down or read them the music is labelled 'primitive') but in the notation, especially owing to the fact that the rhythmic patterns depart from the divided-by-two regularities favoured by the notation. Generation after generation of musicians have been so conditioned by the neat arrangements of black dots on the stave that they can think of music only in those terms; Harry Partch points out that 'Composers can "think" only in Equal Temperament for just that one reason: because it is all they have to think in.'[19] It is only in our own time that many musicians have tried, with varying degrees of success, to break away from the conditioning and have devised either extensions of the old, or radically new, means of notation.

A highly developed notation system such as ours permits the coming into being of classics, musical works that have outlived their creators to become apparently permanent features of the musical landscape. We take it for granted that it is a good thing to be able to preserve the whole conspectus of musical history, to perform, in some fashion, the music of all periods, and to conserve the 'immortal' music of Machaut, of Bach, of Mozart, Beethoven, Brahms and Schoenberg, but we should be aware that this classicizing tendency is unique to our musical culture and depends upon our notation system. Further, it could be that the continued domination of the musical environment today by these classics is not necessarily an unmixed blessing in terms of present creativity. It could be that we are clinging to them in the fearful certainty that nothing will ever be quite as good again as Mozart or Beethoven; it could be that we would be better occupied in making and performing our own works of art than in continuing the endless repetition and contemplation of the works of these long-gone masters, however much we may love and revere them, and that we shall regain our lost confidence and creative power only in rejecting them, albeit lovingly, as a young man may need to reject his over-dominant parents before he can grow to full adulthood.

Finally, the existence of a notation system permits the development of musicology, that bastard child of music and science, which caters to our passion for 'authenticity' of performance, a passion which once more reflects our lack of confidence in our own creativity. A truly confident creative passion takes the great work of the past and remakes it constantly, thus renewing the act of creation through the generations, as the seventeenth century reworked the plays of Shakespeare (themselves largely reworkings of earlier writings to suit the temper of the time) and as Stokowski reworked the organ works of Bach to suit his essentially nineteenth-century sensibility. These reworkings, tasteless as they may seem to our generation, may be truer to the creative spirit than our carefully researched urtext-edition attempts to restore the letter of the original, attempts whose degree of success we have in any case no means of assessing. The next generation may well mock the musicological temper of today as a pedantic fettering of creativity, and believe, rightly, that it is perfectly possible, even necessary, to approach the works of the past directly, without the intervention of musicologists.

I shall be developing this and other themes referred to in this chapter later, while trying to ascertain what the nature of our classical tradition has to tell us of the culture which brought it to birth. Before doing so, however, let us examine briefly some musics from outside our own culture, to see what music means to other members of the human race. Such other musics, fascinating and beautiful as they are in their own right, can also provide us with a mirror through which we can come to see, or rather to hear, our own music more clearly, and to appreciate it better not merely as an aesthetic experience but as an institution and a potential force within society.

Chapter 1: Bibliography

1.　PARTCH, Harry: Sleeve note to recording of *The Bewitched,* CRI SD 304 (1973).

2. LANG, Paul Henry: *Music in Western Civilization,* New York, Norton (1941), p. 711.
3. PARTCH, Harry: *Genesis of a Music,* 2nd edn., New York, Da Capo Press (1974), p. xvi.
4. SACHS, Curt: *The Wellsprings of Music,* The Hague, Martinus Nijhoff (1962), p. 222.
5. MELLERS, Wilfrid: *Caliban Reborn: Renewal in Twentieth-Century Music,* London, Gollancz (1968), p. 18.
6. MANN, Thomas: *Doctor Faustus,* transl. H.T. Lowe Porter, 1949, Harmondsworth, Penguin Books (1968), p. 271.
7. CROCKER, Richard: *A History of Musical Style,* New York, McGraw Hill (1966), p. 224.
8. POUSSEUR, Henri: *Fragments Théoriques sur la Musique Expérimentale,* Brussels, Editions de l'Institut de Sociologie, Universitaire Libre de Bruxelles (1970), p. 87. Author's translation.
9. MELLERS, Wilfrid: op. cit., p. 19.
10. SACHS, Curt: op. cit., p. 218.
11. LOCKSPEISER, Edward: *Debussy: His Life and Mind,* Vol 1, London, Cassell (1962), p. 29.
12. Quoted in MITCHELL, Donald: *The Language of Modern Music,* 2nd edn., London, Faber (1966), p. 22.
13. ECO, Umberto: Programme note to first performance of *Passagio* by Luciano Berio, Milan (1963).
14. MITCHELL, Donald; op. cit., p. 77.
15. SACHS, Curt: op. cit., p. 124.
16. POUSSEUR, Henri: op. cit., p. 88.
17. BERNSTEIN, Leonard: 'Beethoven's Fifth Symphony' in *The Joy of Music,* London, Weidenfeld and Nicholson (1960), p. 81.
18. CARDEW, Cornelius: *Treatise Handbook,* London, Peters (1971), p. xix.
19. PARTCH, Harry; op. cit., p. 194.

A fish is not aware of the water, since it knows nothing of any other medium. Until quite recently, this has been the position of European culture vis-à-vis the rest of the world; the complete and invincible certainty of the axiomatic superiority of European art to that of the rest of the world ensured that Europe was cut off, for more than three centuries, from the fertilizing influence of other cultures, cultures which to Europeans were at best strange and exotic, at worst primitive and unworthy of notice.

The first obvious break with this attitude came with the great Paris World Exhibition held on the Champ de Mars in 1889 where, for the first time in Europe, the gamelan of Java and the musical theatre of Cochin China were to be heard. The effect of these new sounds was sensational; enthusiasm for their exoticism and mystery was unbounded, yet of those who heard and were excited by the fascinating play of metallophone, gong and drum only one western musician really understood their significance: the twenty-seven-year-old Claude Achille Debussy. Many years later, in 1913, he recalled, 'Their conservatoire is the eternal rhythm of the sea, the wind among the leaves and the thousand sounds of nature which they understand without consulting any arbitrary treatise. Their traditions reside in the old songs, combined with dances, built up over the centuries. Yet Javanese music is based on a type of counterpoint by comparison with which that of Palestrina is child's play. And if we listen without European prejudice to the charm of their percussion we must confess that our percussion is like primitive noises at a country fair.'[1]

I shall discuss in a later chapter the direct influence which these wonderful sounds had upon Debussy's music; here we notice only that Debussy was in fact the first western musician to recognize and acknowledge the fact that here was a musical culture that was on its own terms fully the equal of that of the west, a culture from which the west might learn. As we shall see, Debussy's mind was prepared for this new experience, and, alone of the musicians of his time, he was able to incorporate the lessons of this new music into his own work with something more than superficial exotic mannerism. And if he did not fully comprehend the deeper significance of the music, of its place in oriental society, this was because he had no opportunity, in those vast exhibition halls under the shadow of the brand-new Eiffel Tower, to hear the music in its natural setting.

In later chapters I shall attempt to view our own, western, music against the background of western society and social attitudes, but before doing so it will be instructive to examine some non-western musics, in so far as we can generalize about them, in order to establish the kinds of music and the kinds of relationship of music to society that are possible in cultures other than our own. The exploration cannot be more than cursory; it is not intended to do more than establish the fact that other attitudes than our own are possible, and that these attitudes are reflected in the technical procedures of the music. We thus give our exploration of western music in its social framework a more solid background against which to work, and become aware of our own tradition as a medium surrounding and supporting us and pervading all our attitudes and perceptions. In becoming aware of the nature of our tradition we can become aware also of the nature and extent of the changes that have taken place in it over the past seventy years or so.

I discussed in the previous chapter various features of western classical music that make it unique in the world's musical cultures. We should not allow our familiarity with this music to delude us into thinking that these features represent the only, or even necessarily the most sophisticated, way of making music; each has been bought at great cost in other ways. The modulatory freedom and expressive flexibility of tonal functional harmony, for example, is gained at the expense of a rigidity of pitch and a type of mistuning, the equal temperament scale, that other cultures would find intolerable, and which we can in fact make tolerable only through the use of vibrato to blur the edges of the pitch, and at the expense of a simplification of rhythm that other cultures might consider childish. Our generation is fortunate in its ability to summon up, through gramophone records, and the occasional visits of folkloristic theatrical companies, virtually all the world's musical cultures, from the apparently simplest and most primitive to the great cultures of the east and Africa. Although this type of listening fails to give us access to what may be the most important aspect of the music – its social aspect – we are nonetheless able to hear how the music *sounds* in a way denied to previous generations. But really to hear this music on its own terms, one must divest oneself of many of the expectations and assumptions of western music – not really so difficult a task as might be imagined – and try to discover its real concerns. Among the assumptions that should be rejected are the following:

1. the idea of music as a self-contained art, to be contemplated for its own sake, usually in buildings or spaces set aside for the purpose, and at times set aside from everyday life, by audiences who are, in the words of Curt Sachs, 'wholly devoted to its artful elaboration';[2]
2. the idea of a musical composition as having an abstract existence apart from the performer and the performance, to which the performer aspires to present as close an approximation as he can, as well as the idea of the composer as one who is set aside from both performer and audience, a man with something of his own to communicate – indeed, the whole idea of music as communication;
3. the idea that the techniques of harmony and harmonically governed counterpoint to achieve the composer's expressive ends are supreme musical resources and that they predominate as musical techniques over all the other elements of music;
4. the prime attention given to pitch relationships and the relative lack of interest in tone colour, texture and timbre, at least as structural elements;
5. the acceptance of the impoverishment of the rhythmic element in music and relative lack of attention to it as an organizing principle;
6. the idea of music as the conscious articulation of time so that one always knows or expects to know where one is in relation to the beginning and the end – indeed, the idea of music as a linear progression in time from a clear-cut beginning to a fore-ordained end; and
7. the idea that it is necessary to use conscious devices, such as the large harmonic forms, to make clear the articulation in time and prevent the listener from becoming lost in time.

In most non-European cultures, music is regarded almost as a part of technology, that is, as one of the skills of staying alive and well. As Sachs says, 'Everything that sounds, be it in the cruder form of frightening noise or the organized patterns of music, bears the brunt of mankind's eternal strife against the forces that threaten his life and welfare.'[3] It is in fact a kind of magic (we can use that word without any suggestion of patronizing the cultures under discussion since belief in magic is as common in our culture as elsewhere, reluctant as we may be to face the fact) to conquer fear, increase communal feeling and come to terms with the environment. Its purpose, as Wilfred Mellers says, is 'not to express but to reveal. There is no audience to be communicated with, since composer-performer and his listeners are both participants in a rite.'[4] The music is not performed as 'me', the composer or performer, addressing 'you', the audience, but as all of us, of whom some may be musicians and some not, taking part in the common ritual or activity, a situation to which the nearest equivalent in western culture today may be that of the choir and congregation in the celebration of the Roman mass. The composer-performer's personality is unimportant; he is merely the vessel through which the music passes (although this is not to deny the existence of outstanding composers or performers in non-European traditions). The idea of a concert or performance in our sense of the word is thus virtually unknown. It would be possible, as do many writers on ethnomusicology, to quote examples from musical cultures across the whole world illustrating differences between non-western attitudes and those of the western tradition as enumerated above. One could cite, for example, the gamut of twenty-two pitches (or *srutis*) to the octave used by Indian classical musicians, whose intervals lack the mechanical regularity of the tempered scale, as well as the *ragas,* or scalic orders, on which the players' improvisations are constructed, each of which belongs to a certain time or season and is not to be used at other times. One might cite the fact that despite the wealth of literary allusion to and theoretical writing about music among the ancient Greeks, and the esteem in which music was clearly held in that enormously sophisticated culture, it was entirely lacking in harmony in any sense that we understand the term. We might consider the Eskimo, a race of singers and poets who settle quarrels by contests in song, and among whom it is a severe insult to assert that a certain person 'cannot even sing', or the Aboriginals of Arnhem Land, throughout whose life, according to William Malm, 'music is used ... to teach him what he must know about his culture, about his place in it and his place in the world of nature and supernature ... His maturation can be measured in the esoteric knowledge he has acquired through song, and as an old man he knows that his honour is based partly on his mastery of the secret sacred songs of the band.'[5] Or ancient

China, where, according to Curt Sachs, 'Correctness in music was not mainly, if at all, a musical concern. It was essential to the cosmos ... in music (man) took the heavy responsibility for either strengthening or imperilling the equilibrium of the world. And his responsibility included the world's truest images, the dynasty and the country; the welfare of the empire depended on the correctness of pitches and scales.'[6] Lest we should think this merely the conceit of a primitive, superstitious people, William Malm reminds us that 'the ancient Chinese were skilled, knowledgeable acousticians. Many of the fanciful legends and terms were actually ancient ways of reporting important scientific and musical findings derived from controlled, empirical experiments. At least two thousand years ago, Chinese scientists knew as much about soundproof research laboratories, the laws of vibrations and tuning as did western scientists at the turn of the present century.'[7]

But a proliferation of such examples of other possible techniques and attitudes in music would serve merely to confuse, and I propose therefore to examine in some detail two important musical cultures, their technical features, their performance conventions and methods of education, as well as the position and role of music in the society which they inhabit, and to try to find what this can tell us of the nature of that society. Both cultures, those of Bali and of black Africa (in the latter, despite a rich diversity, many features are to be found which enable us to view it as a single culture), are abundantly documented both in print and on record; although the performance traditions and social relations of the art need to be studied at second hand, we have nonetheless a number of reliable observers who can flesh out our speculations and lend them confirmation or refutal.

First, Bali, that tiny populous island lying to the east of Java across a narrow strait, and boasting one of the richest artistic traditions of all the human race. So all-pervasive in fact are the arts that the Balinese have no word for art, or artist — art is not regarded as in any way a separate activity but simply as part of the Balinese concern for 'doing things as well as possible'. It is in a sense difficult to discuss even music as a separate art, since it is inextricably mingled with the ceremonies of the Balinese, the innumerable temple festivals, the dance, the night-long dramatic performances using either live actor-dancers or shadow puppets, the riotous funeral ceremonies, and simply their daily lives. One must regretfully qualify any observations with the caution that they refer to traditional Balinese life, which is fast disappearing, like so many of the other cultures of the world, under the impact of western economic colonization; wherever western capitalism and consumer values go, western music is there also, and there are few eastern cities today that do not boast their western-style symphony orchestra, military bands or innumerable night-club and café groups, playing too often in poor imitation of the gestures of late-romantic symphonic music or middle-European café music, which local musicians have been persuaded, or forced through economic necessity, to accept as superior to the indigenous music.

Thus, we read that in Java tape recordings are replacing live gamelans at village ceremonies, while the gamelans themselves are kept mainly for display to tourists. The idea of villagers using tapes to accompany their age-old shadow plays and dances would be comic were it not so clear an indication that here, as in the rest of the world, interest has shifted from the creative process to the production of music as a commodity, and that the values of the consumer society are coming, even in these paradisiacal islands, to dominate the culture. In much of Africa, too, as the highly sophisticated tribal organization dissolves to be replaced by the cruder functional relations of commerce and consumerism, so the values and conventions of western music are coming to dominate, while the inherited music and ways of performing are relegated to the picturesque past and the tourist trade. Africans have of course always proved immensely adaptable, and the collision between their music and that of Europe has been one of the few good and fruitful consequences of the disaster of slavery. Similarly, the imposition of western values on present-day Africa has produced some extremely vigorous hybrid growths, as well as a few stunted monsters (as much where Africans have tried to imitate the ways of western classical music as where Europeans have tried to ape African ways); as is almost invariably the case where two cultures collide the most vigorous growths are to be found among the unregarded music of the people rather than among the more consciously sophisticated music of their social betters.

Bearing these facts in mind, then, we must regretfully confine our discussion to the music of the traditional African and Balinese cultures, music that dates from before the principal impact of western ways was felt. I shall speak of the music, and of society, in what is known as the 'anthropological present', using the present tense, inaccurately but usefully, to describe the culture as it was in the period when Europeans were able to encounter it without materially changing it. This 'anthropological present' may in fact refer to a real present in certain remote parts, or may refer to a period that ended anything up to fifty years ago in areas that succumbed quickly to European influence. As far as traditional Balinese music and society are concerned we are fortunate that a number of sensitive artists, musicians and anthropologists lived in Bali over a long period in the thirties, when the society was still largely untouched, at least outside the governmental and administrative centres, by western influence. These included the anthropologists Margaret Mead, Gregory Bateson and Jane Belo, the artists Walter Spies and Miguel Covarrubias, and the composer Colin McPhee, whose monumental *Music in Bali* remains the classic in this field.

The primary, and most famous, musical body of Bali, as of Java, is the gamelan, an orchestra of up to thirty players, who use bronze-keyed metallophones with tuned bamboo resonators, bronze gongs, both tuned and untuned, cymbals, one or more flutes and a pair of hand-beaten double-ended drums, one of which is played by the leader of the group. This orchestra produces sonic structures of great delicacy, rhythmic vigour and intricacy whose organizing principle is that of simultaneous variation on a simple, slow-moving theme; this 'nuclear theme' is carried by the low-pitched instruments and doubled one and two octaves higher by smaller metallophones which play ingeniously varied and embellished variations on it. The flutes usually double the nuclear theme, the drums give a regular beat, while the phrases of the music are punctuated by strokes on the various gongs. The music is generally built on one of two pentatonic scales, each extracted from a notional seven-tone scale, neither of which is exactly the same as our familiar 'black-key' scale; one, called *slendro*, is practically an equal division of the octave into five intervals, while the other, *pelog,* approximates to our notes C sharp, D, E, G sharp, A. It will be seen that the latter scale, unlike the black-key scale, incorporates both semitones of our diatonic scale, and this gives rise to much more dissonance than the black-key scale, which has no semitones; this feature the Balinese apparently enjoy, since they emphasize it by a slight deliberate mistuning of the higher, doubling instruments. The music is of course completely non-harmonic; the concourse of several simultaneous sounds is due entirely to the interplay of the various instrumental 'parts' and their elaborate heterophonic interweaving, so that there is nothing of that sense of anticipation, of being drawn towards a climax, which one finds in western harmonic music. We find ourselves, to use McPhee's words, 'in a state of music'; he says, 'the primary utilitarian nature of this music ... emphasizes a conception rather different from ours – that music may be something which is *not to be listened to in itself* ... Never will it become personal, or contain an emotion. At a ceremony its presence is as necessary as incense, flowers and offerings. Here a *state of music* is required for a certain time, nothing else.'[9] (McPhee's italics). In fact, the whole concept of climax and resolution, so central to the western arts that exist in time, is completely lacking in Balinese music, which McPhee describes as circular, in which 'each section of a composition returns to the opening note and repeats immediately, the final note generating a new beginning.'[10]

The music is almost never played in a concert performance, but exists always as accompaniment to the temple ceremonies, the dance dramas that retell in highly stylized form the ancient Hindu myths and legends, the *wayang* shadow plays in which the shadows of intricately-designed leather puppets are thrown on a screen, the antics of the Barong, that strange benevolent but capricious beast animated, like an enormously lively pantomime horse, by two men, as he engages in his endless and forever inconclusive struggles against the evil witch Rangda and her minions, the noble and virile *baris* dances, or the *kebyar,* a twentieth-century dance in which the dancer remains seated throughout, accompanied by a brilliant tempestuous virtuosic music (*kebyar* means to flare, to burst into flame). The forms and styles of Balinese music are many, but the purpose is always the same: to provide a 'state of music', a background against which the dances, the ceremonies and the dramas are enacted, and without which they would be useless.

There are few professional musicians in Bali; the music is created and performed by farmers, merchants, even princes and children, who form themselves into clubs and play wherever and whenever they are called upon to do so, for amounts of money that barely cover the expenses of maintaining the gorgeously decorated instruments. McPhee reports that in one village where he lived, with a population of about two thousand, there were no less than ten of these clubs, each of which specialized in one aspect of the ritual music. The lead in artistic matters tended to be given by the large gamelans supported by the local princes, who were likely to take part on a completely egalitarian basis in the orchestra or dance group; differences in age, profession and caste disappear in the gamelan. Beryl de Zoete reported that one of the finest gamelans in

Bali was headed by a chauffeur, while his assistant was a boy of about five.

Gamelans rehearse in the evenings after the day's work, but even the concept of rehearsal is different from ours. The composition to be learnt is taught by imitation by a musician, perhaps from another village or from a princely gamelan, but each player has a creative contribution to make, offering suggestions which may or may not be incorporated into the music. Unlike amateur players in the west, who are aware that they are attempting something that has been done innumerable times before, and vastly better, by others, these performers are making their creative contribution to the very substance of what will eventually be uniquely their own piece. Rehearsals are public, and watched with interest by the other villagers or townsmen, who comment with perception on the performance and will often offer suggestions. The piece thus grows under the eyes of all, and the actual 'performance' is very little different in atmosphere from the rehearsals. It takes not infrequently six months for a gamelan to work out the intricate details of a piece and attain the precision of ensemble that is the hallmark of a good performance. Each player has in fact a fairly uncomplicated part to play; it is in the interaction of the various parts that the complex musical texture arises.

The education of young musicians takes place, not in academies or schools, but within the gamelan itself. Children are always to be found in the front rank of any group watching rehearsals or performances and in an all-night shadow play they will doze off, awaken, and loudly applaud the more exciting passages. It is in fact not necessary during these performances to observe every detail, as we in the west feel obliged to do; as Beryl de Zoete says, 'Watching dancing ... is almost a state of being, a feeling rather than an action. We gaze and gaze with an earnestness that fatigues us long before the dance is over. The Balinese ... enters into the atmosphere of the dance and remains there as in a familiar landscape. Nature does not make perpetual demands on one's attention, nor does a dance performance on the Balinese. It is just there to be enjoyed in a variety of ways.'[11] Children are accustomed from the very beginning to the intricate rhythms and elaborate non-harmonic polyphony of the music, and many begin to play at an early age. More than one writer has described how a member of a gamelan, during a performance, would take his small son on his lap, putting the metallophone keys into the tiny hands and guiding them to the proper keys at the proper time.

Margaret Mead sums up a great deal of the position of music in traditional Balinese society in four paragraphs which I make no apology for quoting entire:

The Balinese may comment with amusement but without surprise if the leading metallophone player in a noted orchestra is so small that he has to have a stool in order to reach the keys; the same mild amusement may be expressed if someone takes up a different art after his hands have a tremor of age to confuse their precision. But in a continuum within which the distinction between the most gifted and the least gifted is muted by the fact that everyone participates, the distinction between child and adult — as performer, as actor, as musician — is lost, except in those cases where the distinction is ritual, as where a special dance requires a little girl who has not yet reached puberty.

In Bali the absence of sequence even in the life-span of the individual and the absence of discontinuity between ritual role and everyday role seems crucial. The artist, the dancer, the priest, is also a husbandman, who tills his rice fields. Occasionally an artist becomes so famous that he lets his fingernails grow as he does no other work, and, say the Balinese, he begins to grow fat and careless and lazy, and his artistic skills decrease. The priest may stand robed in white during the ceremony, officiating at the long ritual of inviting the gods down to earth, dressing them, feeding them, bathing them, presenting them with dance and theatre, and then sending them back for another two hundred and ten days in heaven. But the day after the ceremony he is a simple citizen of the village, only owing the land he cultivates to his work on feast days as guardian of the temple.

Nor is there any gap between professional and amateur. There are virtually no amateurs in Bali, no folk dancing in which people do traditional things without responsibility to an artistic canon. There are enormous differences in skill and grace and beauty of performance, but prince and peasant, very gifted and slightly gifted, all do what they do seriously and become, in turn, critical spectators, laughing with untender laughter at the technical failures of others. Between the audience that gathers to watch the play and the players there is always the bond of professional interest, as the audience criticizes the way the actor or actress who plays the princess postures or sings, rather than identifying with her fate — however lost she may be in some dense theatrical forest.

Nor is there any gap between rehearsal and performance. From the moment an orchestra begins to practise an old piece of music, there is a ring of spectators, aspiring players, substitute players, small boys and old men, all equally engrossed in the ever-fresh creation of a new way of playing an old piece of music.[11]

We see thus that music in Bali is an intensely communal art. Compositions are not notated, but are carried from one community to another by admired musicians, to be re-created as each community builds its own variations on the piece. Gamelans move around a good deal, especially during festive seasons, carrying their music with them. The pacesetters are in general the old princely courts, which vie with one another in the splendour and excellence of the spectacles, but their creations are not cut off from even the humblest of the peasants who crowd into the courtyard to see and hear. New ideas very quickly become common property, though always with the individual accent of each village or town; new clubs are constantly forming and reforming, according to the presence or absence of gifted and enthusiastic individuals. A village may decide to have a Barong and set out to make costumes and masks, as well as to rehearse the music that accompanies him. Strolling players go during the festivals from one village to the next, taking with them their Barong, who is received as a god; as Margaret Mead says, 'Thus the strolling players who carry from one part of Bali to the other new forms and old forms, newly refurbished, are given dignity and security.'[12]

It will be clear that improvisation plays no part in a gamelan performance; compositions are worked out in rehearsal, parts added and removed, variations invented, new instrumental timbres tried out, but once they are decided upon and rehearsed they are fixed, and no deviation can take place without upsetting the precision and clarity for which, despite the intricacy of the texture, each musician strives. And indeed the precision of a good gamelan performance is to be marvelled at; the players negotiate lightning changes of tempo, dynamics and the lively but subtle rhythmic patterns with an accuracy and panache that would do credit to a professional symphony orchestra in the west. There is not much scope, either, for individual virtuosity. Each individual instrumental part, in itself, makes no great demands on the player; the skill lies in the integration of each part into the whole, the precise timing of the beater stroke, the interaction of two instruments which may share the same melodic line — all demanding communal rather than individual virtuosity, social rather than individualistic skills.

This does not, however, mean that pieces are fixed for all time in the manner of a classic in western music; the Balinese have little respect for the idea of note-for-note fidelity to an original, and, as a new piece is learnt, each musician will have his chance of making modifications, so that the same piece may exist in as many forms as there are gamelans which play it. Since the delight of the musicians is as much in the invention of new ornaments and variations during rehearsal as in actual performance, the pieces are constantly evolving. The players revel in the process of creation and care less about the finished product, which may well disappear unmourned when the musicians become tired of it. Their contact with the past is not through a number of fixed classics as in western music, but through the continuity provided by gradual change. They care nothing for the idea of progress. It is quite possible that a certain innovation may in fact be a revival of something that was done in an earlier time and lost, but this does not concern the Balinese; as with many other oriental peoples their concept of time is not linear but circular. Consequently, there can be no point in trying to hold on to a work from the past, since the past is not, as we believe, irretrievably lost; it will recur, and, when the time is ready, so will the appropriate art forms. This circularity of time is revealed not only in the music but also in many of the rituals and social customs of Bali. For example, the terms for great-grandfather and great-grandson are the same; since these are those most distant ancestors or descendants a man is likely to encounter in his lifetime, the identification of the two generations suggests the idea of generations recurring and recurring in endless cycles, a notion that is reinforced by the fact that when a man dies his great-grandchildren, should there be any, are forbidden to mourn him.

The calendar similarly reflects the circularity of the Balinese sense of time. It measures, not the elapsing of time, but the characteristics of the various parts of time-cycles. The Balinese do in fact keep a solar-lunar calendar, as one might expect of a mainly agrarian people, but it is of less importance in their lives (the fact that they are a tropical people naturally makes the changing of the seasons less emphatic than in temperate climates) than a second calendar, which marks off the rotation of a number of cycles of day-names. These are cycles of from two to ten days, and, as the various cycles coincide (eg the five- and six-day cycles will coincide every thirty days) so festivals are held. As the most important cycles are those of five, six and seven days, so the major festival of the year takes place once every two hundred and ten days; this is called Galungan.

Clifford Geertz notes, 'Details aside, the nature of time reckoning this sort of calendar facilitates is clearly not durational but punctual. That is, it is not used (and could only with much awkwardness and the addition of some ancillary devices be used) to measure the rate at which time passes, the amount that has passed since the occurrence of some event, or the amount which remains in which to complete some project; it is adapted to and used for distinguishing and classifying discrete, self-subsistent particles of time – "days". The cycles and supercycles are endless, unanchored, uncountable, and, as their internal order has no significance, without climax. They do not accumulate, they do not build, and they are not consumed. They don't tell you what time it is; they tell you what kind of time it is.'[13]

The absence of climax is a frequently remarked-upon feature of Balinese life; we have already noticed it in Balinese music. As Gregory Bateson says, 'In general the lack of climax is characteristic of Balinese music, drama and other art forms. The music typically has a progression, derived from the logic of the formal structure, and modifications of intensity determined by the duration and progress of the working out of these formal relations. It does not have the rising intensity and climax structure characteristic of modern Occidental music, but rather a formal progression.'[14] Bateson finds a direct relationship between this characteristic of Balinese art and Balinese character in general, remarking, for example, on Balinese child-rearing habits which are directed towards lessening the sense of climax, by breaking off stimulation as it approaches climax, or by teasing, which also has the effect of diminishing the child's tendency towards competitive behaviour. He remarks that quarrels in Bali seem rarely if ever to come to a head, but fizzle out, and be dealt with in society by a formal acknowledgement of the positions of both parties. Even wars, to the extent that they did take place, were conducted on a kind of Duke of Plaza-Toro basis, with the sides making every effort to keep clear of each other (it is no wonder that they fell such easy prey to the Dutch in the early years of this century!) This easy adaptation is, however, not perfect or complete, and some of the tensions of Balinese life (Margaret Mead compares their grace to that of the tight-rope walker) find expression in socially accepted form in trance-dances where self-mutilation is not unknown, and occasionally in unacceptable form when an individual runs amok, in an orgy of killing and destruction, and often has himself to be killed.

This absence of the sense of climax is closely allied to one of the most important characteristics of Balinese life, one which must surely be a vital formative influence on Balinese music: activities in general are carried out not as a progression towards some desired but deferred goal, but as inherently satisfying in themselves. The valuing of the moment for its own sake does not necessarily make for improvidence (any gardener will agree that planting is every bit as satisfying as harvesting) but is quite at variance with that western habit of thought which was called by Max Weber the Protestant Ethic; this habit of putting off present satisfaction for the sake of future advantage will be discussed later. The Balinese temper shows itself, for example, in a highly developed and subtle kinaesthetic sense, a concern for physical elegance, an urge to do things well, that is, with the utmost possible grace, even panache, and a preoccupation with ritual and ceremonial, private as well as public. It does not lend itself to long-term acquisitiveness or to the embarkation upon large enterprises entailing lengthy sacrifices whose realization may not be seen for some years (this may or may not be a bad thing) or to willingness to work factory hours or make the sacrifices of spontaneity necessary for the growth of industrialization. Its relation to Balinese music, with its lack of harmonic tensions and absence of climax, designed as it is to be enjoyed moment by moment, is clear.

I must emphasize again that since the end of the second world war these values have become severely eroded as western commercial values and consumerism take over; the change from artistic creation as a process involving the whole community to art as a commodity made for sale by a few professional artists has happened here, as throughout the non-European world, staggeringly quickly. As the Balinese are taken over by industrial values time becomes itself a scarce commodity, to be spent carefully, so it comes about that gamelans become played only for the benefit of tourists in the main centres, while the villages use time-saving tape recordings to accompany the remaining ceremonies and their instruments themselves lie rotting in a shed. Meanwhile, colleges and universities throughout the west have acquired their own sets of gamelan instruments, and earnest students, under the tutelage of a Balinese or Javanese musician, are maintaining at least something of the ancient art — ironically, it is in our society only students who find it possible to suspend industrial time. It is possible that these young musicians are seeking in the patient process of learning the techniques of the gamelan something of the old ethic of Balinese society, its continuity, its communality and disregard for western notions of time, as an antidote to the malaise of our own driven society. In this they are unlikely to find anything more than temporary solace; divorced from its ritual and ceremonial roots and performed under western concert conditions the music simply becomes another exotic sensation, another kind of musical experience to add to the dazzling variety available to listeners in our own time, another influence on the contemporary composer of concert music, fascinating and beautiful, but offering no promise for the longed-for renewal of western musical art.

By contrast, the meeting between European and African music has been one of the most fruitful exchanges in the entire history of music. I refer not only to the well-known forms of blues and jazz but to the whole culture of Afro-American music as it exists today along the entire length of the American continents and the Caribbean, everywhere in fact where African slaves were taken. This may be, as Gunther Schuller suggests,[15] because there were enough similarities between the two musics to make a synthesis possible, but I believe it is even more because the Africans, torn abruptly from their native soil, subjected to innumerable hardships and degradations, were obliged to remake a culture from whatever shreds and fragments that were to hand. African music was, and is, by no means a primitive art (whatever that might be) but a foremost expression of a subtle and spiritual people who had colonized the entire vast and often inhospitable continent and evolved political structures that in the main succeeded where our own have so signally failed: to contain the unbridled ambition of individuals and to keep the structures of society small enough to be workable (tyrannies and empires such as those of Dingiswayo and Shaka were mainly a response to the disruption of African ways by European colonization). As Basil Davidson says, 'Where, after all, lay the precedent for the social and ideological structures built by the Africans, so various and so resilient, so intricately held together, so much a skilful interweaving of the possible and the desirable? Where did these systems draw their sap and vigour except from populations who evolved them out of their creativeness?'[16] That creativeness shows itself most prominently in the arts; 'In a deep sense,' says Davidson, 'the arts of non-literate Africa composed its holy books and testaments.'[17] And of all the arts of Africa, the most pervasive and richly developed is its music. Even among the slaves, as one Reverend John Davies of Virginia reported in a letter to John Wesley about 1735, 'I cannot but observe that the Negroes, above all the human species I ever knew, have the nicest ear for music.'[18] Indeed, so all-pervasive is music in African culture that many African languages, as Francis Bebey observes, have no word for it; they have words for musical forms and types, but the great art itself is so much part of the environment that it is not seen as possessing a separate identity.

We should remember, too, that Africa never was the 'dark continent' of popular imagination; it has a history, which is today being pieced together, of sophisticated, humane culture which is as long as that of the human race, of which it is in all probability the cradle. Travel was free and trade flourished, not only with the Arab world, but also with ancient Greece, and even China and Indonesia (it was probably from Indonesia that the African xylophone was imported). It had great cities also, not only Benin, which was visited in the 17th and 18th centuries by many travellers who declared it to be as splendid as any European city, but also a chain of trading cities which astonished Vasco da Gama after he rounded the Cape of Good Hope with their 'wealth and urban comfort, their tall ships ... and commerce in gold and ivory' (Davidson[19]), and which he and his successors promptly proceeded to loot and burn. As Africa is an enormous continent, it is not surprising that it is not culturally homogeneous, or that its music should show great variation, not only between the Arab north and the Negro centre and south, but also from region to region, country to country and tribe to tribe. Nonetheless, there are certain features that are common at least to the music of black Africa, and it is these that I shall now discuss briefly.

First, we should rid ourselves once and for all of any idea that African music is primitive; when western musicians speak of 'primitive music' they are generally discussing a music which is interested in other matters than those with which our music is concerned. Where the main interest of European music, as we have seen, is pitch relations and especially harmony, that of Africa is rhythm. Some western commentators have not been slow to suggest that this is in itself proof of a primitive character, since rhythm is of all the elements of music the most corporeal, the closest to the body, and it is true that most black people are on the whole less alienated from their physical being than most Europeans; but to label this state primitive says as much about those who do the labelling as it does of those who are labelled. At any rate, our concern here is to look at African music on its own terms, not in relation to any criteria that non-Africans might care to erect, and to try to learn what it can teach us about the nature of our own musical culture.

As in Bali, as indeed in nearly all non-European societies, music is not separate from everyday life but is an integral part of it; to listen as we do to, say, a symphony, is as unknown in traditional African culture as it is in Bali. That is not to say that Africans do not perform to one another or to themselves purely for entertainment; such music forms an important part of African life. Nor does it mean that everyone is an expert performer or that there are no professional musicians in traditional African culture, but the relation between performer and listener is of an entirely different kind, since both are intimately connected within a community. The detachment with which a western listener contemplates an orchestral performance plays no part in their musical life and customs, and in most music there is opportunity for participation, singing choral parts, handclapping and dancing. Even when listening to a performance the listeners will react loudly and actively to the music without inhibitions, since, as J.H.K. Nketia says, not only does motor response increase enjoyment of the music, but it also provides opportunity for social interaction in a musical context.[20]

Music is found in all the situations of life, from everyday activities to the great rituals of chiefs and kings. Apart from more obvious examples such as cradle songs, work songs and the like, of a kind familiar from western folk song, there are songs which form part of initiation rituals, as well as carrying gossip or news, praise or insult, warnings or exhortations to their listeners. The 'songs of the elders' remind people of their past and of the values of a society, chronicle the history of the people and reassure them of the legitimacy of their chiefs and kings. Other songs deal with religious and philosophical matters, while various occupations such as hunters, fishermen or herdsmen have their own songs telling the praises of those whom they hunt or husband. Kings may employ professional singers to tell their praises; these usually belong to an hereditary caste, called *griots*.

Even more than the drum, the human voice is at the heart of African music; few performances lack some part for it. The voice is never 'trained' in the western sense to produce sounds remote from those of speech; the vocal music of Africa bears a very intimate relationship to speech (especially is this true of those peoples whose

language is tonal, depending for its meanings, as does Chinese, on·
vocal inflections as well as on actual word forms), and their
technique is devoted to as faithful a rendition as possible of
heightened speech. They use a dazzling variety of types of singing,
depending on the dramatic situation required: head tones, chest
tones, grunts, whispers, whistles, amazingly realistic imitations of
bird, animal and other natural sounds, ululations and yodels; all are
part of their repertory of sounds. Unlike western singers, Africans
deliberately cultivate strong differences between the various
registers of the voice, even emphasizing the breaks between them,
from a growl to a falsetto, even almost a scream, as well as using
with virtuosity the various harmonic and non-harmonic sounds of
which the human voice is capable.

All writers agree that, to an African, a beautiful voice does not
make a good singer; indeed, whether a singer has or has not a
beautiful voice is irrelevant. Rather, it is the artistic use he makes of
what he has. The nearest parallel in our culture to this concept is
perhaps in the orator, who will discover and make use of his own
peculiarities of voice, appearance and deportment, not according to
any accepted canon of taste or vocal quality but in a way which
helps him to communicate what he is as well as what he has to say
in the most effective way possible. We find it, too, in popular and
folk singers (Bob Dylan, Rod Stewart, and, in another field, Rex
Harrison are three who spring to mind) who may have no 'singing
voice' in the classical sense but have made their voices into telling
and eloquent expressive instruments.

Pre-eminent as the voice undoubtedly is, African musicians also
play a wide range of instruments. Most Europeans in thinking of
African music think of drumming, but in fact nearly every type of
instrument we know in European music, with the exception of the
keyboard, has some kind of counterpart in Africa — fiddles, lyres,
lutes, a curious and beautiful hybrid harp-lute called the kora,
horns, flutes, as well as idiophones such as xylophones, rattles, bells
and the like, even metal castanets and tuned stones. There is also an
instrument which is unique to Africa (although a Europeanized
version has recently been placed on the market) which is indeed
almost universal throughout black Africa under various names:
mbira, kalimba, sansa, ikembe, or, in English, African piano or
thumb piano. This consists of a small sounding board a few inches
long to which is attached a number of metal or wooden tines, fixed at
one end, passing over a bridge and free at the other. Like the guitar it
is a very intimate instrument; the player holds it close to him in both

hands and strokes rather than plucks the tines with his thumbs (Europeans trying the instrument for the first time almost invariably pluck too hard and spoil its delicate tone). A small instrument may have only half a dozen tines, but a large mbira may have as many as forty-five, arranged often in two or three manuals; the sounding board may be mounted on a hollow box or placed inside a gourd, both of which act as resonators, and the instrument gives a gentle, haunting sound (there is a great and surprising gentleness in most African music) that is like no other instrument on earth. To take a musical instrument in one's hand will often tell one much about its culture of origin even before one strikes a single sound from it, and the mbira shows this well. First, it personifies the intimate relationship that exists between an African musician and his instrument; the chances are that he will have made it himself, since there are few professional instrument makers, or if he has received it from another it will most likely have been a gift or an inheritance. Selling an instrument is rare; Francis Bebey tells how he tried to buy an instrument from a fine local musician, to be told, coolly, that he, the musician, had come to town to play his drum for the dancing, not to deliver a slave into bondage.[21] The instruments are not mere objects, but colleagues in the work of creation, and symbols, as Bebey says, of the time when God imbued man with life and speech.[22]

Secondly, around each tine of the mbira is wound loosely a piece of metal, which when the tine is plucked buzzes with a non-harmonic sound that lies like a sheen over the music. It is a kind of sound which, if a western classical musician heard it in his instrument, he would take the instrument apart to find and eliminate. Yet Africans seem to love it, as they fill their music with non-harmonic sound, from drums, rattles, scrapers and the like. Even the Chopi of Mozambique, of whom I shall have more to say later, place across the mouths of the gourd resonators under the keys of their xylophones the egg-cases of certain spiders, as thin and flexible as rice paper, to superimpose a buzzing sound on the notes of the instruments. The love of non-harmonic and percussive sounds shows itself too in the predominance of plucked over bowed stringed instruments, and above all in the love of drums and drumming. The love of drum sounds, allied with the emphasis on rhythm as the primary organizing principle, is responsible for some of the most exciting and beautiful of all music.

Thirdly, each individual instrument differs slightly from all others. Instruments do of course fall into broad types, but each is an individual with its own characteristic virtues and defects. Musicians also emerge much more as individuals than do their western counterparts; this is due partly to the individuality of each instrument but also to the fact that formal training is usually very brief. The musician may be taught the rudiments of his instrument, but after that he pays little attention to technical matters for their own sake. He does not practise; he plays. As Nketia says, 'Traditional instruction is not generally organized on a formal institutional basis, for it is believed that natural endowment and a person's natural ability to develop on his own are essentially what is needed. This endowment could include innate knowledge, for, according to the Akan, "One does not teach the blacksmith's son his father's trade. If he knows it, then it is God who taught him." The principle ... seems to be that of learning through social experience. Exposure to musical situations and participation are emphasized more than formal teaching. The organization of traditional music in social life enables the individual to acquire his musical knowledge in slow stages and to widen his experience of the music of his culture through the social groups into which he is slowly absorbed and through the activities in which he takes part.'[23] This of course does not mean that the techniques of African music are to be acquired quickly or casually; a man may play his drum for years before he is accepted as a master drummer, if indeed he is ever so accepted. It does, however, mean that the same kind of instrument may be played in a multitude of different styles; as Bebey points out, technique is very much a matter of individual taste. He says, 'The absence of technique – in the western sense of the term – does not imply a corresponding absence of artistry. Art is a utility, and, as we have already seen, music is a necessity – a vital function. Music is the outward and audible manifestation of inward biological functions; it is the support and realization of their metaphysical purpose.'[24]

The highest achievement of African music is undoubtedly in the field of rhythm. 'Rhythm', says A.M. Jones, whose *Studies in African Music* is the classic of its field, 'is to the African what harmony is to the European, and it is in the complex interweaving of contrasting rhythmic patterns that he finds his greatest aesthetic satisfaction. To accomplish this he has built up a rhythmic principle that is quite different from that of Western music and yet is present in his simplest songs ... Whatever be the devices used to produce them, in African music there is practically always a *clash of rhythms*; this is a cardinal principle. Even a song which appears to be mono-rhythmic will on investigation turn out to be constructed of two independent but strictly related rhythmic patterns, one inherent in the melody and one belonging to the accompaniment.'[25]

It is child's play to an African to sing (to use European terms) in a constantly changing metre while preserving a strict hand-clapping pattern of the type *1 2 1 2 1 2 3 1 2 1 2* 3; often there are anything up to half a dozen or eight different patterns made by drums, handclaps, other instruments and voices, all making not only different patterns but working in different metres with different points of accentuation, so that downbeats do not coincide. Moreover, the master drummer, to whose beat all other musicians must conform, may be continually changing his patterns. The only element holding the performance together is the beat, which is identical for all the lines; around this one constant factor are built complex and fascinating rhythmic structures which most Europeans can scarcely comprehend, much less perform.

The emphasis on rhythm does not, however, mean that African music is melodically deficient. There is a wide variety of scales (though African musicians do not think in those terms), not only of four, five, six or seven tones to the octave (the pentatonic being the most common) but also in a large number of different tunings. Very few, if any, coincide exactly with the tones of the western tempered scale (which many Africans find intolerably out of tune); each area, even each tribe or village, has its own minute shading of pitch, some even tending towards an equal division of the octave, as in our whole-tone scale. These tunings are not random or accidental, but are argued over, worked on and adjusted with methodical accuracy; a man of the Chopi, for example, moving from one village to another will need to retune his xylophone if he is to play in the orchestra. But the basic pitches, at least in vocal music, are regarded as points of reference from which the singer might move, 'bending' the pitches and sliding from one tone to the next as a jazz cornettist might – the real tones are always there by implication.

Melodic phrases tend to be short, and repetition is common; in fact repetition is one of the characteristics of African music. Improvisation is less common than one might imagine, and free improvisation without any framework whatsoever almost unknown. A call-and-response sequence may go on for several hours, with apparently monotonous repetition of the same short phrase sung by a leader and answered by the chorus, but in fact subtle variations are going on all the time, not only in the melodic lines themselves but also in their relation to the complex cross-rhythms in the accompanying drumming or handclapping. It is difficult at first for western listeners to distinguish melodies in much African vocal music; it often seems like mere exaggerated speech inflections with its slides and bendings of pitch and its unfamiliar pitch relations, but that is exactly what the melodies set out to be. The style of most African vocal music is intended 'to echo the speech and thoughts of the people as faithfully as possible and without embellishment' (Bebey[27]), and it takes Europeans some time before the different melodic contours become clear, individuated and expressive. Melody is rarely used in a personal expressive way; a poem may lament the death of a child, but it will probably be set to a lively music. 'They do not seek to evoke the reflective emotions which we associate with our sentimental ballads composed in some distant theatre land. They seek the trance-like experience of complete participation in music and dance, their own common grief. So they dance together and share together.' (Tracey[27]). The repetitions of African music have a function in time which is the reverse of our own music – to dissolve the past and the future into one eternal present, in which the passing of time is no longer noticed. A performance may go on for several hours or all night, and will have no formal beginning or end; rather, it will take some time to gather momentum and probably just fizzle out at the end when the musicians run out of energy or enthusiasm. There is no time limit set.

The music of Africa that is in general most pleasing to European ears is that which functions purely as entertainment; one is haunted by the sound of two Baoulé flutists from Guinea engaging in a polyphony of rhythms as well as of tones, by a single mbira played by a Shona musician of Rhodesia, by the sound of a Hutu shepherd breaking the silence of the night with his flute (and incidentally giving warning to prowlers that the cattle are guarded) – all these sounds and more can be heard on the increasing numbers of fine recordings now available to show the richness of African music. It is of course such contemplative music that comes off best in disc; more active ritual and communal music is reduced on record to a mere shadow of itself through the absence of action and spectacle, and above all of *involvement*.

Before ending this very brief description of African musical culture, it would be worthwhile to examine in a little more detail one group of African musicians whose particular musical skills and attitudes challenge many western notions not only about African music but also about the very basis of music and musical technique themselves. These are the Chopi, who live near the coast of Mozambique to the north of the port of Lourenço Marques. Their music was studied thoroughly in the 1940s by the ethnomusicologist Hugh Tracey, whose book *Chopi Musicians*[29] is the source for my information, although the conclusions I draw are my own.

Each of the larger Chopi villages has its own *ngodo* or orchestra with singer-dancers, presided over by its own resident composer and musical director, who is responsible for the composition of musical works of symphonic size, lasting up to an hour, for voices and *timbila* or xylophones — both words and music — which are then set to dance by a dance director. These works are in several movements, each lasting up to five or six minutes each, including an orchestral introduction (sometimes more than one) and a finale, and climaxing in the Mzeno, or Great Song, which is the heart of the work. When Dr Tracey was in Mozambique, in the mid-1940s, there were two outstanding musicians, Katini weNyamombe and Gomukomu weSimbi (to whom, in a touching gesture, he dedicates the book), and he reproduces the texts of several of their works in Chichopi and English, with an elucidation of the local and topical allusions without which even the English would be incomprehensible. These texts are ousntanding examples of the allusiveness and obliquity of African poetry, cunning mixtures of mirth and sadness, political comment and protest and just plain gossip, outbursts of vitality which remain indissolubly linked to the concrete lives of the people from whom they arose, and yet at the same time bearing a universally human and spiritual message. Tracey describes the composer's way of working (completely uninfluenced, he insists, by European music), how he builds his text first of all (which, he says, 'performs a highly social and cathartic function in a society which has no daily press, no publications, and no stage other than the village yard in which publicly to express its feelings or voice its protests against the rub of the times'[30]) then begins the musical settings, first in his mind, then developing the melodic and rhythmic ideas at his timbila, working out counter-melodies and cross-rhythms. He then calls in his fellow-musicians of the orchestra, all of whom are of course fellow-villagers, many of whom in the 40's were conscripted to work in the mines of the Rand; between them they work out the various accompanying figures and textures, usually in the form of variations on a ground, all under the leadership of the composer, who is the final arbiter of which ideas are used, and who puts the final touches to the musical composition. Then the dance leader is called in; the work is played over and he devises the dance routine to fit, calling on occasion, like any other choreographer, for a little more here, a little less there, until agreement is finally arrived at. Thus one movement of the new ngodo is completed, and movement by movement the whole work is created in this way.

The music, to judge from the few available recordings, is by any standards of a noble and satisfying richness of melody, rhythm and texture. It is complex to a degree, full of incident; it is fully composed music, yet not a word or musical sign is written down. The ability of these musicians to imagine a work of symphonic scale without putting pen to paper challenges not only many western notions of the limits of musical memory but also assumptions concerning the necessity for notation; whatever it *is* needed for, it does not seem necessary for the working-out of a composition.

But an even more important challenge to European ideas lies in the way in which these works are used. The new work is inserted into the existing work, movement by movement as it is completed, finally replacing the old completely. The old work is then forgotten; however fine or masterly it might have been (Tracey describes the musical idiom of Gomukomu as 'mature and compelling', a view which the recordings bear out), it has served its purpose and can be let go. Tracey says that Katini, who had composed at least ten mgodo, could remember only the last two or three and fragments from earlier ones, and seemed quite unworried by the fact. There was, it seems, plenty more where that came from, and like the Balinese the Chopi see no need for 'classics' to keep them in touch with their past, no need to take refuge in the past from the pressures of the present. To these African musicians it is the process of creation that is important; the product is relatively unimportant and can be discarded without compunction, a sign of a self-confidence on the part of these richly creative artists that seems to be lacking in the west.

Finally, although they are greatly admired and respected by the village communities in which they live, these composers do not stand in any way apart from it. They are supported to an extent by the community, it seems, but are certainly not professionals in any European sense. Their function is not to provide completed art works for professionals to play and the community to listen to, but to act as leaders and pacemakers in the communal work of musical and choreographic creation. It is a situation that many European composers might envy.

The two different yet in many ways similar musical cultures of black Africa and of Bali will have to stand as representatives of the innumerable cultures and societies across the world which exhibit features not shared by our own. I must emphasise that my aim in describing these musics and these societies has not been to prove them superior to that of Europe (although they undoubtedly possess features from which we might learn), but to challenge the often unexamined and even unconscious assumptions through which we view our own music and our own society. These assumptions concern not only technical features such as harmony, rhythm, tone colour and the articulation of time but also performance conventions, social relations and the function of the art in society, indeed its whole philosophical foundation. I have suggested ways in which these non-European musics might relate to their societies; I shall use these ideas later to reveal what our own music can tell us of the foundations of our own culture. First we must examine another activity which is characteristic of western society, which originated within it and has transformed not only it but latterly virtually the whole world. I refer of course to western science, which has given us a paradigm of knowledge which, while it has proved in many ways liberating and invigorating to western thought and society, at the same time bewitches us with an enchantment that is as profound and mysterious as the Mindanao Deep.

Chapter 2: Bibliography

1. LOCKSPEISER, Edward: *Debussy: His Life and Mind* Vol 1, London, Cassell (1962), p. 115.
2. SACHS, Curt: *The Wellsprings of Music,* The Hague, Martinus Nijhoff (1962), p. 124.
3. SACHS, Curt: ibid., p. 83.
4. MELLERS, Wilfrid: *Caliban Reborn — Renewal in Twentieth-Century Music,* London. Gollancz (1968), p. 6.
5. MALM, William P.: *Music Cultures of the Pacific, Near East and Asia,* Englewood Cliffs, Prentice-Hall (1967), p. 2.
6. SACHS, Curt: *The Rise of Music in the Ancient World, East and West,* New York, Norton (1943), p. 112.

7. MALM, William P., op. cit., p. 111.
8. McPHEE, Colin: *Music in Bali,* New Haven, Yale University Press, (1966), p. 15.
9. McPHEE, Colin: 'Dance in Bali' in BELO, Jane (ed.): *Traditional Balinese Culture,* New York, Columbia University Press (1970), p. 311.
10. de ZOETE, Beryl and SPIES, Walter: *Dance and Drama in Bali,* 2nd edn., London, Oxford University Press (1973), p. 16.
11 MEAD, Margaret: 'Children and Ritual in Bali' in BELO, Jane (ed): op. cit., p. 199.
12. MEAD, Margaret: 'The Strolling Players in the Mountains' in BELO, Jane (ed.): op. cit., p. 145.
13. GEERTZ, Clifford: *Person, Time and Conduct in Bali: An Essay in Cultural Analysis,* New Haven, Yale Southeast Asia Studies (1966), p. 47.
14. BATESON, Gregory: 'Bali: The Value System of a Steady State' in *Steps to an Ecology of Mind,* London, Paladin (1973), p. 86.
15. SCHULLER, Gunther: *Early Jazz: Its Roots and Musical Development,* New York, Oxford University Press (1968), p. 43.
16. DAVIDSON, Basil: *The Africans: An Entry to Cultural History,* Harmondsworth, Penguin African Library (1973), p. 36.
17. DAVIDSON, Basil: ibid., p. 137.
18. Quoted in CHASE, GILBERT: *America's Music,* 2nd edn., New York, McGraw-Hill, (1966), p. 80.
19. DAVIDSON, Basil: *Africa in History: Themes and Outlines,* London, Paladin (1964), p. 180.
20. NKETIA, J.H. Kwabena: *The Music of Africa,* London, Gollancz (1975), p. 207.
21. BEBEY, Francis: *African Music – A People's Art,* transl. Josephine Bennett, London, Harrap (1975), p. 120.
22. BEBEY, Francis: ibid., p. 120.
23. NKETIA, J.H. Kwabena: op. cit., p. 58.
24. BEBEY, Francis: op. cit., p. 132.
25. JONES, A.M.: 'African Rhythm', *Africa,* Vol XXIV, No 1, January 1954, p. 26-7.
26. BEBEY, Francis: op. cit., p. 132.
27. TRACEY, Hugh: *Chopi Musicians,* 2nd edn., London, Oxford University Press for the International African Institute (1970), p. 4.
28. TRACEY, Hugh: ibid.
29. TRACEY, Hugh: ibid., p. 3.

Just as western classical music occupies for many music lovers the whole field of musical experience, so to many thoughtful people the methods and approach of western science provide a paradigm for the acquisition of all knowledge. To such people, scientific method is the only valid means of exploring the universe, the scientific eye the only valid means of viewing it. And indeed, the spectacular achievements of European musicians from the seventeenth to the nineteenth centuries run in striking parallel to those of men of science in the same period, men such as Newton, Lavoisier, Gauss, Pasteur and Darwin. Like the music of the period, indeed like the whole of western culture of the period, it is characterized by a superb self-confidence, a certainty of its ability to subsume to itself the entire universe of knowledge. But, again like the music of the time, its methods, and in fact the nature of the knowledge gained, rest on a set of attitudes and assumptions which are not necessarily of universal validity, and which are often concealed from or only imperfectly understood by its practitioners. Just as the significance of a work of art lies deeper than its overt subject matter, so that of science lies deeper than its actual discoveries, important and influential on our thinking as those may be; both give clues to the real concerns of the culture, and I propose to devote this chapter to a consideration of the underlying assumptions and attitudes of western science.

In doing so I am painfully aware that I am challenging the expertise of many who know a great deal more about science than I; nevertheless I believe the project must be undertaken if we are to become aware of, and thus free our minds from, the limitations of the scientific worldview which has such a powerful hold on our culture, limitations which are built into the very structure of scientific thinking, in particular the universal scientific practice of transforming everything upon which it is brought to bear into an object, as something to be observed, not experienced. I should not, even so, dare to make such a challenge were I not convinced that the matter is as much a moral as an intellectual one. It is the right, if not the duty, of all to challenge on these matters the authority of experts, whom we have for too long allowed to do not only our thinking but also even our feeling for us.

We have seen that the 'classical' period of western music lasted roughly from 1600 to 1910, during which time it was characterized by a degree of logic, abstraction and isolation from everyday life that makes it more or less unique among the world's musical cultures. It is interesting, and, I believe, significant that the 'classical' period of western science (it is sometimes even known by that name) occupied almost exactly the same time-span. Whether scientific thinking or science existed before about the mid-sixteenth century depends on how one defines science. If one defines it strictly as the interrogation of objectified nature by means of controlled and repeatable experiments, and the attempt to formulate the answers in mathematical form as causal 'laws' and 'theories' (both words having a very precise meaning in the scientific context), then the middle years of the sixteenth century certainly mark its beginnings. The investigations of the ancient Greeks and the Arabs into the nature of the physical world, which have been called 'first' science in contradistinction to the 'second' science of the period we are discussing, were based on different assumptions about nature and man's relations with her. This is true also of Chinese science, which I shall discuss briefly later. To the Greeks nature was alive and permeated by mind, and man had therefore an intellectual and spiritual kinship with the whole of nature and with all creatures – an idea which, as we shall see, made impossible the development of science in its modern form, but which did perhaps make it more easy actually to *live in* the world. The methods of Greek science were accordingly different; as the questions they asked were different from ours, so were the answers they received. Second science took what it could use from those answers, Euclid's geometry for example, and consigned the rest to the realm of 'proto-' or 'primitive' science (ignoring the fact that its concerns were completely different), in much the same way as western musicians have been accustomed to dismiss non-western music.

Modern science as a way of investigating nature really began with the work of Copernicus and Giordano Bruno, and its philosophy was first made explicit in the writings of René Descartes and Francis Bacon; the first assumed the supremacy of reason over all other human functions – 'I think, therefore I am' (what kind of knowledge might arise from the seemingly more basic proposition

'I *feel,* therefore I am'?) — while the second proclaimed the possibility, if not the veritable human duty, of gaining mastery over nature through the uncovering of her modes of operation, and gave, in one majestic sentence, a key to the purposes and methods of science: 'Nature to be commanded must be obeyed'. At around the same time it was Galileo who first conceived the idea that a natural phenomenon might be susceptible to reduction to a mathematical expression, while Newton later in the seventeenth century triumphantly proved Galileo's case by his formulation of the universal law of gravitation, while admitting, uneasily, that his formula did nothing to explain the true nature of forces such as gravitation which act at a distance. Newton, who was still close enough to the beginnings of second science to have practised alchemy as well as science (the distinction is visible only by hindsight), was worried by the separation of knowledge from experience implicit in scientific work, and in his own notes to the *Opticks* puzzled over the reduction of the experience of colour to a mathematical expression.

The roots of Copernicus', of Galileo's, Bacon's and Descartes' thinking lie deep in the past of the Judaeo-Christian tradition, not merely in the famous passage in *Genesis* in which Jahweh gives Adam dominion over the whole world of nature, but, more subtly and profoundly, in the almost obsessive hatred observable throughout not only the Jewish and Christian but also the Moslem tradition, of what was called idolatry, the worshipping, as they saw it, of a natural object. A cooler eye might see this 'idolatry' as a recognition of the sacredness which suffuses the entire physical world; in a state of almost wilful obtuseness, however, these traditions failed to comprehend that what, to quote the old hymn, 'the heathen in his blindness' was bowing down to was not mere 'wood and stone' but an all-embracing divinity manifested throughout nature and brought into focus in the physical object, that the world the 'idolater' inhabited was suffused through and through with divinity (St Francis of Assisi has always been an embarrassment to the Church, but his Christian pantheism, it seems, will not go away). They failed to see, too, that the attribution of divinity exclusively to a being who resided outside the cosmos was to strip the cosmos itself of its sacredness and reduce it and all our companion beings within it to the status of mere objects, and that the attribution to the human race of an origin different from that of the rest of nature was to make us lonely intruders in a world with which we could have no relations other than those of aggression, even antagonism. Finally, the Protestant devaluation of revelatory experience and of its involvement of the total being — mind, emotion, sensation and all — as well as the construction of' elaborate theologies ('sciences of God') completed the splitting-off of man from nature, and of intellect from experience, which was necessary before 'second' science could take shape in the minds of the early thinkers. R.G. Collingwood describes this splitting-off as 'the denial that the world of nature, the world studied by physical science, is an organism, and the assertion that it is devoid of intelligence and of life.' He continues, 'It is therefore incapable of ordering its own movements in a rational manner and indeed incapable of moving itself at all. The movements which it exhibits and which the physicist interrogates are imposed upon it from without, and their regularity is due to "laws of nature" likewise imposed from without. Instead of being an organism, the world is a machine: a machine in the literal and proper sense of the word, an arrangement of bodily parts designed by an intelligent mind outside itself. The Renaissance thinkers, like the Greeks, saw in the orderliness of the natural world an expression of intelligence; but for the Greeks this intelligence was nature's own intelligence. For the Renaissance thinkers it was the intelligence of something other than nature.'[1] Important here is the implication that western science, far from being able to claim access to absolute truth, is in fact as bound by the assumptions and belief systems of its culture as is any other system of knowledge.

The implicit claim of western science to be pursuing, and gradually uncovering, portions of absolute truth brings us to the third aspect of the split that gave birth to science: that between truth and value. This may be found as far back as the later Athenian thinkers, most notable perhaps Aristotle, who was, interestingly enough, the Greek philosopher most admired by the medieval Church. Modern western science comes down heavily on the side of the idea that truth must be pursued regardless of consequences; what can be discovered must be discovered, and what is discovered is said to be value-free, being neither good nor bad. It is up to us, says the physicist as he presents us, unasked, with the split atom or the artificial gene and the consequent developments of his curiosity, to decide how we use his discovery; if it turns against us it is due to the irredeemable wickedness or stupidity of our nature. But I believe, and shall argue later, that the knowledge gained by western science is by no means morally neutral; the worldview that animates it, the motivation for its acquisition and the method of acquiring it all serve to give it a particular character.

Nature, being reduced to the status of object, has in the first place no rights in any conflict of interest with the needs, or even wants, of the human race (even this statement, we notice, implies that we have by now lost any sense of belonging to the natural world at all), and in the second place as a machine it is viewed as finite, like all machines, and therefore as ultimately and completely knowable by the human mind. The confident assumption made by the early scientists was that if a sufficiently large number of humans devoted their energies for a long enough time to the matter, even though, as Bacon put it, 'these things require ages for their accomplishment', eventually every last secret of nature would lie revealed. Nature would hold no further mystery and man would be total master. That this idea would have been inconceivable within a world view that perceived nature as living and sacred and the human race as inseparably part of her is obvious; nature had to die and ourselves become split off from her before true science could be born. The very nature of the scientific experiment depends on this attitude. The experimenter forces matter, animate or inanimate, to behave in a way unnatural to it, and in so doing obtains information concerning a certain aspect of its operation, usually one aspect at a time. He stands outside, and apart from, that on which he is experimenting and has no concern for the experience of that on which the experiment is being conducted, be it a tube of gas, a flask of acid, an amoeba, a rat, a beagle – or a human being, as witnessed by the recent sensational but surely wholly superfluous demonstration by Dr Stanley Milgram of human willingness to obey orders, however repugnant to conscience they may be.

Indeed, experience as such has no place in the scientific worldview. Scientific knowledge was – and is – viewed as an abstract body of knowledge and theory existing outside, and independently of, the person knowing, such knowledge increasing quantitatively over time, so that each generation knows more than the preceding; knowledge that took Galileo, for example, much of a lifetime to gain is now part of the mental furniture of any schoolboy. The experiences that Galileo underwent in order to obtain that knowledge are irrelevant to the nature of the knowledge itself; we are concerned, not even with the mental processes which went into it, but only with the final product of the thinking. We may be vaguely aware that he was brought before the Inquisition for his views, we may find his lively and vigorous personality interesting, even attractive, but this has nothing whatsoever to do with the knowledge which he brought into being; it exists in a different world. The history of science is of no concern to scientists as scientists. Few mathematicians have read Newton's *Principia Mathematica,* or astronomers Copernicus' *Revolution of the Heavenly Orbs,* nor is there any reason in the practice of their science why they should have done so. The discoveries, once made, can usually be summarized in a formula, a few paragraphs or pages at the most in a textbook; it may even be that reference to the original material may prove confusing to the scientist since, as Thomas Kuhn points out, a succession of scientific revolutions taking place since the original work was done will probably have altered unrecognizably the contextual world of the knowledge. Here we see a major difference from the practice of the arts in the modern west, in which, by common consent, some knowledge of the experiential world of the creative artist is considered necessary for an understanding of his explorations, and in which no summary can hope to convey the meaning intended by the artist.

The view of scientific knowledge as simply cumulative is, however, as Kuhn also observes, not necessarily valid, but a consequence of the necessary rewriting of textbooks in the wake of each scientific revolution. In so doing, says Kuhn, textbooks 'inevitably disguise not only the role but the very existence of the revolutions that produced them.' Scientists of earlier ages are presented as 'having worked on the same set of fixed problems and in accordance with the same set of fixed canons that the most recent revolution in scientific theory and method has made to seem scientific.'[2] And since the training of scientists takes place largely through the medium of textbooks (what better way, one might ask, could one find for the transmission of this seemingly objective body of knowledge?), they themselves, no less than laymen, are generally caught in the same conceptual trap and come to see science as simply the gradual and essentially orderly accumulation of fact and explanation, with controversy when it does occur taking place within the context of a generally agreed set of basic concepts and values, a general agreement as to what is the legitimate material of science. Kuhn demonstrates that this is by no means so (Newton's alchemical studies, for example, and his obsession with the *Book of Revelation,* would make him strange company for a modern scientist), but it is nonetheless little wonder that this view of science is generally accepted without question by scientists and scientific laymen alike; and since what people believe to be true is as potent an influence as what actually is true, and since scientific knowledge is taken in our culture as the paradigm of all knowledge, the idea of the gradual orderly growth of knowledge has come to dominate our thinking. The existence of histories of music, for example, under such titles as *The Progress of Music* and *The Growth of Music,* both written by respected musical scholars, shows how easy it is for us to allow our thinking to be shaped by quite inappropriate ideas of scientific progress, while most of us are not entirely immune to the kind of thinking which assumes automatically that when European painting acquired the techniques of linear perspective it became better, or at least more sophisticated, than medieval painting; similarly in music with the elaboration of harmony and orchestral resource.

This cutting-off of scientific knowledge from the realm of experience is of course essential to the idea of knowledge as cumulative over time, since the most efficient way of transmitting fact and theory is by making it independent of the irrelevant experiential world of the individual. Experiences are unrepeatable, unique to the individual and in the long run untransmissible (except, in a limited way, through the medium of art); if scientific knowledge is to be transmitted exactly it must be divorced from experience, and the more exact the transmission the more completely divorced it must be. In any case, the nature of atomic and subatomic processes, of cell biology and the evolution of galaxies is inaccessible to human senses, and can be inferred only from dial readings, photographic plates, fluoroscope traces and the like. The scientist's way of objectifying his experience (since even to read a dial or examine a photograph is indubitably an experience) is to reduce it as far as possible to those sets of abstract relationships we call mathematics, but in doing so he imposes severe limitations upon the kinds of knowledge with which he can deal, limitations which we would see more clearly were we not so infatuated with the undoubted degree of mastery over nature which this knowledge has permitted and the material benefits which it has delivered. An examination in elementary physics, for example, may set the candidate a problem which goes something like this: 'An elephant weighing two tons is sliding down a hillside sloped at 60 degrees. How fast will it be going after it has slid three hundred yards?' Sir Arthur Eddington, who invented this rather ludicrous example, goes on to say, 'The experienced candidate need not pay too much attention to the elephant; it is merely put in to give an impression of realism.'[3] The important matters here, of course, are the quantities involved and the relationships between them. What Eddington does not point out is that the problem is not in the least concerned with the equally interesting questions of how the elephant happened to be sliding down the hill, whether it was frightened and how it was reacting to the situation. We are concerned, not with any experiential quality, but only with quantities; everything that does not lend itself to quantification is ignored, and is in fact mostly not susceptible to investigation by the methods of science at all. It is a corollary of this fact that those sciences which are most involved with quantification are viewed as the most intellectually respectable – the 'hard' sciences, of which physics is of course the prime example. Just as, according to the old saying, all arts aspire to the condition of music, so all sciences aspire to that of physics; the comparatively recent accession of the biological sciences to the status of 'hard' science bears witness to the extent to which they have succeeded in reducing the living flesh to the abstraction of mathematics. Academic psychologists and sociologists, on the other hand, react to the patronism of the hard sciences with a passion for the quantification of human experience and behaviour (assuming that they admit the existence of the former), thus showing the classic Adlerian symptoms of inferiority complex.

It has often been remarked that the seventeenth century was the great age of clock-making, and it is not surprising, therefore, that the earliest mathematicizing scientists should have found in the clock the most inviting model of the universe as they perceived it. Virtually down to the end of the nineteenth century – with a few dissenters – the idea of the cosmos as an enormously intricate, if finite, machine, comprising innumerable separate parts interlocking with one another in accordance with strict laws of cause and effect like trains of gears, from which one could isolate individual elements and examine them, dominated the imagination of western man – and still largely does today, even though it has long been abandoned by most scientists. The simultaneous development of clocks and of the 'clockwork' model of the universe carried with it the implication that time was a dimension of reality external to human consciousness, flowing along in the regular, homogeneous way characteristic of the movement of clock hands, independent of our perception of it, a dimension that could be measured by a clock in the same way as length could be measured with a ruler. Time came to be thought of as a linear progression, which had a beginning and would undoubtedly have an end, just as space had extremities, an absolute length, breadth and depth.

Once this mechanistic universe was accepted as the true model of reality it was possible to obtain a vast amount of knowledge, and extend vastly the area of speculation, about the physical universe. So successful was it that the mechanistic view overflowed into areas of knowledge where its validity was, to say the least, doubtful, that of living creatures, and, in particular, man; the behaviourist ideas of Watson, and more recently Skinner, which see the experiencing 'I' as the mere epiphenomenon of a large and complex system of chemical and mechanical, or at best physiological and biochemical, reactions, derived from this carry-over. The mechanistic viewpoint when applied to the living world produced also a portrait of the biological cosmos as fixed and stable rather than as dynamic and evolving, and made it possible to develop the taxonomic and classificatory system of Carl von Linné, or Linnaeus, the eighteenth-century Swedish botanist, who himself refused to believe that the plant or animal kingdoms could be in a state of change. The extremely stratified and hierarchical European society of the time fostered the idea of the biological universe which most resembled it — a kind of pyramid with the simplest forms of life at the base and, of course, man himself alone at the top like an absolutist king, without relatives or friends in this mechanistic universe into which he seemed almost to have strayed by mistake. This attitude survives, amazingly, among some biologists even today; the late C.H. Waddington, at the time Professor of Animal Genetics at the University of Edinburgh, in his extended and fascinating study of the relations between science and the visual arts in our century, says, 'If you look at the animal kingdom in general — the whole system engaged in evolution — it defines its own criterion, by which it is clear that animals like lions, horses — and men — are improvements on worms and cockles.'[4]

Of course, the scientific model of knowledge proved enormously successful, both in terms of its liberating effect from the cramped worldview imposed by the beliefs of the Christian Church, which insisted that its sacred events be placed in a strictly historical context instead of the limitless time of myth, and then proceeded to limit the extent of history to conform with events occurring in the Eastern Mediterranean in the first century BC (universal creation according to the famous Bishop Usher took place in 4004 BC), and in terms of the material benefits and power over nature that it awarded to European society. As the knowledge accumulated, as the concepts became subtler, the earlier conceptual tools of science proved inadequate to deal with the new phenomena they themselves had revealed, or to provide the means for further speculation. The metaphors changed; it was no longer possible to think of electricity as in any way analogous to the flow of water in a pipe, or of atoms as resembling tiny billiard balls. By the early years of this century, Einstein and others had overturned the Newtonian clockwork universe, and Darwin and Lamarck the stable biological universe of Linnaeus, while the work of Freud and his disciples was beginning to reveal the whole world of psychic life lying beneath the apparently smooth surface of rationality. Their revolution in scientific thinking was clearly of immense importance, ushering in the new era of 'third' science, and introducing a completely new model of the physical universe — but the basic nature, aims and methods of science remained, and remain today, unchanged. Science as an activity, as a mode of thought, still concerns objective, non-experiential knowledge, its aim remains the total domination of nature through the uncovering of her secrets, and its approach involves the transformation of the 'observed other' into an object.

A further element was added to the situation by the fact that the new discoveries and concepts in physics, notably quantum theory, relativity, the principles of complementarity and of uncertainty, and the substitution of the idea of probability for that of rigid causality, not only made the mechanical model of the universe impossible to sustain, replacing it gradually with a model which conceived of the universe as a vast unified field where everything is part of everything else, more in the nature of an integrated electronic circuit than of a machine (but still, we note, inanimate and needing some outside prime mover), but also, through their sheer complexity, effectively placed them beyond the participation or even comprehension of the most assiduous scientific 'layman' (an interesting word, suggesting the complementary idea of a scientific priesthood, in possession of esoteric knowledge denied to others), if not, indeed, of many physicists also. This was not always so; in the eighteenth and even the nineteenth centuries science was not normally a profession at all (the very word 'scientist' is a surprisingly recent coinage, appearing only in the mid-nineteenth century) and the interested amateur had an important part to play. Today, however, specialisms have become narrower and narrower; the sheer bulk of information to be assimilated prevents any one person from knowing what is going on in more than a tiny fraction of the field. The layman's ignorance of science is matched by the average scientist's lack of concern for the arts and what are known as the humanities, producing a condition in our society mistakenly called the 'Two Cultures'. There are not two cultures, but one, though it is seriously, and increasingly, schizoid.

Among the proliferation of specialisms (or 'disciplines', to use another interesting word, suggesting a role as a soldier in the service of order against chaos) a fascinating feature has been the burgeoning of new fields of study known as the social sciences, which aspire to treat humans in their society with the mathematical strictness, and thus the status, of the hard sciences. These, not unnaturally, in taking over the approach and methodology of the physical sciences without questioning their appropriateness, take over also, more or less unexamined, their ideology, their ethic of mastery. Roy Willis makes this point in an illuminating article on anthropologists. He discusses the shock and feelings of desolation which the anthropologist experiences when he first begins his field study, and describes his gradual acceptance among the people he is studying through their sympathy, even pity for his helplessness, and recognition of their common humanity. They treat him, in fact, somewhat as they would a motherless child. 'But the importance of this initial "acceptance" of the anthropologist is magnified even further by the fact that established social anthropology has *nothing* to say about it. This glossing over of the real relations between the anthropologist and the "natives" seems connected with the ruling assumption of western thought that knowledge is essentially cerebral; and that consequently the practical experience of the anthropologist is irrelevant. Social anthropology *disembodies* the anthropologist, denying him his full humanity as relentlessly as colonialism denied or diminished the humanity of the colonized ... So, paradoxically, it is precisely in that society where the western anthropologist experienced himself as most fully human – as most free, integrated, autonomous and "growing" – that he was *at the same time* used by his society and culture as a passive means of increasing western scientific intellectual mastery of the world.'[5] (The italics are the author's, but I would have placed them in exactly the same places.)

The urge to domination and mastery over the world may arguably be justified in the case of the physical sciences (though there is, equally, a good case to be made against it – and in the most practical terms, since we should all have been able to sleep more soundly had the atom never been split), but the situation becomes morally ambiguous, to say the least, in the case of the social and psychological sciences. If knowledge is to be sought, the question may fairly be asked, Who is the knower and who the known? and if power is sought, one may ask, Power for whom? and even Power over whom? Too often the psychologist assumes a similar relationship to his 'subjects' (yet another interesting word) to that which a physicist assumes over his inanimate materials. The gross and cynical deceptions often practised by psychological experimenters on their subjects (who are often students and in no position to refuse their professor's invitation to take part in his games) in the name of knowledge give one to wonder what kind of knowledge could possibly be generated by such methods. On the other hand, the obsession with quantification produced by aspirations to the status of exact science has obliged psychologists to ignore those aspects of human experience and behaviour that cannot be quantified; as these include practically all the most interesting and important aspects it is scarcely surprising that psychologists find themselves less able to say anything significant about human mental life than any competent novelist. Again, the methods of physical science may be justifiable on its own ground in terms of the spectacular advance in knowledge about and power over nature, while the application of these methods to the study of the human mind has produced nothing of value, save the restatement, generally at great length and in less intelligible form, of small truths which are conventional wisdom in any village culture. The citing by psychologists of mutually contradictory proverbs such as 'Too many cooks spoil the broth' and 'Many hands make light work' simply will not wash as a defence of their methods; the wise man does not need psychology to tell him that both these saws are right in different contexts or how to choose the correct one for a given situation, while the foolish man is only confirmed in his folly by blind reliance on the statistical platitudes to be found in textbooks of social psychology.

The quest for knowledge for its own sake is a chimera, no less than is the pursuit of art for art's sake, and despite the protestations of such undoubtedly distinguished and humane men as the late Jacob Bronowski, always has been. There are just two possible motivations for the pursuit of knowledge: love and the quest for power. Scientific knowledge has so far been motivated almost entirely by the latter, and has been successful to the extent that it has been able to produce power. Those physicists in Germany in the twenties and thirties whom Bronowski in his television spectacular and book *The Ascent of Man*[6] lauds as having been disinterestedly seeking knowledge of the atom for its own sake were deluded, but it is a delusion shared by all who divorce knowledge from experience, truth from value, and, above all, themselves from nature.

Resources are allocated for scientific research for the sake of power, and most resources go where most power is to be gained, while history suggests that most scientists will work for whoever makes resources available to them; nor are they, in their own terms, necessarily wrong to do so, since if the knowledge they win has, as they believe, nothing to do with values it does not matter who pays as long as the knowledge is gained. But science is about power. As Leslie Sklair says, 'The function of science and technology in urban societies is nothing if not to increase the economic and military capacities of those societies. Despite the stated intentions of some of those who decide the finances of science and technology, and of many of those who work in them, the utilitarian consequences cannot be denied.'[7]

But knowledge gained for the sake of power is by its very nature limited. He who would gain control over a person or group for his own purposes may study them intimately, as does the advertising man, the political manipulator, even, alas, some psychologists and sociologists — and many gain much power-oriented knowledge of them to use for his own ends, but he will never learn of them what lovers learn of each other. The loving and reciprocal investigation of loved one by lover is a universe away from such researches, and the knowledge gained is neither more nor less, but of a different order. Orthodox scientific research, motivated as it is by the quest for power and disregarding the experience of that which it investigates, will yield much knowledge of a specific kind, but never the final secrets of the universe. Only those who will submit to nature, will wait for her to reveal himself, those who will ponder over her secrets as the lover ponders on the beloved, will ever gain that true knowledge which *is* experience.

It would be easy at this stage to assert that the only way in our society that one can obtain that knowledge which is experience is through the work of artistic creation, but this is not the whole truth. The Balinese say they have no art, but just do things as well as possible, while the Greek word for art, *techne,* was also the word for making and is of course the root of the word 'technology; we shall explore these ideas later. For the moment, just as we explored other musics in order to clarify some of the assumptions of western music, let us look very briefly also at a concept of science in the one culture apart from our own which developed a substantial body of knowledge about the physical world and an advanced technology, that of China. It will, I hope, remind us that even in a field which we consider to be concerned only with objective knowledge there remains still a great amount of subjective assumption and culturally conditioned attitude, and that other attitudes are possible than our own.

Joseph Needham has made a lifelong study of Chinese science, and addresses himself to the problem of why Chinese science, which until the seventeenth century was so decisively ahead of that of the west (he lists not only such well-known achievements as explosives, the study of magnetism, and printing, but also the technology of cast iron, the stirrup and harness, many advances in public health and epidemiology as well as the recognition of deficiency diseases, much astronomical knowledge and many other crucial developments, as having been imported from China to the west) failed (his word) to keep pace subsequently. He points out that one of the key concepts of western science, which has no parallel in traditional Chinese culture, is that of laws, principles which govern the workings of nature independently of the physical substance of the things governed, an idea that Needham traces back to the Old Testament idea of Jahweh as divine lawgiver to the whole of the universe (we see here once more the idea of the divine being residing outside the order of nature) — a concept which the Chinese, with their ancient distrust of precisely formulated and codified law, never developed. Their concept of law, says Needham, was concerned rather with good and accepted custom, and their view of the cosmos was not that of things obeying the orders of a superior authority (so potent an idea in the west that in the seventeenth century a cock that had laid an egg was prosecuted in court for violating divine law) but with things simply obeying the dictates of their own natures. With both society and the cosmos, they were inclined to leave things alone, to go with the grain of things, letting nature take its course with minimum interference, like the good magistrate who interfered as little as possible in community affairs.

Thus, observation, of a remarkably patient and accurate kind, rather than experiment was more in accordance with the Chinese temper, and though their technology was highly sophisticated it never attained the runaway pace, never came near the stage of upsetting the processes of nature as it has in the west. The great inherent stability of Chinese culture and society enabled it to absorb with scarcely a ripple discoveries in science and technology that had such an explosive effect on European society.

Secondly, Chinese philosophy, being perpetually inclined to what Needham calls an 'organic materialism', never developed the mechanistic model of the universe which, as we have seen, proved so decisive in western science. They knew nothing, either, of Euclidian geometry, a fact which, while probably preventing growth in some directions (and we should remember that the great mathematician Poincaré pointed out that Euclidian geometry is not 'true', only convenient) at least saved them from the centuries-enduring misconceptions of the Ptolemaic model of the solar system.

And thirdly, the Chinese never felt that separation of knowledge from experience, or of man from nature, which was the necessary push that started western science on its headlong course. While bowing with the deepest reverence to Dr Needham's scholarship, I cannot help feeling that it is a mistake to view the absence of developments parallel to those in Europe after the seventeenth century as a 'failure'. From his own account[8] it would seem that the Chinese had in fact got things just right; the leisurely development of knowledge of the physical universe has a different 'feel' from the frantic pace of western science, and implies a loving respect for the processes of nature that is lacking in the west. The leisurely pace enabled the knowledge to be assimilated into the fabric of society (there is no evidence, says Needham, in that vast and labour-intensive society, of technological unemployment, or even of the fear of it) without the kind of upset and confusion that we have come to accept as endemic to our society. It is a science that is devoted not to mastery of nature but to the unifying of man with nature.

It is interesting to see, in a recent issue of *New Scientist,* an account of how the Chinese continue, even after the Cultural Revolution which aimed at the destruction of Confucian ideas, in this way of thinking. Under the heading 'China goes its own way in industry', we read that people's communes in rural areas have established their own factories and workshops to serve their immediate needs, making drainage and irrigation equipment, farm machinery and the like; they have built small iron-smelting plants and small workshops, which must be not unlike the small rural blast furnace illustrated in Needham's book,[9] their purpose being to fulfil a need rather than to make a profit.[10] Needham quotes a phrase collected by Bertrand Russell during his time in China: 'production without possession, action without self-assertion, development without domination', which summarizes the traditional aims of Chinese science; they are, it seems, still alive today.

Perhaps the nearest that western science has to the unassertive, traditionally non-dominating science of China is in the relatively new sciences of ethology, the study of animal behaviour in its natural setting, and ecology, the 'subversive science', the study of the relations between living things and their environment. Both have been so mistreated by the media that even to mention them is to court the reader's boredom, if not irritation, but it is necessary to do so, if only to point out that their 'subversive' nature, if such it is, with regard to orthodox science lies less in their findings than in their approach. Those who study living creatures in their environment — Jane Goodall, for example, with ape communities, Leonard Williams with his monkey colonies, Konrad Lorenz with his greylag geese and jackdaws (I intend no comment on the validity of the latter's extrapolations from animal to human behaviour) — must be prepared to sit still and passively (strange how that word has become almost a term of abuse in our culture) letting them and their sets of relationships reveal themselves in their own time. The knowledge thus gained is of a different order from that gained by experiment, and it is this, rather than the concepts of relativity, complementarity and uncertainty, that may constitute the true scientific revolution of our time. One cannot love animals and at the same time be prepared to induce cancer in them, insert electrodes in their brains or subject them to various forms of physical and mental deprivation; on the other hand, it is necessary to love them if one is to sit still and become part of their environment, even their society. The knowledge obtained by such researches may not be readily quantifiable, and does not necessarily confer power, but it has led to at least one important conceptual change.

This concerns the western attitude to the subconscious and instinctual processes of human life. Freud is an interesting, almost tragic, figure in this respect; he recognized the importance of the subconscious mind and courageously set out to map it, but one has the feeling that he did not really like what he had found, and in his last, almost despairing book *Civilization and its Discontents,* he came to the conclusion that the continuance of civilization depended upon the ruthless suppression of this instinctual life, which he thought of as a kind of chaotic steamy swamp, a jungle inhabited by dark monsters forever preying on one another. In this, of course, Freud is only representing a tradition of European thought that goes back to the Old Testament; it is a view that does scant justice to either the subconscious mind or the jungle, and is largely, if unconsciously, based on the concept of the jungle that was illustrated at perhaps its most hilarious in the old film *King Kong,* which depicted everything in the jungle as at war with everything else, gorilla with alligator, lion with anaconda (in blissful disregard of even the facts of geography) and man with himself and everything else. It is a view which is frequently advanced by the defenders of capitalism and the 'free market' system, and without capitalism, second science, as Needham remarks, would in all probability never have got off the ground.[11] Today, largely thanks to the work of these careful and loving researchers, we are coming to see the jungle as far from chaotic, in fact as an orderly place, perhaps more so than many a big western city, and the 'savages' who live in it, once we forget our preoccupation with hardware, as at least as civilized in their relations with one another and with their environment as we are. (We need not think of these insights, however, as progress, since, as we read in Colin Turnbull's *The Forest People,* 'primitive' peoples understand these matters perfectly well without the benefits of western science.[12]) To this new insight runs in remarkable parallel the perception that the subconscious mind is not the region of chaos and disorder that Freud and his followers imagined, but a vital source of creative energy and the indispensible basis of reason and consciousness.

Despite what must be my obvious mistrust of the aims and methods of science, at least as at present generally practised, this chapter is intended, not as an attack on the scientific world view itself; it is rather an attempt to make explicit some of the implicit assumptions upon which it is based, and to point out its limitations. This is a matter of great importance, since the scientific approach has so taken over the mind of western man (and, increasingly, that of the rest of the world also) that it becomes the only acceptable means of dealing with the problems and opportunities of our world. 'In our own lives', says Professor R.S. Silver in a recent article, 'the concepts of objectives, design, planning, optimization and many others, all clearly taken from the practice of engineering and science, are now routine in sociology and economics. Indeed it is hardly too much to say that the major political confrontations and divisions of our time concern different interpretations of, and attitudes to, the role of planning and design in society as a whole.' He goes on, 'The root cause of the distrust and disillusion with which so many of our contemporaries now regard science and technology is not actually due to the technical results but to an ill-defined yet powerful feeling that human affairs are now conducted largely on attitudes which are scientific and technological in origin and which somehow fail to satisfy many important facets of human reality ... this feeling is well-founded; it is the adoption of science-based attitudes into human affairs which is a major cause of many of our problems.'[13] That it should have so taken over is in part understandable in view of science's undoubted ability to deliver the material goods, at least to the more prosperous members of the human race, but such ability cannot explain the deference afforded to pronouncements made by academic psychologists, sociologists and economists who, as has already been remarked, have after a century or more of ceaseless activity afforded us scarcely a single significant insight into ways of conducting our personal, social or political lives. (Nor, fortunately, do they seem to have succeeded in placing in the hands of those who would manipulate us for their own ends any significant tools that a mixture of native cunning and unscrupulousness had not already provided for them.) Insight in these fields remains a matter of observation, intuition, experience and empathy, and without these the greatest academic distinction is worthless, as the recent sad but ludicrous and even somehow reassuring spectacle of the disintegration of the Santa Barbara Center for the Study of Democratic Institutions demonstrates. As the London *Observer* reported on June 1 1975, 'Credited with nearly two decades of important work on world problems (*important to whom, one wonders*?) and a magnet for the great minds of the day, the Center is falling apart amid charges of financial mishandling, spying, back-stabbing and "academic watergating".' (A similar, though fictional, account of the uselessness of conclaves of high IQ's is given by Arthur Koestler, who of all people ought to know, in his novel *The Call-Girls*.[14]) The popular fear of the 'mad scientist' exploited so enjoyably in thrillers from Dr Moriarty to Dr Strangelove, has strong intuitive justification, and finds its natural contemporary target in the hubristic fantasies of Herman Kahn (whose IQ is reported to be 200), and his Hudson Institute. Neither intellect nor the power of logical thought is any guarantee of insight, a fact that remains as true for today's scientists as for the medieval schoolmen, who must have been no whit less intelligent, and probably rather better at logic.

A crucial limitation of the scientific world view lies in its assumption that all phenomena of nature, including those of the mind, are, at least potentially, accessible to conscious thought and reason. Freud is reported to have said, 'Where Id was, let Ego be!', thus proclaiming his belief in the perfectability of conscious awareness, but in fact the conscious mind can no more be aware of all the mind's workings than can the television tube, to use Gregory Bateson's vivid analogy, show all the workings of the TV set of which it is a component. 'Suppose', says Bateson, 'that on the screen of consciousness there are reports from many parts of the total mind, and consider the addition to consciousness of these reports necessary to cover what is, at a given stage of evolution, not already covered. This addition will involve a very great increase in the circuit structure of the brain, but will still not achieve total coverage. The next step will be to cover the processes and events occurring in the circuit structure which we have just added. And so on. Clearly the problem is insoluble, and every step in the approach to total consciousness will involve a great increase in the circuitry required.'[15] It is in fact in principle impossible that we should ever be aware of all the workings of our minds; the rational mind simply has no access to the total mind.

It is only our European passion for finding out that sees this inescapable fact as ground for dismay or even as necessarily a difficulty; other cultures are content to accept it and to allow religion, art and the study of dreams to guide them in the exploration of this vast hinterland of the mind. Freud, as Bateson points out, had it all wrong in viewing the conscious mind as given and self-explanatory; it is the subconscious that is the given and consciousness the mysterious, the inexplicable phenomenon.[16] It is perhaps possible through the methods of science to carry out some fruitful exploration of conscious processes, but the deeper levels can be reached only by other means. Reach them, however, we must and give them their due; three centuries of exclusive attention to conscious processes and rationality resulted in the terrible outburst of irrational destruction that lasted, on and off, from 1914 to 1945 and is probably not over yet. The tool proper to that task is not the methods of science, at least not as we know it, but art.

It is understandable that our culture, placing emphasis as it does on conscious processes, with its model of knowledge as a body of fact and theory existing outside of and independently of the knower, should view education as primarily the transmission of that information to the new generation, and the activity of education as concerned exclusively with the conscious level of existence. We shall see in a later chapter what the consequences of that view have been for education in our society. Let us now turn to a consideration of what the nature of western science on the one hand and of western music on the other over three centuries of spectacular achievement have to tell us of the nature of western culture.

Chapter 3: Bibliography

1. COLLINGWOOD, R.G.: *The Idea of Nature,* London, Oxford University Press (1945), p. 5.
2. KUHN, Thomas: *The Structure of Scientific Revolutions,* 2nd edn, Chicago, University of Chicago Press (1970), p. 137.
3. EDDINGTON, Arthur S.: *The Nature of the Physical World,* Cambridge, Cambridge University Press (1928), p. 251.
4. WADDINGTON, C.H.: *Behind Appearance,* Edinburgh, Edinburgh University Press (1969), p. 107.
5. MASON, Roy: 'Is the Anthropologist Human?', *New Society,* March 27 1975, p. 778.
6. BRONOWSKI, Jacob: *The Ascent of Man,* London, British Broadcasting Corporation (1973), Chapter 11.
7. SKLAIR, Leslie: *Organized Knowledge,* London, Paladin (1973), p. 71.
8. NEEDHAM, Joseph: *The Grand Titration; Science and Society in East and West,* London, Allen & Unwin (1969).
9. NEEDHAM, Joseph: ibid., p. 104.
10. 'China goes its own way in Industry', *New Scientist,* March 25 1976, p. 675.
11. NEEDHAM, Joseph: op. cit., passim.
12. TURNBULL, Colin: *The Forest People,* London, Jonathan Cape (1961).
13. SILVER, R.S.: 'The Misuses of Science', *New Scientist,* June 5 1975, p. 555.
14. KOESTLER, Arthur: *The Call-Girls,* London, Hutchinson (1972).
15. BATESON, Gregory: 'Style, Grace and Information in Primitive Art' in *Steps to an Ecology of Mind,* London, Paladin (1973), p. 116.
16. BATESON, Gregory: ibid., p. 108.

A culture is a unity; that we may take as an axiom. The fashionable notion of the 'Two Cultures' picturing our society as split into those who know about science and those who do not, with the Second Law of Thermodynamics as touchstone, is a convenient fiction; while it may be taken as indicating the increasingly schizoid nature of our society, we should remember that, as with a schizoid personality, even the most apparently contradictory features of a culture stem from a unified source. In this chapter I propose trying to see what kind of culture it could be that produced, over three centuries, the spectacular achievements of both second science and classical music (I continue to use that term, for want of a better, for the art music of the period roughly 1600 to 1910). It might be possible, as the first chapter suggested, to examine any of the arts other than music from this viewpoint; nonetheless, because of its highly abstract nature, its almost complete lack of explicit verbal or representational content, music is perhaps the most sensitive indicator of the culture, and of all the arts is the most closely tied to the subconscious attitudes and assumptions on which we build our lives within a society — which must be why, in all cultures, music is the art most closely associated with the practice of magic. It will, I hope, be clear that I am not trying to ascertain whether second science 'caused' classical music or vice versa; I am trying to show that the natures of both stem from deep sources within the European psyche.

Second science became possible only when the rational on the one hand, and on the other the emotional, experiential and sensual lives of westerners became split off from each other. Further, it needed the enthronement of reason and logic as the highest human functions, and the complementary devaluation of those other mental processes, before the scientific world view could come to dominate our thinking. I must emphasize that, within its limitations, there is nothing necessarily wrong with the scientific world view itself, *as long as those limitations are recognized*. It has often been remarked that the earliest and most spectacular achievements of second science were made in Protestant countries or by members of Protestant minorities in Catholic countries; this is not only because of the Catholic Church's early opposition to scientific thinking but also because the Protestant is committed in his religious life to the subduing of the emotional, sensual and instinctual processes and to the rigorous maintenance of his religious life on the conscious level (this, surely, rather than overt doctrinal matters, is the crucial difference between Catholic and Protestant). It is interesting in this regard that D.C. McClelland found that physical scientists tend to come from puritan backgrounds, and to be intensely masculine in their sense of identity.[1]

The mind absorbed by the scientific world view goes further, to the devaluation, even mistrust, of the emotional, sensual and instinctual aspects of our lives, which are thought of as generally misleading, even dangerous. The paranoic persecution of witches in the seventeenth century, at the moment when science was beginning to take over the western mind, can be seen as symbolic rejection of those processes whose irrationality those unfortunate women seemed to represent. Freud was not alone in thinking that the continuance of civilization depended on the repression of instinct and emotion; it has long been implicit in our social institutions, and underlies much of our educational theory and practice. It is no accident that tonal functional harmony began to take over western music precisely at the start of the seventeenth century; the daylit rational world that this music was to inhabit almost exclusively for the next three centuries, despite the efforts of the Romantics to break out of it, is the same world as that of scientific rationalism.

The elevation of the intellect and the exultation of abstract logic, as well as the devaluing of experience (we *will* know, we *must* find out, regardless of the cost in experience) and of the less conscious mental processes, are in fact revealed not only in the nature of western classical music itself but also in common attitudes to it. In the first place art, being essentially experience, and having as much to do with intuitive and emotional life as with the intellect, has been relegated to a marginal position in our society. For the overwhelming majority art plays no essential part in life; it is a spare-time activity, to be engaged in, if at all, when there is nothing more pressing to be done. It is split off from the everyday world, placed in a frame, its only relation with everyday life being one of antithesis; the music lover turns to his music not as an exploration of life but as a respite from it. It thus becomes possible, for example, for a man to be a sincere lover of art and yet, without any awareness of incongruity, be capable of constructing a working or living environment for himself or others of surpassing visual, auditory, tactile and olfactory ugliness; many of those who endowed our great art collections and musical institutions in the nineteenth century were just such.

It is a truism that in our culture our lives are fragmented. We separate our work from the rest of our lives, which we call leisure, the time when we think ourselves to be really living, so that work comes to be defined as that which we do when we would rather be doing something else. For most, the time of work is the time of boredom, frustration and unfulfilment, to be got through as best they can in order to provide the means for living. Again, we divide knowledge into self-contained compartments (or rather, we try, since the real world constantly overflows such categories) which we call 'subjects' or 'disciplines', and which themselves become further and further subdivided. We divide the age groups one from another and incarcerate the two extremes, the younger in schools and the elder in geriatric wards. We expect our children, at the sound of a bell or, more recently, a buzzer (the latter in most schools being of a startling, but perhaps appropriate, auditory offensiveness), to forget their real lives and enter a world of isolated rooms in which in succession they study the various 'subjects', each subject and each child isolated from the others and from the total world in which he lives the rest of his life. Children live in school an abstract existence divorced from their natural experiential matrix.

We have seen how the splitting-off of man from nature, of observer from observed, was necessary before science could begin its work of discovery and conquest. Similarly, the abstract and logical nature of classical music, its careful balance of phrase with phrase, sentence with sentence, period with period, would not have been possible without the ability of the composer to separate himself, to distance .himself, from his composition. Indeed, when Paul Henry Lang says, 'The essence of all these types of music is causal relationship achieved by the grouping of many small units into larger ones and finally into a great system of architecture,'[2] he might equally have been a nineteenth-century physicist expounding his essentially mechanistic view of the cosmos. The analytical passion is common to this music and to science; we dissect out first and second subjects, ritornelli and the like much as the zoologist dissects out the digestive system, the nervous system, the urinogenital system, both without regard for those qualities which emerge only in the total living system.

It may seem strange to speak of classical music, whose essence seems to be the expression of personal emotion, as abstract and logical, but this, as we have already seen, is the case. The logical transparency of this music parallels the vision of nature held by practitioners of second science, as does the emphasis laid on the subduing of the sound materials (the latter a metaphor for the subduing of nature herself) by the composer, and his view of those materials as so much recalcitrant matter to be worked on, shaped and put in order by the power of human will and intellect. A composer's attitude to his sound materials in any culture is a fair indicator of that culture's attitude to nature; the highly stylized and even arbitrary order imposed on the sound materials in this music speaks of a certain unease towards nature, such as is exemplified by Freud's unease about the subconscious. It is a fear, largely unfounded, that nature left to herself will revert to chaos that is at the root of this unease, and so scientist and artist alike come to view themselves as if they were soldiers in the service of order against chaos. Like other soldiers these are expected to undergo long and arduous training, involving many kinds of frequently mind-destroying drill (learning of formulae and all the other elements of what Bernard Dixon calls 'the strait-jacket of the science degree course'[4], practice of scales, exercises and studies, exercises in harmony and counterpoint) before being considered fit to go into battle; we are reminded once again of Erik Satie's comment on his certificate in counterpoint from the Paris Scola Cantorum 'authorizing him to engage in the practice of composition'. We shall see later, by contrast, how many present-day musicians, including such disparate personalities as Messiaen and Morton Feldman (who once advised Stockhausen to 'leave the notes alone, Karlheinz; don't push them around') are quite explicit in their attitude to both nature and the nature of sound, both of which they aim to treat in a non-exploitative manner.

A desire, even a need, for mastery runs through our culture, and has done so at least since the Renaissance. The stance of modern western man to nature and to his environment is one of aggression; to him everything represents a challenge. We speak of the conquest of the air, the conquest of the seas, of disease, of Everest (our approval of Mallory's famous reply when asked why he wanted to climb it – 'Because it is there' – must sound strange to those Sherpas who lived in its shadow for generations and never thought to climb it, or to the follower of Zen, who would see the mountain as lifting the climber and thus as an indispensible partner in the ascent). Daniel Bell voices clearly the European attitude:

> In existentialist terminology, man is 'thrown' into the world, confronting alien and hostile powers which he seeks to understand and master. The first confrontation was with nature, and for most of the thousands of years of man's existence life has been a game against nature: to find shelter from the elements, to ride the waters and the wind, to wrest food and sustenance from the soil, the waters and other creatures. The coding of much of man's behaviour has been shaped by his adaptability to the vicissitudes of nature. In the nature of societal design, most of the world's societies still live in the game against nature.[4]

I wonder how many 'primitive' peoples would recognize themselves from that description; I wonder too whether Professor Bell really believes that the 'confrontation with nature' has been resolved for western man!

The energy and strength of will of western man have enabled him to impose his values on the rest of the world — not, to say the least, always to the rest of the world's advantage. This restlessness and urge to power through conflict pervades all aspects of our lives: our social relations, our official religion, with its theme of life as an endless struggle against evil, and naturally our arts. In music it reveals itself metaphorically not only in the composer's struggle with his materials but also in the nature of the art work itself. From the seventeenth to the nineteenth century, all the music of the western classical tradition has contained some of the characteristics of opera, that is, of drama. Every musical work of the period is a drama, whether cast in the language of comedy or of tragedy, whether ending in apotheosis, dissolution — or a shout of laughter; a symphony is a psychodrama, the inner struggle of an individual (it was Tchaikowsky who first realized that a symphony did not have to have a happy ending), the concerto an exciting representation of the individual confronting the crowd — or, on a lower level, of the cowboy riding the bucking bronco. For the majority of music lovers the criterion of value in a musical work is dramatic; does it excite us, move us, make us weep, inspire a triumphant or a melancholy state? The values of formal perfection, balance and harmonic and contrapuntal ingenuity such as are esteemed by critics are in truth mere servants of those dramatic values. But the violent contrasts, sudden changes of mood and extremes of emotional tension of our music are not universal musical values; to the Confucian they would seem the work of a vulgar-minded man. In the words of Confucius himself, 'The noble-minded man's music is mild and delicate, keeps a uniform mood, enlivens and moves. Such a man does not harbour pain or mourn in his heart; violent and daring movements are unknown to him.'[5] This judgement would immediately rule out of court the overwhelming majority of works of western music, including most of those which we consider masterpieces.

One may see the development of western music over these three centuries as the product of the tension produced when abstract logic is placed at the service of personal drama. Each new development made in pursuit of ever more 'violent and daring movements' was a bolder step which placed further strain on the logical links holding the structure together and the tradition finally collapsed when the demands of drama overwhelmed the power of logic to sustain it any longer. The next chapters will deal with the decay of musical rationalism and the revolt against the concepts of both drama and logic in music. The fact that the music of this revolt is not yet fully accepted by the conventional concert audience tells us clearly that the attitudes that gave birth to the classical tradition are still overwhelmingly strong. Heads of state wishing to impress their visiting counterparts take them, not to hear a new piece of music, but to concert or opera performances of the most routine classical works – which may tell us also something of the inability of politicians to ask the really important questions in their society.

The methods of experimental science depend on the assumption that all the samples of nature which are investigated are also interchangeable; if it were not so, no experiment would be repeatable. This assumption applies not only to gas molecules, or samples of copper sulphate but also to rabbits, cats, dogs and other laboratory animals (of whom over 100,000 die weekly in its name at British laboratories alone), and even on occasion to men. While there is justification, in varying degrees, for this idea, it is nonetheless one which belongs very much to the tradition of western thought in general. A more mystical regard for the uniqueness of all things in creation would have made modern scientific thinking impossible; the purely instrumental attitude towards nature shown by experimental science means that it is possible to value things not for themselves but only for their functional usefulness in serving our purposes.

Similarly, I have already remarked how classical music is not concerned with sounds themselves at all, but only with the relationships between them; the classical composer, in fact, viewed sounds as valuable only in so far as they could be made to serve his expressive purposes (hence the rejection of non-harmonic sound by the classical tradition), just as the mind dominated by the scientific world view thinks of nature as being of value only so far as she can be made to serve human purposes. The one ignored any sound whose pitch could not be accurately controlled, while the other ignores any phenomena which do not lend themselves to quantification. Neither attitude would be possible in a culture that viewed nature as sacred, and every part of her as unique and of value for its own sake.

The methods of mass production, similarly, are based not only on the idea of the production of large numbers of interchangeable objects, but also on the use of a large number of interchangeable people to produce them. One might speculate that the constant unrest among heavy mass-production industries, such as the automobile industry, which depend on the interchangeability of people to serve the production line, is due primarily, if not always consciously, to a distaste among the workers for being so regarded, their distaste taking outward form in the only way they can formulate – the demand for higher wages. But higher pay, though acknowledgement of a kind, can do little to satisfy the need for recognition as an individual, and so the discontent continues. The interchangeability of people pervades our entire culture. It is to be found, not only in the anonymity of the shop assistant, post office clerk or milk roundsman, but even among those professions where personal relations are, one would imagine, vital, for example teaching, where a proliferation of audio-visual aids and assorted hardware attempts to fill the gap left by the lack of any real relationship between teacher and pupil. Most children learn the interchangeability game very early. They enter the school and come into contact with the infant teacher, with whom they soon enter into a quasi-filial relationship. They discover that this seemingly close and loving relationship is more apparent than real when the time comes to move up to the next class and the next teacher; if it were real both quasi-parent and child would be heartbroken at the parting (this is not criticism of infant teachers, who usually manage to inject some genuine human warmth into what is essentially a false situation – but they have no option but to play the game). Some children, of course, *are* heartbroken, since they have not yet learnt the interchangeability game, and some will never learn it; these will travel a hard road, but their obstinate humanness could be a leaven in the lump of society.

Those who think at all of these functional relationships between human beings are accustomed to view them as a consequence of the growth of populations and as an adaptation which protects us from having to enter into personal relationships with too many people. Perhaps, however, the truth is in the reverse; a society which did not treat nature (including human nature) in such a functional manner would not have allowed itself to grow so large in the first place. Many societies, including many traditional African societies, have (or had) very sophisticated mechanisms built into them serving the express purpose of preventing them from becoming too large, as well as for preventing the unbridled ambition of individuals from taking over the society. In any case, the evidence in our society for such functional, instrumental attitudes is clear from both science and music.

In western classical music, performers too are interchangeable. A work is composed, not for a person, but 'for voice and piano', 'for violin and orchestra', 'for oboe and tape', and so on. True, each performer will bring his own special skills and his personality to bear on the written notes, but he has very little room for manoeuvre, since the essence of the music lies in the notes, not the performer. We take this situation for granted, but it has not escaped comment from musicians of other cultures. The Sufi musician Iniyat Khan some fifty years ago observed:

> Every man and woman has a certain pitch of voice, but then the voice-producer says, 'No, this is alto', 'soprano', 'tenor', 'baritone' or 'bass'. He limits what cannot be limited ... Besides this, the composer has probably never heard the voice of that particular singer, and has written only for a certain pitch, either this one or that one; and when a person has to depend upon what the composer has written and has to sing in a pitch that is thus prescribed, then he has lost the natural pitch he had.[6]

An Indian musician, for whom a performer has only to play a few sounds on the sitar to reveal his personality, is of course especially likely to notice this depersonalization of the performer, a depersonalization which is emphasized by the performance conventions of western music: a uniform style of dress, for example, uniform bowing in the string section or the distance placed between players and audience. Within the ensemble, too, musicians are interchangeable, given an acceptable level of technical competence, and even whole orchestras can be exchanged one for another, leaving the Beethoven symphony, the Bach suite or the Mozart concerto essentially unchanged.

I commented earlier on the contrasting attitudes to time in western and other musics, as well as on the mechanistic concept of time held by scientists of the classical tradition. The notion of 'time, like an ever-rolling stream', coming from somewhere and going somewhere, time as a linear progression from a beginning to an end, is paralleled by the purposive nature of a work of classical music, as it progresses from a clear-cut beginning to its fore-ordained end, occupying a precisely predictable segment of time (homogeneous time), each section articulated in an additive manner with the preceding and the succeeding, each punctuated by the ceaseless periodicity of the I-IV-V-I cycle like the swinging pendulum of a clock.

The complex temporal articulation of a classical work has as one of its functions the protection of the listener from being lost in time, from not knowing where he is in relation to the beginning and the end of the music. The proliferation of clocks, watches and time-checks in our society bears witness to a need, certainly over and above the actual requirements of everyday affairs, to know what time is is; articulative devices in music such as introductions, perorations, transitions, recapitulations, as well as whole temporal structures such as sonata, rondo, da capo aria and so on, are all devices for helping us to keep our bearings in time. The listener to an unfamiliar work, as long as he is familiar with those devices – and he need not be able to put a name to them to be familiar with them – will always know where he is in the music; not to be able to do so will induce unease and discomfort. In my experience many concert-goers are ill at ease with much modern music simply because 'you don't know where you are in it'; they cannot let go and cease to worry about their orientation in time.

Unlike most non-European musicians, a composer of post-Renaissance music plays with the time sense of his listeners. The music does not exist purely in the present tense, taking each moment as it comes, but leads the listener forward to coming events, often in passages which are themselves of no great intrinsic interest (the tensions created on the large and the small scale by tonal functional harmony, as well as by introductions, for example, and variations). We have seen that much of a classical movement exists simply to space out and point attention towards important events; these are, so to speak, not fully present, only those elements we call themes existing fully in the musical present.

This linear, dynamic view of time is at variance with what we have observed in other cultures, and just as our classical music exists more in the past and the future than in the present, that is how we live; indeed, we seem to have largely lost the ability to live simply in the present. What Max Weber called the Protestant Ethic is obviously related to this attitude; crudely put, it means that we are prepared to have a bad time in this world in order to have a good time in the next. Translated into secular terms, the Protestant Ethic becomes the motivation behind the industrialization of society and the boring alienated drudgery that for most people today (and not only on the shop floor – it is to be found no less in the manager's office), passes for work. We need to get through so many days a week (as few as possible) doing something which, to put it no more strongly, we would rather not be doing, in order to enjoy during the rest of the week the material comforts which our labour and that of others has bought, and to get through the fifty (or forty-nine, or even thirty-nine – it makes little difference) weeks of this in order to enjoy annually a few weeks of leisure or package tourism. Daniel Bell points out the dichotomy in modern society which demands that a man observe the Protestant Ethic in work and be a swinger in his leisure time so that both production and consumption may be maximized.[7] The trouble is that once we neglect the God-given present we quickly forget how to enjoy it; leisure time becomes somehow self-conscious and lacking in that spontaneous enjoyment which seems to be the happy lot only of the models in travel brochures.

Living time, time as we actually experience it, is not homogeneous, does not progress at the constant rate suggested by the movement of clock hands. A watched pot never boils, days go by faster when we are busy and happy, Christmas Eve is endless to a five-year-old, and the years go by faster as we grow older – although television with its half-hour packages of material probably conditions today's youngsters much earlier than previous generations to homogenized clock time. We are nonetheless borne along willy-nilly by the demands of the clock. We clock in, clock out, make and keep appointments; the school day is parcelled out mechanically and inexorably in equal chunks which must be filled even when no-one is gaining anything from them and curtailed even when enjoyment and learning are in mid-flight. So the symphony is borne along on its evenly spaced accents, its ceaseless cycle of I-IV-V-I, from clear-cut beginning to fore-ordained end. We cannot linger over some ravishing sound or repeat some cunningly-shaped melody; all is subordinated to the demands of the temporal design, all is carried along in the stream of linear time. The ear of the musician, like the eye of the scientist, cannot allow itself to be seduced by the beautiful, the appealing, the awe-inspiring; it must get on with its purpose of building the grand design.

The consequences for education of this supreme position in our society of the scientific model of knowledge will be dealt with in a later chapter; we note here simply that one of the consequences of this view of knowledge, as abstract and as existing apart from the experience of the knower, is the coming to power of the expert, of the person with knowledge in a particular field (since it is impossible for anyone to be an expert in everything) at his disposal. His authority is to all practical purposes absolute, despite the fact that his verdicts are liable to constant change; one need look no further than the successive and often mutually contradictory fashions in education and medicine, each supported with apparently God-given authority by squads of experts. The ways in which intelligent and presumably well-informed people can differ radically on every imaginable issue are explicable only if one views knowledge, not as an abstract and absolute thing, but as a relationship between the knower and the known, as a function as much of the knower as it is of the known. Were this not so, the agreement of intelligent and well-informed people on everything of importance would be complete. But notwithstanding this commonsense view, our lives at every turn are become the property of experts, through whom our experience is to be mediated. We have experts to tell us we are sick, and to tell us we are well again (thus arrogating to themselves the individual's right to his own bodily experiences), experts to tell us we need a new motorway or supersonic airliner, experts to tell us how to decorate our houses, what our sex lives should be like, how to educate our young, experts to paint our pictures and compose and perform our music for us, and finally experts to tell us which of the products of the composing or performing experts we should be listening to.

The last examples remind us how remote the act of artistic creation has become from the majority of people. While we pay lip-service to the creativity of the common man, it is in fact only a tiny minority of the population who think themselves capable of writing a poem, painting a picture, making a piece of music — not to mention a film or a television programme – or designing and making a chair or a radio receiver. The essential process of art – creation – is inaccessible to most, who must content themselves with the contemplation of someone else's finished work; assessment and criticism become vital adjuncts of art since the receiver of the art, lacking the experience of creation, lacks also confidence in his ability to distinguish what is worth his contemplation from what is not. In handing the creative function of art over to professionals, we reinforce the schismatic tendency of our society, the division into those who produce and those who consume. All of us, of course, are consumers of something we have not produced, but today a greater and greater number of people produce nothing, in the physical sense, being concerned entirely with handling symbolic material – clerks, most professional people, salesmen, businessmen generally. We are expected, for the good of society, to consume ever more of what others produce, and society employs some of its sharpest wits to persuade us to do so.

In this consumer society the artist is forced willy-nilly into the role of producer of a commodity which he hopes others will want to consume. He is obliged to adopt the tactics of the advertising man, albeit more discreetly, employing agents, publishers and dealers to put his product before the public, occasionally himself engaging in stunts to gain attention. Dali's lectures given in a diving suit and David Hockney's bleached hair and round glasses are two modern examples that spring to mind, while Beethoven's famous public refusal to doff his hat to 'a mere king' has long struck me as the best publicity stunt in the history of western art. In order to become known it is necessary to engage the attention of a critic, who will write eulogistic articles praising the artist's work, often at the expense of rivals for the public's attention (for example: 'Mr A's computer-generated stochastic methods reflect a much more profound understanding of the basic processes of music than the total serialism of Messrs X and Y' or 'Mr B, in continuing to write tonal music, has no truck with the fashionable excesses of the avant-garde, as represented by Messrs A, X and Y' and so on); indeed, the world of publishers, agents and impresarios is as cut-throat as that of Madison Avenue or The City. Those who have listened in on conversations among young composers will know that discussion centres more on the scramble for performances, commissions and publications than on purely musical matters.

The producer-consumer polarity in art, reflecting the polarity that pervades our society, means that ever more value is assigned to the products of the art process and even less to that process itself. Just as in our economic life we fix attention on the product rather than on the means of production — who would guess that the beautiful shiny dream-car in the motor show, surmounted by a topless model, could have been born in the fiery hell of the blast furnace and the clattering nightmare of the assembly line? — so in art we value the art object — the painting, carefully restored and cleaned and sold for hundreds of thousands of pounds, the early opera, restored by devoted scholarship to its original orchestration and embellished with authentic ornaments of the period, the first edition of the play, stripped of all its traditional accretions, and, in our own time, the musical work recorded under the composer's direction in an attempt to fix the art object for all time — and we ignore the creative abilities of ordinary people. The art objects which most of us are capable of producing may not compare with those of a Beethoven or a Rembrandt, or even of Grandma Moses, but the creative process satisfies as deep a need. Our passion for preservation contrasts strongly with the way of the Chopi, who are quite willing, after making and performing a work (in which the entire community has been involved) for a year or so, to let it go and replace it with a new creation.

So long as we view the created object, rather than the creative process, as the essential element of art, we are committed to the work of preservation of everything that the past has produced. And yet — people die, despite all efforts to keep them alive, and will continue to do so. Death is an unspeakable presence in our society; we cannot accept it as a fact and cannot mourn, and behind much medical research is an unspoken and unexamined hope for immortality. In the meantime we use the apparent immortality of a work of art as a surrogate for the immortality we desire and cannot obtain.

If an art work is thought of as in any way alive it should be allowed to die when its time comes, and, if necessary, to be mourned. Just as, if no-one were to die, there would be no room for new life, so the art works of the past that we do not allow to die are leaving us insufficient room for new creative life. Our art galleries, and especially our concert life, are choked with past works, many of them, like Leonardo's *Last Supper,* being kept alive by methods that do as much violence to the artist's vision as do the oxygen tent and drip feed used to prevent the dying nonagenarian from ending his life in peace and dignity. The Greeks who sacked Troy, the soldiers of the Commonwealth who smashed the cathedral windows and those of Henry VIII who razed the monasteries may have had a truer concept of the function and the power of art than the most assiduous preservationists, ministers of tourism or producers of *son et lumière*. Anatol Holt says: 'All of you will probably remember the disaster that took place in Florence with the floods and the great damage that was done to those stored artworks. I had very mixed feelings about it. I thought, from a certain point of view, that it could be regarded as good rather than bad; that is — yes, it's an occasion for mourning, but on the other hand it makes room. You know, there can only be so many masterpieces in the world, quite apart from the physical space in which they're stored, and new masterpieces must be produced, ones whose relations to your old masterpieces are perhaps hard to understand.'[8]

I am not advocating the deliberate destruction of works of art, any more than I advocate the murder of old people. We need, however, to recognize their natural life span and respect it, not try to render them immortal. A work of art has its moment of greatest glory at the moment of its creation, whether or not its own time recognizes it; it serves its time for perhaps many generations, and should be allowed, lovingly, to die. The triumphant exhumation of yet another baroque oboe concerto or nineteenth century French ballet runs counter to the very nature of the creative process. Even the music of Bach and of Beethoven will one day have served its time and die, and that day may be closer than we think. In our love for the processes of art and of life we should be prepared to let them go. New life can be created only if enough space is left by the old, as the world's present desperate state of overpopulation, largely brought about by the western refusal to face the fact of death, demonstrates so tragically; new art, likewise, can flower only when people can see and hear it with eyes and ears uncommitted to earlier masterpieces. And only by letting go of it can we regain the true relationship with our past which the preservers of past masterpieces try so unsuccessfully to achieve, and which other cultures seem to manage so effortlessly.

The labour of musicologists has had another effect, related to the passion for abstract knowledge: we know more about past music and its history than perhaps any other generation in history, yet our experience of it is seriously vitiated. The musicological temper pervades our concert life; the performer compiling a programme will automatically arrange his items in chronological order, and any other arrangement will need to be the result of conscious decision.

Music programmes on radio tend to be constructed around a musicological or historical idea – a comparison between two composers or performers, the way a composer developed from Op 1 to Op X, the relation of an artist to his literary sources, and so on. The whole concept of a 'well-balanced programme' depends upon such considerations, as does the more recent idea of the well-balanced record collection; both assume tacitly that knowledge about music is more important than the direct experience of it, and in neither case do considerations of sheer enjoyment appear to play much part.

It has thus happened, in music as in other aspects of our lives, that we have passed our experience into the hands of experts, not only those who compose and perform our music for us but also those who tell us what we should be listening to, and who filter our experience through their expertise. Those who know nothing about music but know what they like are indeed fortunate; the majority of those who are not expert in music do not dare to make such a claim, being often afraid even to say whether they enjoyed a certain piece of music without finding out the expert's opinion first. This is the trap waiting for the society that worships abstract knowledge; such knowledge, instead of being diffused through society, can be accessible only to a few, and gives those who *know* power over those who do not. Since no-one can know everything, not only do we find those who know, or claim to know, increasingly difficult to control, but also those who know do so in such small areas and are so ignorant of everything outside those areas that they are incapable of making sensible decisions on matters affecting society as a whole. Highway engineers are the last people to pronounce on the need for motorways, or teachers on the need for education, while musicologists are the last to be able to speak with authority on the enjoyment of music.

The separation of producer from consumer is confirmed by the ever greater and greater technical skill of performers. One after another, in piano, violin and other competitions, young players come forward to display a dexterity that would have made Liszt or Paganini blench; the fact that every now and then one comes forward with real musical abilities and insights does not alter the fact, that in setting standards of technical proficiency that non-professionals cannot begin to approach, they are removing the practice of music ever further from the ordinary citizen and confirming him even more completely in the role of consumer. The process is paralleled in many areas of society that we have turned over to professionals: not only education, in which the young are mere consumers of knowledge, but also medicine, in which the patient passively (the words 'patient' and 'passive' being derived from the same Latin verb) accepts the treatment offered, neither he nor his family having any part to play in his own healing, as well as accepting without question the various social services, to which society turns over its feelings of responsibility for its weaker members. All are commodities which are bought and paid for by society, and all are currently becoming too expensive for us to afford, at least in their present forms. The problem remains in principle insoluble until the community takes back to itself its rights and responsibilities for education, healing and social care — and the right to make music and other arts for itself.

We participate, in the words of Jean Duvignaud which form the superscription to this book, 'through the symbols offered by a work of the imagination, in a potential society which lies beyond our grasp'. Over the three centuries of the triumphant scientific world view there have been many works of the imagination which have offered just such a potential society as an alternative to the existing; the entire romantic movement can be seen in this light. In the twentieth century, however, the vision of the potential society gained strength and cogency through the forging of a new language, in poetry, in painting, music and drama as well as the new art of the film. The following chapters will attempt to trace the main outline of this new movement in music; it makes no claim to be comprehensive as history, but intends simply to suggest a way in which the history of music in our century may be considered. Whether the new movement has in fact been any more 'successful' in its critique than the romantic movement is beside the point; what is to the point is that we can find, here as in all art, the dimly perceived shapes of ideas that have not fully emerged from the matrix of society.

Chapter 4: Bibliography

1. McCLELLAND, D.C.; 'On the Psychodynamics of Creative Physical Scientists', in HUDSON, Liam (ed): *The Ecology of Human Intelligence*, Harmondsworth, Penguin (1970).
2. LANG, Paul Henry: *Music in Western Civilization*, New York, Norton (1941), p. 1020.

3.   DIXON, Bernard: *What is Science For?*, Harmondsworth, Pelican (1976), p. 60.
4.   BELL, Daniel: *The Coming of Post-Industrial Society: A Venture in Social Forecasting,* London, Heinemann Educational (1974), p. 487.
5.   Quoted in SACHS, Curt: *The Wellsprings of Music,* The Hague, Martinus Nijhoff (1962), p. 220.
6.   SUFI INIYAT KHAN: *Music,* Lahore, Sh. Muhammed Ashraf (n.d., reprinted 1971), p. 51.
7.   BELL, Daniel: op. cit., p. 477.
8.   Reported in BATESON, Mary Catherine: *Our Own Metaphor,* New York, Knopf (1972), p. 310.

One needs only to look around to see that our society as a whole still firmly espouses the post-Renaissance scientific world view, even though that view may be somewhat on the defensive. As a recent article in *New Society* says, 'As recently as the 1960s, to call an argument "scientific" was a compliment; it is fast becoming a slur.'[1] The article, however, is itself based on several unexamined assumptions of the kind discussed in Chapter 3, and concludes, 'Science as the repository of all objective knowledge and the crucial concept of objective reality, must not remain rigidly attached to its historical "method" if it is to survive the persuasive attacks of the anti-scientists.'

It is not disputed that science is the repository of all objective knowledge (in so far, that is, as such a thing is presumed to exist); indeed, the words 'science' and 'objective knowledge' can be viewed as to all intents and purposes synonymous. What is disputed is the assumption implicit in the scientific world view that objective knowledge, knowledge divorced from him who knows, is the only valid way by which reality may be apprehended. It is a principal thesis of this book that the reality of experience, a reality in fact of even greater significance in our lives than the structure of atoms or of galaxies, is inaccessible to scientific method, and that it is this reality that art proclaims and explores.

The revolution that took place in scientific thinking in the early years of this century, though of great importance, was essentially superficial as far as the basic attitudes and assumptions of science were concerned. True, nature has come to be conceived in terms ever further removed from our everyday experience, making science increasingly remote from the culture of ordinary people. True, the cosmos has come to be thought of as a unified field in which everything is part of everything else, and the concept of strict causality has had to be abandoned, and, true, the uncertainty principle and the principle of complementarity has caused some scientists to wonder with dismay if the universe may not be ultimately un-knowable after all (the artist has never doubted that it is so). C.H. Waddington makes an interesting case for an interrelation between these scientific ideas and certain movements in the visual arts (complementarity and the all-round view of cubism, for example, or the over-allness of Pollock, Tobey and the Abstract Expressionist painters and the holistic field view of modern physics[2]), but, in the first place, this would require the artists to have read, and understood the implications of, the scientific literature (a highly unlikely supposition as even among physicists few understood it at the time), and secondly, the real revolution of art in our century is more profound than this, being nothing less than a revolt against the whole scientific world view and its ethic of domination. We have seen how classical music reflects the world view that gave rise to science; so the destruction of that tradition, whether deliberate or inadvertent, reflects a rejection on a profound level of its world view, its attitudes and its values.

The rejection began in fact much earlier, with the Romantic movement in poetry, painting and music. In music, traditionally much slower to pick up new artistic currents than the other arts, we hear the first pre-echoes of Romanticism perhaps in Mozart's poignant chromaticisms and subtle dissonances, but the revolt is sounded loudly and clearly first in Beethoven. It was in fact Beethoven, so generally thought of as the supreme exemplar of post-Renaissance musical attitudes, who made the first serious attempt to transcend them. That he did not succeed completely is due not only perhaps to his comparatively early death but also to the fact that, lacking any experience of alien musical culture against which he could view his own, such as Debussy was to encounter sixty years later, not even his supreme genius could escape the 'Mindinaoan depth' of his musical conditioning. Nethertheless in his last years, alone of his age, he had turned his back on the central myth of European culture and was furiously composing his way through to a new world, whose outlines he could have perceived only dimly, where time, power and conflict had no meaning. He died before the vision could fully take form. It is easy, even customary in conventional criticism and biography, to think of Beethoven as having completed some divinely-appointed destiny in his life, to have shaken his fist at the heavens and died, his work more or less complete. He was, however, only fifty-seven at the time, with a host of uncompleted projects, and was no great age in comparison with Haydn, who was spared to seventy-seven, Handel (to seventy-three) or Verdi (nearly ninety). He was on his way to

unimaginable musical discoveries which one is tempted to assert
would have changed the course of music in the nineteenth century,
but has to admit would probably not have, since he had already left
his contemporaries so far behind him that they thought him either
senile or mad or both; it took almost a hundred years for musicians
to learn to hear and play those final works which he did complete.

It was not simply the musical world that was not ready for him;
Beethoven had turned his back on the whole set of myths and
assumptions, not just of music but of that culture for which western
music is a metaphor. And so the last works were for years rejected,
dismissed either as over-intellectual or, conversely, as lacking in
intellectual coherence, the work of a madman, or of a man who had
put all sensuous beauty behind him in pursuance of some abstract
ideal of truth. Of course we can now hear that the reverse is true;
those last quartets are among the most sensuously beautiful music
of the entire western tradition. It is not until Debussy that we again
hear music written with such a keen and loving ear for sound
quality, such pure delight in sound itself.

It was suggested earlier that the forms of the classical tradition
can be seen as a defence against becoming lost in time. Beethoven
was the first composer of the European tradition to conceive the
possibility of going out of linear time altogether. In the last
quartets, sonata-movements, movements which are based on
drama and contrast, play a minor role, their place at the centre of
gravity being taken by fugues and variations. A fugue can induce a
sense of timelessness, as we can hear both in the huge fugue of the
Hammerklavier Sonata, Op 106, and in the *Great Fugue, Op 133*
which originally concluded the *B flat quartet, Op 130*; he seems in
these works to be setting out to make us lose ourselves in the
torrent of sound he creates. The fugue that opens the *C sharp
minor quartet, Op 131*, is timeless in a different way; here we feel
ourselves to be floating in an infinite space. Variations in these last
works, as well as the marvellous set in the *Archduke Trio, Op 97*
and the last *Piano Sonata, Op 111*, break down finally into static
repose. Even tonal harmony itself is all but abandoned in the great
Heilige Denksgesang of the *A minor quartet, Op. 132*.

Even Beethoven, however, could not complete the rejection of
the European myth, and, probably, even if he had, he would have
remained an isolated figure. The cycle had to complete itself, to run
down of its own accord; music in post-Renaissance Europe is too
marginal a phenomenon to have exerted any great leverage on the
course of affairs in society. As we know, nineteenth-century

European music was dominated by Beethoven, but it was the Beethoven of the great middle-period works, the symphonies and concertos and of *Fidelio*. It could be that the meaning of his music is less personal, more universal than we realize. When he said that 'He that divines the secret of my music is delivered from the misery that haunts the world', might he not have divined, with the intuition of the supreme artist, that the source of that misery lay in the pain of the post-Renaissance consciousness, from which his music was trying to break free?

The revolt against the dominance of the scientific world view, which was at its most triumphant in the nineteenth century, can be perceived again and again in Romantic music; its failure – a noble failure – lay in its inability to propose a new language for the discourse. The Romantic rebellion couched itself in the language, the rhetoric and the gestures of tonal functional harmony, of the formal structures of symphony, concerto, sonata and opera which arose from it, and it remained within the social conventions of the concert hall and opera house for its performance, a fact that was noticed by the ever-perceptive Debussy when he remarked, 'Romantic – a label that to my mind has no significance. The language of Schumann, Berlioz and Liszt is the classical language. I hear in them all the same kind of music.'[3] It was thus possible for the revolt to be assimilated effortlessly into the prevailing aesthetic of the time.

And yet, when one is attuned to it, what power is contained in that criticism! Richard Wagner must surely have been aware of the implication of his dramatic themes, in *Der Ring,* for example, where the central situation of his vast drama of the destruction of a world derives from the renunciation of love for power by the dwarf Alberich, and from the manipulation by Wotan, also for the purposes of power, of the forces of nature, symbolized by the giants Fasolt and Fafner, which sooner or later demand the price of their services and must be paid. All else in the cycle derives from these premises; what better metaphor could there be for the choices made, all unawares, by western society? Again, *Die Meistersinger* is described as a comedy, and is indeed richly funny, so why, then, should I find myself weeping through the entire first act if it were not that the work is a hymn in praise of all that western society has discarded in its pursuit of power: continuity, community, respect for the uniqueness of the individual and, above all, education in its truest sense, education of the emotions, for that is what happens to Walther von Stolzing in the course of the drama. *Die Meistersinger* is wonderfully funny, infinitely sad and painfully beautiful; it is perhaps significant that it is set in the period of a society which immediately afterwards was to be destroyed by the scientific world view. Behind the scenes, one feels, is a living community that cares about Sachs, about the Mastersingers' contest, about Eva, Maddalena and David, even about Beckmesser and the intruder Walther. The message is too clear, too explicit, to be unintended, yet present-day audiences confine their attention to the vocal abilities of the singers and details of production and musical direction. The criticism, like the whole of Romantic music, has been effortlessly absorbed and trivialized by the mainstream middle-class culture. The language is familiar; the conductor raises his baton, tonic moves to dominant and back again, the spectacle remains safely in its frame and distance is comfortably preserved.

It was not until the closing years of the nineteenth century that a new language began to be evolved which was to make possible the revolt against post-Renaissance sensibility itself. As with many revolutions, some of the leaders were conscious destroyers of the old, while many others, probably the majority, were caught up in it against their conscious will, believing themselves to be merely opening up the *ancien régime* a little. It is always well to remember that few truly creative artists are consciously concerned with making revolutions; mostly they are thinking simply about their current creation and perhaps sketching out the next. Few concern themselves with history and their place in it; those who do usually occupy, as does Schoenberg for example, a very special historical niche. Yet, on the other hand, it was Schoenberg who eloquently and consistently voiced his reluctance to be cast in the role of revolutionary.

It is in fact this ability of our society to absorb into itself and neutralize revolt that has characterized the history of music – and not only art music – in our century. This is also true in other fields; an avant-garde theatre director recently observed disgustedly that 'Middle-class audiences these days consume Brecht like a new breakfast cereal.' One after another, the great revolutionaries are being absorbed into the mainstream of the concert repertory and their revolt is neutralized. We have seen in our own time the domestication of Debussy, of Satie and Stravinsky. Schoenberg (some of his music at least) and Webern are gaining a degree of acceptance by the middle-class concert goer, Ives is losing much of his power to disturb, while Mahler and Berg are becoming concert and opera-house favourites. Yet each in his time had something of importance to say about and to our culture, and one can still today feel something of the force of that message. What they had to say is not revealed by the surface of the music, by its overt message or subject matter; Wozzeck's sad fate may move the audience to tears but not to give away their goods to the poor, any more than will the *Ode to Joy* induce listeners to the *Ninth Symphony* to embrace one another. No; just as we found in our examination of the classical tradition, we shall discover that the meaning lies within the techniques themselves. While it is an exaggeration to say that the medium is the message, it is true that the medium carries a message, which is, as with so many spontaneous gestures, often of more significance than those which we deliberately make.

If tonal functional harmony, as I suggested earlier, is a syntactical system of chord relationships by which expectations are created and satisfied, tensions aroused and resolved, and if its historical development can be viewed as the progressive increase of the tension by the use of ever more dissonant sounds (acceptable so long as they can be shown finally to relate to the logical structure of the discourse) and an increase in the level of expectation by delaying for as long as possible its satisfaction, then both tendencies reach their climax in the works of Wagner, and most obviously in *Tristan und Isolde*.

With the intuition of the great artist, Wagner saw (if not perhaps completely consciously − the borderline of conscious activity is impossible to draw in artistic work) the analogy between the story of lovers whose passion was so intense that it could only be requited in death, and the techniques of tonal harmony stretched to breaking point. At the opening of the famous *Prelude* a dissonance is sounded, which resolves on to another dissonance, and so on through the course of the entire drama. This famous dissonance, which has come to be known as the *Tristan chord*, finds resolution only in the last moments of the drama, three enormous acts and nearly five hours later. The lovers are both dead, and just as it is only in death that their love can be satisfied, so it is only at the moment of the representation of their death that the dissonance can be resolved.

This seemed to be about as far as the resources of tonal functional harmony could stretch without breaking altogether. If we see in tonal-harmonic music a metaphor for the rationalistic and individualistic temper of western man, then Wagner presents to us, in genuinely mythic form, his situation in the later years of the nineteenth century, which was about as far along the rationalist-individualist road as it was possible to travel at that time. Debussy, thirty years later, said that Wagner was a sunset that thought it was a sunrise, and we can see now that he was right; Wagner stands at the end of an old tradition, not, as he himself thought, at the beginning of a new.

Wagner was, of course, writing a music drama, not proving a technical point. But he presented his successors with a terrible problem. Given the twin tendencies of tonal-harmonic music, if the resources of the tradition had been stretched to breaking point, what further could a composer do and still remain within the domain of rationalistic western culture? Here we again see something of the prophetic nature of art, since the dilemma of musicians in the last years of the nineteenth century was a metaphor and a model of the situation which has faced western man throughout the present century, although it has reached crisis point only in our own time. Just as, in tonal-harmonic music, the relaxation that the music seeks to achieve by logical means becomes ever more elusive, so, too, the more western man seeks peace, security and the satisfaction of needs through the proliferation of material means, with the products of will and intellect divorced from values, the more does he find them receding from him; the more he tries to progress, the more he destroys that which he wishes to attain. The dilemma appeared in metaphorical form decades before the problem itself emerged from the matrix of society.

When Debussy was astonished by the performances of the Javanese and Annamese musicians in 1889, he must have been only one of thousands who heard this music and marvelled at it. Nevertheless it was he, and only he among the musicians of his time, who found that it spoke intimately to him; his mind was prepared. We read of him as a student improvising at the piano and mocking the dismay of his fellow students who, he said, could not hear a chord unless they could put a name to it. His temper was already turned against the rationalistic, abstract nature of tonal-harmonic music and symphonic composition; the gamelan merely served to confirm what he already knew, that other kinds of musical thinking were possible, and indeed, since the music of Wagner, even necessary.

Debussy was born in 1862, and thus grew up in the 1870s and 1880s, when the high tide of Wagnerism was sweeping over French musical culture. He was for a time thoroughly immersed in it, but emerged finally with the help not only of his friend Erik Satie but also of his own infatuation with sound. It may seem odd to describe a composer as in love with sound; one should expect such a state to be characteristic of any musician. But, as was pointed out earlier, the classical tradition was interested, not in the actual sounds themselves but in the relationships between them, the patterns into which they could be organized and the intellectual and emotional weight they could be made to bear. Debussy, on the other hand, loved sound for its own sake; it was the immediacy of the sensual experience that fascinated him. He once remarked that he would exchange all the symphonies of Beethoven for a single sunrise – an unguarded remark, perhaps, and not to be taken too literally, but indicative of a frame of mind.

Debussy is not to be written off as a limp-wristed aesthete wallowing in a sensual warm bath; on the contrary, he had a fine, disciplined and deeply perceptive mind. What we hear in his music is a new-found – or new-regained – respect for nature, which meant for him the nature of sounds. Sound is no longer inchoate raw material to be put into the service of human communication by the force of will and intellect, but is to be listened to and loved for its own sake. In parallel, nature in his music is portrayed not merely as the background and sustainer of the human drama (as in, for example, Beethoven's *Pastoral Symphony,* Smetana's *Vltava* or Wagner's overture to *Der Fliegende Holländer*) but as an autonomous entity, independent of human values. In *La Mer,* for example, unlike those earlier sea- and land-scapes, there are no human figures, no sailors, no shipwrecks, no menace (a human concept) – in short, no drama. It is the innocent sea, as it was before the human race appeared and will be after it has gone, the only dialogue being between the wind and the sea, the only play that of the waves.

Even in the earlier works, where Debussy had not yet emancipated the individual sound from its position as a link in a logical chain, we hear his delight in the sound for its own sake – not perhaps an entirely new phenomenon in the closing years of the nineteenth century but new in having a structural, rather than a purely decorative function in the composition. Consider, for example, the wonderful opening of the *Prélude à l'Après-midi d'un Faune,* with its unaccompanied low-pitched flute sounds and sweeping harp glissandi leaving a dissonant chord unresolved, superficially not unlike (and definitely on the conscious level influenced by) the *Tristan chord,* but lacking in any urge to resolution, and therefore inhabiting a different world from that of

Wagner. This music, for all its air of spontaneity, is as precisely calculated as a Bach fugue, its very precision of concept and execution precluding any trace of sentimentality or nostalgia. Despite its overt subject matter, the sensual musings of a faun on the slopes of ancient Etna, it does not look back to any lost world, but is rather a manifesto for a 'potential society which lies beyond our grasp', a society living happily in the present, free from the constraints of clock time and the urge to domination. No wonder Pierre Boulez said that 'modern music awakes with the flute of the Faun'.[4]

To Debussy a chord was not merely a link in a logical chain, an instrument for an expressive end; it was almost an end in itself. We have seen how the dominant seventh chord, for instance, had in classical practice a clearly defined function as leading strongly to the tonic, but in the piano prelude *La Cathédrale Engloutie* of 1910 we find a descending chain of dominant sevenths (bars 62-64) which never resolve on to a tonic, or show any urge to do so; they are not functional dominant sevenths but rather sonorities, chosen for their concrete sound alone. They do not resolve because Debussy does not perceive them as dissonances; in fact the concepts of consonance and dissonance have here no more significance than they have in a peal of bells.

Another passage in the same prelude (bars 28-40) represents the chanting of monks; here Debussy takes a simple triad (in its second inversion, itself a dissonance according to classical practice) and moves it bodily around, treating it as a sound in itself, not as a member of a harmonic sequence. The very low C that punctuates the phrases is especially significant. An earlier composer would have been likely to regard it as a harmonic bass or pedal point, and, to obtain the utmost weight and strength of sonority, would have added the C an octave above. But the two Cs in combination produce a sound which is much more precise in pitch, whereas Debussy wanted the sound of the very low C, which on the piano is apt to be ill-defined, to represent the sound of a very deep bell, whose pitch is also vague. That low C, all alone, far below the rest of the music, is a sonority which belongs exclusively to the piano and will not transcribe for the orchestra or any other instrument or combination of instruments. Only the hand on the keyboard can produce the *sound* (rather than the pitch, although the pitch is of course one aspect of the sound) that Debussy imagined.

A consequence of this new interest in sound for its own sake is that the forward impulse of harmony disappears. The music no longer creates expectation, no longer pulls us forward into the future; it remains firmly in the present, to be experienced moment by moment. We live in the *now,* holding ourselves passive, letting the sounds enter into us — passive but not supine, with the passivity of him who watches nature with a lover's concern, at work in her own time, not coerced into action in a laboratory. Without the impelling power of the harmonic progression, without the regular swing of the I-IV-V and its patterns of regularly recurring accent, we once more regain something of the rhythmic freedom of medieval — or indeed of Javanese or Annamese — music.

What Debussy did, in fact, was to liberate European music from sequential logic. Chords in his usage, regardless of whether they are in classical usage 'consonant' or 'dissonant', become entirely new kinds of material; the ear no longer attempts to analyse them or to discern the direction in which they are tending, but simply accepts them, as one does a peal of bells, the sounds of the wind or the sea, for their own sakes. In his music, too, instrumental timbres enter into the substance of the discourse, acquiring a completely new importance in their own right, rather than a mere decorative function. We find ourselves much closer to the sonorous experience, in much more sensuous, tangible contact with sound, than in tonal-functional music. Nature (in this case the nature of sound) is treated with a lover's joy.

Debussy worked a quiet revolution, in that in his work the engine of European tonal-harmonic music ran down and stopped. Sound qualities rather than harmony, or sometimes even melody, become factors in the construction of a work, and accordingly the whole classical apparatus of closed forms — themes, development, modulations and all the other devices for the articulation of time — disappears. Even regular rhythmic accent may vanish.

It is in the ballet *Jeux* that we find the most complete realization of his techniques. This has been an unlucky work, and even today it is not well known to concert audiences. Debussy wrote it for Diaghelev's 1913 Paris season. He disliked the subject and was unhappy with Nijinsky as choreographer; its success at the time was only moderate, and was swamped by the scandalous première of *Le Sacre du Printemps* only a fortnight later. It has only recently been perceived as the masterpiece it is. Boulez has written the sleeve note for his own recording of the work. He says,

> *Jeux* marks the advent of a musical form which *instantly* renewing itself involves a no less instantaneous mode of listening ... the usual

categories of an exhausted tradition could not be applied to his work ... Debussy repulsed all hierarchy except the musical event itself ... the moment and the mobile erupt in his music; not only in the impression of the instant, or intangible, to which it is reduced, but a relative and irreversible conception of musical time, and, more generally, of the musical universe. In the organization of sound, the conception is expressed by a refusal to acknowledge existing harmonic hierarchies as the unique data of the world of sound.[4]

What I take Boulez to be saying is that Debussy cut through all the traditional techniques of harmony and organization of time to a world where the moment, the *now*, is all-important, looking neither forward nor backward, using none of the devices of anticipation or reference back that had previously characterized western music. His music has in fact a hypnotic quality that takes us out of time.

If the revolutionary significance of Debussy's music was long overlooked, the reason lies in the simple fact that it is so easy on the ear. Although the music often contains surprising and sharp dissonances, they are so cunningly placed and so couched in ravishing instrumental and vocal sound that everything is subsumed into consonance. It is therefore difficult to realize that an important divide has been crossed, in that dissonances no longer bear within them any urge to resolution. They exist, like natural objects, as things in themselves rather than as a means to an end. So in Debussy nature is readmitted in her own right to the tonal world, nature, admittedly, still playful and sunny, as Pousseur says, a garden rather than a jungle, invoking pleasure rather than awe;[5] Debussy's is in fact among the most joyful music ever written.

But, once nature is allowed to return on her own terms, there is no reason to stop at that point. Once we admit that sound (that is, nature) has an autonomous value, once we admit the significance of sounds or sonorities as objects in themselves, once we negate the harmonic argument, why should we content ourselves with those sounds which conform to the canons of taste decreed by the society of the day? Can we not open our ears to all sounds and every sound, however mysterious, however inexplicable in harmonic terms they may be? In so doing we acknowledge, and even celebrate, the mysteriousness and the final unknowability of nature.

It was, thus, Debussy who established a language for the argument against the scientific world view, of a kind which the Romantics, noble as their achievements were, never succeeded in forging. But it was not a western European who understood the significance of Debussy's work, but the young Igor Stravinsky, newly arrived from what to the sophisticated Parisians were the semi-barbarous wastes of Russia.

There is little doubt that it was his acquaintanceship with Debussy, whom he had met in 1910 after the sensational Paris success of *L'Oiseau de Feu*, which liberated Stravinsky from the constraints of functional harmony (though, being Russian, and having therefore received the Renaissance tradition at second hand, his feeling for tonal functional harmony being less bred in the bone, he had less of the European tradition to weigh against. He also had Mussorgsky in his inheritance, who, as Debussy acknowledged, had gone more than halfway there.) He and Debussy had played through parts of *Le Sacre du Printemps* on two pianos long before the première in July 1913.

The dissonant chord which opens the *Danse des Adolescents* has become almost as famous as the *Tristan chord* or the four notes which open Beethoven's *Fifth Symphony*. It has *almost* lost its power to disturb, *almost* reached the stage of cosy familiarity with which we greet Beethoven's *Fifth*, or the statue music in *Don Giovanni*, yet in that chord lies the even more complete reversal of the tonal-harmonic aesthetic than Debussy had imagined. Logic, clarity and transparency were the ideals of that aesthetic, and this chord is not clear, not is it logical or transparent. It consists of two quite ordinary chords superimposed, an F flat major triad underneath and a dominant seventh based on E flat on top, the two in perfectly arbitrary association, probably found by Stravinsky's fingers as he explored the keyboard of his piano, and while each element taken alone is perfectly clear, in that one can hear one's way through it, the two superimposed become quite impenetrable to the ear. One can no longer identify the elements, and certainly the chord can play no part in any logical tonal-harmonic sequence.

If there is in the harmonies of *Le Sacre du Printemps* no longer any logic in the internal organization of the sound, there is even less in the relations between them. The harmonic textures — and they are more often textures of sounds than harmonies in the traditional sense — are static and repetitive. Melodies, and the work is rich in melody, are usually short, lacking in harmonic implication, like folksong; they do not develop, and frequently centre almost obsessively around one note in the manner of Russian folk tunes. The violent corporeal rhythms with their continually shifting patterns of accents stand in their own right, independent of melody and harmony, like those of African drumming.

Much, perhaps too much, has been made of the fact that *Le Sacre du Printemps* appeared on the eve of the first world war; if, however, we view that cataclysm as representing an upsurge of irrationality after three centuries or more of repression in the name of reason, we can see in Stravinsky's early masterpiece a hint of a way out of the impasse of western man. In *Le Sacre,* nature, not well-behaved and playful as in Debussy, but mysterious, unknowable, even menacing, is restored to the realm of the sacred, from which it had been so rudely torn by the efforts of western man from the sixteenth century onwards. Here, as in *Tristan und Isolde* and in Schoenberg's *Erwartung,* indeed in any truly great art, technical means and overt subject matter come into perfect focus one with the other; the spring rituals of prehistoric Russia and the voluntary sacrifice of a young girl as propitiation to the forces of nature are depicted in a musical language which runs completely counter to the rationalistic and logical bias of western music. *Le Sacre,* in fact, celebrates the mystery that remains at the heart of nature.

Stravinsky knew what it was that he was doing. He said in later years, 'Practically no tradition lies behind the creation of *Le Sacre du Printemps,* and no theory. I heard, and I wrote what I heard. I was the vessel through which *Le Sacre du Printemps* passed.'[6] Such language resembles that of the shaman or priest rather than of the artist as commonly thought of in the western tradition. One is reminded indeed of the words of an Eskimo shaman-poet quoted by Sir Maurice Bowra: 'But it will happen that the words we need will come of themselves. When the words we want shoot up of themselves — we get a new song.'[7]

Stravinsky never attempted to repeat the success of *Le Sacre du Printemps,* although *Les Noces* is in a sense a re-statement of the same theme in terms of a Russian peasant wedding, which blends Christian and pagan rituals. Just as in both of these works he created a ritual, so the idea of ritual runs like a thread through all his work to the very last. Our age is starved for ritual, for that unemotional rehearsing of actions that are known to the whole community, which for all their impassivity and lack of external expressiveness carry a powerful emotional charge, grounding it like a lightning conductor, enabling us to celebrate our common humanity, shared beliefs and communal feeling. The secular tendencies of the last three hundred years have demythologized our lives, and without a significant myth no significant ritual is possible.

But if we throw nature out through the front door she comes in through the back, and our false and trivial myths are celebrated by false and trivial rituals. Our myth concerning the nature of knowledge, for example, is celebrated in written examinations such as the English *General Certificate of Education,* which, like other written examinations, probably does not examine anything worth examining (except possibly the candidate's ability to pass examinations), but is a kind of debased adolescent passage rite (debased since we deny our young the consummating experience of ritual rebirth which is the real conclusion of such rites), an ordeal to which we subject our young to conclude their adolescence; if they fail the ordeal or do not present themselves for it they forfeit their right to a place in the affluent society. Similarly the myth of the power of money is celebrated by dozens of petty business rituals: the key to the executive washroom, the name on the door rating the carpet on the floor, the expense-account lunches; these are small but significant examples. (I use the word 'myth' not to suggest falsehood but in its strict sense of a story by means of which men shape their lives and actions.)

Stravinsky's music generally lacks any form of outward emotional display. It presents, like an African ritual mask, a deadpan face, with all the impassivity of a priest performing the mass, and just as, for the Christian believer, the ceremony can be a powerful emotional experience, so can this music. Its frequently-noted features all contribute to this ritual impassivity: the mosaic-like juxtaposition of often disparate elements which makes impossible the developmental techniques of earlier western music, the adoption of varying stylistic manners from the past, now drained of any dramatic quality, and finally the composer's acceptance in his later years of that most objective of technical methods, the twelve-tone series, as a basis for composition. One need consider only three works from widely different periods in the composer's life to see the persistence of this ritualistic quality and understand the unity that underlies the sudden stylistic twists that so puzzled and infuriated his contemporaries: the *Symphonies of Wind Instruments* of 1921, written appropriately in memory of Debussy, the *Symphony of Psalms* of 1930, which has more affinities with Byzantine and medieval psalm settings than with those of the great classical and romantic composers, being concerned not so much with the composer's own religious emotions as with the creation of a state of mind in which some revelation might occur, and thirdly, the *Requiem Canticles* of 1965, whose terse impassivity has more to tell of life, death and eternity than all the emotional fireworks of the Berlioz or Verdi *Requiems.*

In every note of his music Stravinsky celebrates the unknowability, the darkness, that lies at the heart of nature, asserting through his intuitive and even partly unconscious perception (and who can fix precisely the boundary of conscious awareness in the process of creation?) a fact that is becoming more and more apparent in our own time. I use the word 'celebrates' deliberately; it is finally a joyful thing to contemplate a mystery, and Stravinsky's music, like Debussy's, induces a joy of a quite different kind from the music of the classical tradition. To know that there are things that one cannot, and even need not, know is to be able to live once more in a world of rich and varied meaning, quite unlike the joyless two-dimensional universe we should inhabit if ever the human race were to succeed in uncovering the last physical secret of the cosmos. W.H. Auden, a longtime friend of Stravinsky's, put it thus, in his cool and fastidious way:

> *This passion of our kind*
> *For the process of finding out*
> *Is a fact one can hardly doubt,*
> *But I would rejoice in it more*
> *If I knew more clearly what*
> *We wanted the knowledge for,*
> *Felt certain still the mind*
> *Was free to know or not.*[8]

Of the three European masters of the early years of this century who forged a new language for the discourse of music the most heroic, and the least regarded in his own time, was Arnold Schoenberg. He faced the tonal problem of the late nineteenth century head on; where Debussy and Stravinsky had felt free to reject the implications of the work of Wagner he, rightly believing himself the heir of both Wagner and Brahms, accepted the responsibilities of his position (he seems almost to have felt himself to have been chosen for the task) and followed those implications through to the final disintegration of the tonal hierarchy and of the tonal language which derived from it.

One can hear the process in early works such as the *First Chamber Symphony* of 1907; this work is in E major, which is to say that it uses E as a base from which the complex polyphony ranges ever wider and wider until in places there occur notes, chords, whole phrases even, that seem to have travelled so far from the key — or indeed any key — as to have severed any connection with it. In this work they are only passing moments, such as one also hears in the work of contemporaries such as Strauss or Reger, before the sovereignty of key is re-established, but they are prophetic. It was in the last movement of the *Second String Quartet,* a work bearing witness to a spiritual as well as a technical crisis, that for the first time in post-Renaissance music the absence of a key signature means not the key of C major but the absence of all relationships with a tonic. Even here the severance is not final, and the movement ends in F sharp, the ostensible key of the work, but the decisive step had been taken, and the possibility of writing music outside the logical framework of key relationships had been established.

The rejection of the tonal hierarchy and the consequent equality of the twelve degrees of the chromatic scale must have seemed to Schoenberg to lead straight to that state of chaos which, as we have already seen, lives as a vague fear born out of distrust for the methods and purposes of nature in the minds of all rationalistic Europeans; it was thus with enormous courage that he accepted that possibility and turned it to his creative purpose. In doing so (and who can tell if the language or the creative purpose came first?) he found himself equipped to explore a region of human experience very different from the daylit world of logical harmonic relationships: that of the subconscious mind, the half-lit area which many contemporary poets, playwrights and painters, as well as Schoenberg's fellow-Viennese Sigmund Freud, were also engaged in mapping.

Freud had said of dreams that they were 'the royal road to the subconscious'; in the works of Schoenberg's middle period, roughly Op 10 to Op 22, we find the same free-associating quality, the same paradoxical associations, the same concentration and condensation as we experience in dreams. Without the need to establish a key and its logical relationships, the material of a piece could be exposed very quickly, sometimes all at once, much as the ideas tumble over one another in a dream. Schoenberg had always liked to work with motives — short and highly plastic groups of tones — from which he constructed his larger melodic and sometimes even harmonic shapes; in these works the motives are extended, shortened, condensed, telescoped, turned upside down and inside out, placed in relationships which no logic can explain (again as in dreams) but which sound right. He himself spoke of a 'subconsciously functioning sense of form which gave a real composer an almost somnambulistic sense of security in creating, with utmost precision, the most delicate distinctions of formal elements'.[9] A dream is an on-going, evolving drama of pure relationships divorced from the logic of objects; similarly this music is in a constant state of dynamic evolution as one motive mingles with others, and is transformed by them. Schoenberg never repeats what he has already stated, but each moment of a work grows naturally out of the preceding and into the following. This is the real meaning of what he called his technique of perpetual variation; it provides a technique for the exploration of the subconscious, free from the demands of formal tonal logic.

This marvellous series of 'expressionist' works, which clearly relate very closely to the work of the Expressionist painters, writers and especially the dramatists of the time,[10] ranges in scale from the *Sechs Kleine Klavierstücke, Op 19,* of which the longest piece is eighteen bars long and the shortest nine, each piece a tiny dream-fragment, through the *Five Pieces for Orchestra, Op 16* and *Pierrot Lunaire,* with its nightmarish images of violence and nostalgia, to the short operas *Die Glückliche Hand* and *Erwartung.* It is perhaps in the last-mentioned of these that the overt subject matter and the technique coincide most closely, since it is, quite simply, a dream (Schoenberg's own comment that 'In *Erwartung* the aim is to represent in *slow motion* everything that occurs during a single second of maximum spiritual excitement, stretching it out to half an hour'[11] emphasises its dreamlike quality). There is only one character and she is the dreamer; we know nothing of her waking life. She is given no name, being called simply 'The Woman', in interesting parallel to that other twentieth-century dream masterpiece *Finnegans Wake,* in which the characters keep changing their names, the name being par excellence the symbol of waking identity. Schoenberg's dream-logic music matches perfectly the hallucinatory intensity of the libretto, which was written under Schoenberg's direction by Marie Pappenheim, an early follower of Freud. The dream is a nightmare, in which the woman wanders alone in a dark and terrifying forest, apparently waiting for her lover (*Erwartung* means waiting or expectation) – though one cannot be sure of anything in this dream. She eventually finds his body, murdered and bloody. The dream of the violent death of a loved one is not uncommon, and was interpreted by Freud as expressing the mixed feelings of love and resentment we inevitably feel towards those to whom we are closest. In the dream the lover had apparently left her for another woman, who is described only as having white arms (a curious inconsequential detail characteristic of dreams) although whether this woman had any waking reality it is impossible to tell. It may be that the woman woke from her dream to find her lover beside her, as loving as ever; it may even be that the lover himself existed only in the dream. We all know this kind of dream, and Schoenberg touches a raw nerve in us. But in her dream the woman comes to terms with her fears and her guilt, and finally, after a succession of outbursts of terror and jealous rage at her dead lover and her rival, she attains a kind of resigned peace, bidding him a tender farewell as the day breaks. She breaks off in mid-sentence: 'I was seeking ...' and the orchestral ending is a miracle – a mere bar and a half of ascending chromatic scales and the music vanishes. It does not end, or even stop, but simply vanishes, much as a dream vanishes when we wake. Such a stroke could not occur within the tonal-harmonic framework, with its need for a perfect cadence to end a work; indeed, tonal-harmonic music lacked the vocabulary to enter such a discourse at all. Constant Lambert once pointed out that Oscar Wilde, 'in his search for the "curiously coloured, scarlet music" that his soul desired could find nothing better than the piano pieces of Dvorak';[12] western music in the nineties simply lacked the language with which to explore the world that literature and painting had inhabited since Poe and Fuseli – though Wilde need have waited only a few more years to hear his curiously coloured, scarlet music in twentieth century expressionist music.

Schoenberg's development of twelve-tone technique in the early twenties is still a controversial matter. It is possible to argue that it reveals a failure of nerve on his part, and it is true that, with a few exceptions, the twelve-tone compositions are less adventurous, both spiritually and technically, than the 'free' atonal works. Nevertheless, the new technique does seem to have been necessary to its creator for two reasons, the one spiritual and the other technical – that the two go hand in hand is the mark of the psychic unity of the great artist.

The technical reason lies in the extreme strain which free atonal composition imposed upon a mind as steeped as Schoenberg's in the rationalistic techniques of tonal harmony which he had acquired with the laboriousness of the autodidact, and from which he strove in vain to escape completely. Without the constraints imposed by the demands of harmonic progession within a key there is no guide to the choice of tones; in theory at least, at any point in a composition the composer can choose any tone of the chromatic scale, in any register or octave. Every semiquaver has therefore to be invented as it were from scratch; nowhere can the composer relax within the guidelines provided by tonality and the resolution of the dissonance. There is no background in the music; everything is foreground and must be invented totally. It may have been this need for total invention that produced the flickering nervous energy and emotional intensity which inform this music, but the five-year silence which preceded the appearance of the first twelve-tone pieces suggests that he felt himself unable (and he was, after all, approaching fifty) to continue composing at such fever heat.

This view is lent support by the fact that it is possible to hear in the first twelve-tone works, the *Five Pieces for Piano, Op 23*, the *Serenade, Op 24* and especially the *Suite for Piano, Op 25,* a new relaxation, a new detachment, after the intense subjectivity of the previous works, an almost neo-classical abstraction and even an ironic wit that recalls much of Stravinsky's work of the same period. His twelve-tone technique had in fact provided a rule that saved him from the strain of total freedom, and, in giving him a rule, a guide for the choice of the pitch material at his disposal, enabled him to relax somewhat.

But allied to this technical point was a spiritual one, which shows that Schoenberg found himself in a position remarkably similar to that of Freud on which I remarked in an earlier chapter. Freud, as I pointed out, took a somewhat ambivalent attitude towards his own discoveries in the subconscious; one occasionally gets the impression that he would rather not have made them at all. Similarly, certain remarks made by Schoenberg in later life lead one to wonder whether he would not in fact have been happier not to have been chosen for his life's task. 'I was not destined', he wrote in 1948, 'to continue in the manner of *Verklaerte Nacht* or the *Gurrelieder* or even of *Pélléas und Mélisande.* The Supreme Commander had ordered me on a harder road.'[13] Again, when asked by his commanding officer in the army if he was 'this notorious Schoenberg' he replied, 'Beg to report, sir, yes. Nobody wanted to be, someone had to be, so I let it be me.'[14] Much of this, of course, reflects the difficulties he had encountered over the acceptance of his music, but one senses also a certain longing for the safe world of tonal relationships from which he had set out long before to explore the new sonic universe and the new territories of the spirit. He followed the road he had chosen (or that he felt had been chosen for him) with courage and integrity, a road which led inexorably towards the destruction of the tradition in which he had grown up, but his music nonetheless remains on a profound level true to that tradition and its ideals. It remains in many respects tied to the rhetoric of tonal music, to its forms and its gestures; we hear in it what often sounds like functional dissonance raised to its highest pitch of tension — but the dissonance never resolves. This contradiction, which disturbs so many listeners, is in fact central to his significance to us today.

We have remarked how the gradual increase in the level of dissonant tension over the history of tonal-harmonic music, and in the delay before the sought-after relaxation occurs, made the relaxation which the music sought to achieve ever more elusive. In Schoenberg's music this relaxation finally becomes inaccessible, as if a road had finally been closed off; and if we accept tonal-harmonic music as a metaphor for European rationalism and individualism, then the tonal impasse revealed presents us with a powerful allegory for the dilemma of modern western man.

Schoenberg, genius as he undoubtedly was, never found a way out of the tonal impasse of western music; indeed, it is not at all certain that one has yet been found. The greatness of his achievement lies in the clarity and honesty with which he faced the musical situation, and in so doing depicted the condition of modern man, decades before it manifested itself in the wider social situation. His music speaks directly to us; with warmth and compassion it tells us that our dilemma is the same as his, and will remain unresolved until we find new questions to ask concerning our nature, our needs and the world in which we live.

It was Schoenberg's friend and former pupil Anton Webern who was able to use Schoenberg's essentially arbitrary and unnatural system to enter a new, or perhaps rediscovered, sound world which Schoenberg himself had only glimpsed, a world in many ways not unlike Debussy's in which the individual sound has an autonomous value, but differing from Debussy's in that the natural and the human are held in harmonious balance. We have seen that the great achievements of tonal-harmonic music were made at the cost of a drastic limitation in the means of sound production, virtually every instrument being excluded which was not capable of producing sounds of clear, definite pitch and simple harmonic structure. We have seen how complex and non-harmonic sounds were reintroduced, gradually, almost timidly, at first always as decorative, never as structural features, how, indeed, tone colour itself remained in a role subordinate to the play of pitch relations, which were the real architectural material of the music. The idea that tone colour might become a structural element was in Schoenberg's mind when he observed that 'pitch is in fact only tone colour, measured in one direction', and speculated that music might be in the future constructed with 'timbre-melodies' (*Tonfarbenmelodien*), but he experimented only briefly and tentatively with the idea, as in his *Five Pieces for Orchestra, Op. 16,* as well as extending it into a synaesthesia of sound and vision in *Die Glückliche Hand,* with stage directions for a 'crescendo' of light from red to green to purple and finally white, to match a crescendo of orchestral sound.

In 1913, the same year as *Die Glückliche Hand,* Webern carried forward his teacher's idea in two characteristically brief works, *Six Bagatelles for String Quartet, Op 9,* and *Five Pieces for Orchestra, Op 10.* These go far beyond Schoenberg's experiments, into a world of sounds that are as concrete as those of Debussy. We have seen repeatedly that a composer's treatment of sound itself is a metaphor for his attitude to nature, and we have seen how the music of the classical tradition treated sounds as subordinate to the needs of musical and dramatic argument, relegating nature to the background of the human drama. Debussy, in reinstating nature to the foreground, all but eliminates the human from his landscape, while Webern treats both the natural and the human as existing in a loving and reciprocal relationship, one with the other. Classical music treated the individual sounds much as the absolutist states of the period treated its citizens, as elements of form, of value only collectively, and meaningless individually (can it be coincidence that modern absolutist states such as the USSR try to preserve the 'classical' values in music?). Webern was too thoroughly European a musician to run to the antithesis, of treating the form only as a frame in which to show off the individual sounds, as some modern Americans have done; rather, the individual sound and the over-all form are maintained in subtle and delicate balance. We relish the total characteristics of each sound as it occurs, but we hear the sounds also as part of a large and complex design. The balance can be characterized as a metaphor for an ideal state, in which the needs of the individual and those of the community are viewed, not as an opposition which needs sacrifice and compromise to preserve an uneasy balance (much as Freud viewed western civilization and its discontents) but rather as complementary, the individual being fully realized only within his social milieu and the needs of the community being most fully met by completely realized individuals. That such a society may not exist is immaterial (though some come closer to it than those whose minds are limited to the western experience might imagine); the music offers us the *symbols of that potential society* which lies still beyond our grasp.

If we listen to, say, the first of Webern's tiny *Six Bagatelles for String Quartet,* we obtain an impression almost of a solid object in sound. The composer organizes not only the pitches but also the tone colours, the densities (the number of sounds going on at a given moment), the intensities of the sounds, their durations (not only the point of onset but also the ending of each sound is important), the way a sound overlaps its predecessor, butts on to it or is separated from it, silence thus becoming not merely the space between the sounds but a rhythmic possibility in itself. Each characteristic of the sounds may be changing at a different rate from, and out of phase with, the others, so that the total effect is of a many-dimensioned object changing its shape constantly, though retaining the same substance (in this case the homogeneous sound of the string quartet). It is like a piece of clay as we knead it between our fingers, or a computer graphic which shows on a video screen the changes that take place in a complex mathematical expression as we alter the variables. And yet the effect is not cold and mathematical, but warm and lyrical. *The Five Pieces for Orchestra* are equally to be admired as sound constructions and as miniature tone poems (the third, for example, surely evokes the Alpine landscapes Webern knew and loved so well).

He adopted the twelve-tone method effortlessly and with no perceptible change of style, using it consistently for the rest of his life, although in a way altogether different from Schoenberg's – a way which is both simpler and more rigorous – in conjunction with almost medieval contrapuntal, especially canonic, devices of the utmost complexity. Yet despite (or even, perhaps, as with Bach, because of) the dizzying complexity of the intellectual processes on paper, what emerges in performance is great beauty of sound, and a lyricism which is all the more telling for being understated. Webern is as concerned with counterpoint of rhythms, of tone colours and densities, of patterns of articulation, as of pitches. The concern for every aspect, every parameter, of every sound that is made results in a music which, although polyphonically conceived, resembles more a band, a multi-coloured ribbon of sound, made by the interweaving of lines and of the spaces between them as they pass in succession from one instrument to another, a band which is thus in a state of constant transformation as it progresses through time.

There is in this music none of the division into foreground and background that we have noted in earlier music, no harmonic tension and relaxation (one of Webern's minor miracles was his draining of the tension out of highly dissonant intervals such as major sevenths and minor seconds and ninths, making them sound as relaxed as do thirds and sixths in earlier music), none of the treble-and-bass pull which imposes upon our hearing of that music, however we may admire its polyphony, the unity of the progression of chords, no transitional or spacing-out material, no rhetorical gestures, no 'melody-and-accompaniment' texture; every voice, every sound, is of equal importance with every other, yet gains its full significance only in its relationships with other sounds, like members of a truly just society.

It was surely this aspect of Webern's work which, however dimly perceived (Henri Pousseur alone has committed the perception to print[15]), led those European composers who had grown up in the terrible years of the second world war and came to maturity in the late forties to look to his work as a model. And certainly it must have seemed as if his whole life, spent in obscurity, virtually ignored by the big-time musical world, polishing, as Stravinsky said, his precious diamonds in mines whose extent only he knew,[16] which finally ended in a grotesque and violent incident when he was shot by an American soldier of the occupying forces three months after the ending of the war in Europe, had been spent in preparing a language which could replace what seemed to those young composers to be a worn-out and discredited classic-romantic tradition. If Beethoven could have been used as a propaganda device by the winning side, if Wagner could have been perverted to support the megalomaniac obscenity of Nazism, if concentration camp doctors could have spent their days performing unspeakable experiments on human beings and pass their evenings peacefully playing Mozart and Haydn quartets, where, then, was the moral authority claimed for the tradition? All the traditional devices of drama, of rhetoric, of harmonic argument, seemed tarnished and tainted by association; even Schoenberg, to the extent that he remained tied to that tradition, could not provide a model. When this quiet unobtrusive music presented itself, Webern became god to the new generation of musicians. That they seriously misunderstood the nature of his genius, and put back for a generation a true understanding of it, is immaterial; the stone that the builders rejected had become the cornerstone. In its simplicity and concision, its economy and discipline, its lyricism and spiritual simplicity, it provided a starting point for the whole efflorescence of post-war European music.

The group of composers who took their point of departure from Webern came, largely through the annual Darmstadt summer course and festival and the support of the newly reconstituted West German radio networks, to dominate European music. But, in their desire to divest themselves of the last remnants of the former tradition, they deeply misunderstood Webern's reticent lyricism, and his attitude to sound, compounding the error by finding features in it that did not in fact exist. In their rejection of the subjectivity of the classical tradition, they saw in Webern, not lyricism and the loving exploration of sound, but objectivity, the objectivity of science and of numbers. Looking through the pages of *Die Reihe,* the occasional publication edited by Stockhausen and Herbert Eimert which acted as mouthpiece for the group between 1955 and 1963,[17] one cannot but be struck by the proliferation of graphs, formulas and diagrams, the paraphernalia of science and mathematics. Most of this is in fact nonsense, and its pretensions were gleefully demolished by a physicist-musician, who concluded that it amounted to 'nothing more than a mystical belief in numerology as the fundamental basis of music'.[18] Such a belief is, of course, not new, and has been found by musicians of many periods to be a fruitful source of ideas, but never before had the deductive logic of numbers been invoked and used so ruthlessly, in the hope of gaining total control, on the intellectual level, over the sounds themselves, and of abolishing the irrational from music. Taking, like Webern, the individual sound as starting point, these composers subjected it to such an extreme form of serial control of all its parameters (we note the borrowing of mathematical terminology), that is to say, of not only pitch but also duration, tone colour, intensity and type of attack, that each piece became simply the logical result of the serial postulates while the act of composition became simply the working-out of those postulates. The aural aspects of the music became subordinate to the ideal of total control, and the paradoxical result was near-incomprehensibility. The more nearly complete the control over every aspect of the music the more random it sounds — but in any case it soon became clear that total control of the kind envisaged was impossible. Boulez in a later essay wrote, 'On the basis of my experience it is impossible to foresee all the meanders and virtualities contained in the material you start with ... Despairingly one tries to dominate one's material by an arduous, sustained, vigilant effort, and despairingly chance persists, and slips in through a thousand unstoppable loopholes.'[19] We have here a restatement of what we have seen to be constant theme of western music – and western thinking – the domination of nature by bringing her under conscious control. (That this theme should have been restated so forcefully in new form after more than forty years is perhaps by hindsight not surprising if one considers how the west, and indeed all the industrialized world, after the second world war, redoubled its efforts towards the scientific and technological domination of the universe, rejecting, on the example of the United States and the German 'economic miracle', the opportunity to construct a society on the Webernian model.) But chance – or the subconscious mind, what Koestler in his telling phrase calls the 'Ghost in the Machine' – trips us up every time, and Boulez was not the first European to wonder what hit him; we have already remarked on the despair provoked by intimations that nature may not be susceptible to total control through the methods of science. (Boulez in the same essay gives in a revealing phrase his definition of the function of art: to 'fix the Infinite'.) Like all attempts to gain total mastery, its failures and its successes alike resulted in an impoverishment of experience; the early music of the so-called Darmstadt School refuses in the most puritanical way to make the slightest concession to the ear. Nearly twenty-five years after their composition, Stockhausen's *Kontra-Punkte* and *Zeitmasse,* Boulez' *First Book of Structures* and *Polyphonie X* as well as scores of lesser productions of the period remain as remote, forbidding and enigmatic as when they were first heard at Darmstadt or Donauischingen.

To say this is by no means to deny the validity of the vision of these composers, which ironically seems to have more to do with Schoenberg's feeling of being driven by historical necessity than with Webern's visionary lyricism and love of nature. Indeed it can be argued that these works were carrying out a necessary purification of style, much as the German novelist Heinrich Böll, for example, writing immediately after the war, felt it necessary to weigh every word in the German language to eliminate any which showed traces of contamination with the imagery of Nazism. It is true, also, that the deductive inevitability of the method revealed new technical devices that are now common currency in western music: extended static passages, pointillist textures, new means of instrumental articulation, new sound combinations, which might not have been discovered had not the method cut across composers' habitual ways of thinking. But it was basically a bleak vision, coming closer to despair (a state which, if attained, would surely prevent an artist from engaging in any creative activity whatsoever) than perhaps any other music of the western tradition. It is a despair which arises from the final recognition of man's inability ever to bring the materials of his art – or his world – under complete conscious control; yet it was already clear, as we have seen in the work of Stravinsky, that such a recognition should be a cause not for despair but for celebration – a view which John Cage also set out to demonstrate, in his life no less than in his art (if indeed he would acknowledge any split between them).

In any case, one cannot live for long with such a vision; the phase of 'total serialism' in its most rigorous form was brief, and the composers of the Darmstadt School have long since gone their own ways and lost any semblance of unity they may once have possessed. Boulez himself in his 1958 article,[19] attacked the total serial concept and explained how he came to 'integrate chance into the notion of structure itself ', to 'tame those potentialities, and force them to render an account, to account for themselves' – in other words, to bring even chance under conscious control like other elements of composition – by allowing elements of choice to the performer. His *Third Piano Sonata,* for example, allows the performer the freedom to rearrange the order of the movements (within limits) and to accept or reject certain material that the composer provides – no great concession to multiple possibilities but clearly to Boulez an important one. It was, finally, his marvellous aural imagination, stimulated by the study of his second idol, Debussy, that enabled him to move out of the Waste Land, but his world remains stubbornly that of the rationalist-Cartesian, and his attempts to accommodate chance seem strangely half-hearted and offhand. The text of his best-known work, *Le Marteau sans Maître,* has a nightmare quality, suggesting what happens when conscious control (the *Maître* of the title) is abandoned; the airy, floating music has an improvisatory quality at odds with the rational strictness of the serial organization. The fact that he has written little since the sixties may testify to the strain of continuing in such a position, although a work written in 1975, *Rituel,* in memory of Bruno Maderna, suggests, with its choruses of gongs, a movement towards the world of his former teacher, Olivier Messiaen.

Of the other former leading members of the Darmstadt School, Stockhausen has retreated into an orientalism of a kind which proclaims loudly, if all unawares, his imprisonment in the western tradition (which does not, however, prevent him from on occasion writing works of power and beauty such as *Stimmung* and *Mantra* – but they remain ineluctably western concert music). Berio, whose intense musicality and Italian ear for sensuous melody never allowed him to travel so far along the road of total serial organization as to lose touch with a considerable audience, uses serial techniques in complex and beautiful theatrical works which implore the significance of the act of making music; every one of his works acknowledges the dramatic nature of western music, whether or not it belongs to the theatre. Nono, on the other hand, like Henze, has become sidetracked into the spurious dichotomy between political commitment and artistic values (spurious in that it exists only when one assumes the importance of the art-object over the art-process).

These composers, all of whom are now in their fifties, along with many of the younger generations, represent what might be called the 'official' avant-garde of European music; they work mainly within the assumptions of the western tradition, using concert halls and traditionally trained professional musicians, and, despite certain innovations, their music is performed to an audience in the traditional manner. It is likely, too, that their music, if it has not done so already, will eventually meet with the approval of the middle-class concert audience and be absorbed into the mainstream of the culture as that of their predecessors has been; perhaps this is finally what they would wish. In so far as they accept these limitations, while seeking always to extend them, they, like other composers discussed in this chapter, present little direct challenge to the concert tradition itself or its conventions and assumptions, although it is, admittedly, often their intention to bring these conventions and assumptions to our notice.

All of the music of our time in fact finds itself confronted with the crucial problem of finding a relationship with the central myth of our society, which I have called the scientific world view. Bartok, for example, confronted the myth of rationality with the musical thinking of pre-industrial European peoples, its free additive rhythms, its non-harmonic modal melodies which he took as the basis of his own work, as well as forms and shapes derived from nature, such as the Fibonacci series, the mathematical principle underlying the growth patterns of pine cones and nautilus shells alike, and the Golden Section, and those sounds of millions of small night creatures that can be heard in many of his slow movements. At the same time, he was not unequivocal in his rejection of classical forms and techniques; right to the end of his life he continued to work within the framework, however greatly enlarged, of classical harmonic progressions, traditional forms and means of articulation of time. Bartok, like Schoenberg, was a musician of genius who sensed the existence of the potential society but was never able fully to enter it in his imagination; as with Schoenberg, much of the power of his music lies in the tension between the two worlds. It has been, on the other hand, an unfortunate characteristic of too much British music of this century that it retreats from the confrontation altogether, taking refuge in a vision of a pastoral England, or of Celtic lands, that probably never existed.

Then there is Messiaen himself, the true French heir of Debussy, who, in the words of Wilfrid Mellers, 'seeks to assert man's validity not in conflict with, but as part of, the principles – if not the "laws" – of Nature.' Mellers continues, 'He, more than any other composer of our time, represents modern man's weariness with a literate, will-dominated, patriarchal culture ... He is concerned with the nature of Matter (in this case sound-matter) in itself; with the possibility of changing matter not through man's will but by way of understanding of its laws; and with the ultimate possibility of man himself being reborn, so that the All becomes the One.'[20] Messiaen is arguably the greatest living European composer, but I intend here not to pursue such an argument, but merely to point out the characteristics of his music that support Mellers' comment.

Central to any understanding of Messiaen is his strong and almost naïvely undoubting Catholicism. To say this might appear to contradict my earlier observations on the role of the Judaeo-Christian tradition in bringing about the schism which afflicts western society, but Messiaen's Catholicism is a faith which sees no discontinuity between the creator god and created nature, between time and eternity, between man, and his own physical, especially sensual, self, and the world of which he is a part. He is in fact nearer to the pantheism of St Francis of Assisi than to any dogma issuing from the Vatican. He is concerned less with matters of Christian doctrine than with the all-involving mystical experience, and his religion transcends the boundaries of orthodox Christian belief.

Just as he has taken the Christian faith as he found it and built on it something wider, less time-bound, more universal, so he has taken the technical means of European music as he found them, its materials and instruments, and made of them something which transcends the western tradition. This we can hear both in his approach to the piano, from which he draws remarkable new sonorities while avoiding outré ways of playing, and in his use of traditional orchestral and instrumental resources. His enthusiasm for the sounds of percussion, especially for the instruments which have been called the 'western gamelan' — xylophone, xylorimba, vibraphone, glockenspiel, chimes, gongs and piano — is no longer unusual among western composers, yet here again he creates a unique sound, of splendour and sensuous beauty, of huge climaxes and intimate moments, a music of almost corporeal presence, which celebrates at once the glory of his God, the splendour of nature and of sound itself, the innocence of birds (which Messiaen treats as symbols of unfallen nature, in that they live outside the 'abyss of Time' into which western man has tumbled). The music is impersonal, ritualistic; like Stravinsky, Messiaen is interested less in personal expression than in the creation of a state of mind in which revelation can take place, but unlike Stravinsky he grounds his music firmly in the physical nature of man and of sound. Time and time again in his music one feels that sound, for example the recurring trio of gongs in *Et Exspecto Resurrectionem Mortuorum,* is meant, not just to make a point in the musical discourse, but to be admired and enjoyed in its own right. How intently one listens to the ever-louder recurrence of the three gongs, noting the change in timbre — the *nature* of the sound they make — as they are struck ever more and more forcefully, and by the power and beauty of the sound as it fades. These sounds are living creatures; the music is pervaded with wonder at and love of their inner nature, at a chord, a sonority, sometimes even a simple triad, perhaps with sensuous added sixth, as it emerges from a complex dissonant texture. Like Webern's, his sound-creatures inhabit a society; they live in a world that is suffused through and through with divinity, or, even more specifically, with love, both human (including sexual love) and divine. Messiaen's is not a faith that bears much resemblance to the God-sciences of the theologians but it would be quite familiar to a Hindu or a Buddhist.

Messiaen has been reported as saying 'I am no Cartesian Frenchman,' and in denying the inheritance of Descartes he denies also the schism to which the scientific world view of the Renaissance committed western culture. The quest for unity pervades the whole of his musical technique; even the famous (or notorious) piano piece *Mode de Valeurs et d'Intensités* in which for the first time serial techniques were applied not only to pitches but also to durations, types of attack and dynamics, was inspired less by a desire for total control than by a desire to unify all the elements of a piece. It was this piece which, by a kind of creative misunderstanding not uncommon in the history of the arts, inspired Boulez and Stockhausen to begin their experiment in total serial control.

It is to be expected that the dualistic processes of tonal functional harmony play virtually no part in his music; indeed, for the most part they could not occur, since his music is largely built, not on the diatonic or even the total chromatic scale, but on various non-diatonic modes of his own devising, which may have more or fewer than seven tones to the octave. There are harmonies, in the broader sense, dissonant and consonant complexes of sound which give colour (for Messiaen himself quite literally as his synaesthetic sense is very strong) to his melodies, sometimes making parallel bands of sound, a development of Debussy's parallel triads, sevenths and ninths. But equally we find long passages of monody, such as the *Dance of Fury* in the *Quartet for the End of Time,* where all four instruments play in unison and the octave throughout, and heterophony, such as the *Epode* in *Chronochromie,* where harmonic relationships between the eighteen real string parts have no more significance than they have in the birds' dawn chorus that the movement represents. Both melodically and harmonically Messiaen favours the tritone (the interval between the fourth and seventh degrees of the major scale) over the perfect fifth; this is an interesting reversal of attitude, in that the tritone, the one irrational interval of the diatonic scale and a perpetual tripwire to musical logic (the old theorists called it *Diabolus in Musica*), represents to Messiaen not a menace but 'the subtlety of radiant bodies, pure as the angels of God in the heavens'. Lacking the alternate tension and relaxation of tonal functional harmony and its forward directional impulse, the music remains in the present, free also from the periodicity of accent and rhythmic squareness of tonal-harmonic music. This enables the composer to put to use his studies of Indian and ancient Greek concepts of rhythm, of Gregorian chant as well as of the music of Debussy, Stravinsky and, surprisingly, Mozart, from whose treatment of the rhythms of speech he finds much to learn, leading him to a rhythmic practice which is based on duration rather than accent, and which is, to use his own words, 'inspired by the movement of nature, a movement of free and uneven durations', placing his music outside the reach of mechanical time and into the time of nature, time as we perceive it rather than as we measure it. His influence in this respect on younger composers has been incalculable.

We would thus seem to find in this music a closing of the gap that opened in our society at the time of the Renaissance (although its origins lie far earlier) and a restoration of the nature of western man to itself. Yet western man continues on his Cartesian way unheeding, and, while audiences come to hear and applaud, and Messiaen's former pupil Pierre Boulez presents his master with the medal of the Royal Philharmonic Society, the musical world goes on unchanged. Messiaen, like those of his predecessors and successors whom we have been discussing, presents us with the vision of a potential society which lies still beyond our grasp; indeed, it seems not to have formulated itself in the minds of more than a very few people. Composers, like other artists, catch ideas and visions that are, as it were, still in solution in society and crystallize them in metaphorical form; they can do no more, and in any case they do not generally see themselves as being in the business of changing the world. All the composers I have discussed in this chapter have continued to work within the context of the western concert tradition, which in fact appears to be extremely difficult, if not impossible, to break away from; to what extent this limits the force of their vision I shall discuss later. The fact remains, however, that although a new language has been forged, most music lovers fail to comprehend it, thus bearing witness to the continuing power of the Renaissance world view. Before considering this matter, let us complement our study of the ways in which European music in this century has erected a critique of the Renaissance world view with some comments on the development of music in the United States of America, a country founded on the ideal of individual liberty, in which that world view has taken a curious and interesting twist.

Chapter 5: Bibliography

1. WALGATE, Robert: 'Breaking Through the Disenchantment', *New Scientist,* September 18, 1975, p. 375.
2. WADDINGTON, C.H.: *Behind Appearance,* Edinburgh, Edinburgh University Press (1969).
3. LOCKSPEISER, Edward: *Debussy: His Life and Mind,* Vol 1, London, Cassell (1962), p. 204.

4. BOULEZ, Pierre: Sleeve note to recording of *Jeux, La Mer, Prélude à l'Après-midi d'un Faune*, transl. Felix Aprahamian, CBS record 72533.
5. POUSSEUR, Henri: *Fragments Théoriques I sur la Musique Expérimentale*, Brussels, Institut de Sociologie de l'Universitaire Libre de Bruxelles (1970), p. 91.
6. STRAVINSKY, Igor: Introductory remarks to his own recording of *Le Sacre du Printemps*, CBS record 72054.
7. BOWRA, Maurice: *Primitive Song*, London, Weidenfeld & Nicholson (1962), Mentor Books (1963), p. 44.
8. AUDEN, W.H.: 'After Reading a Child's Guide to Modern Physics' in *About the House*, London, Faber (1966).
9. Quoted in MITCHELL, Donald: *The Language of Modern Music*, 2nd edn., London, Faber (1966), p. 39.
10. See for example RITCHIE, J.M. (ed): *Seven Expressionist Plays*, London, Calder & Boyars (1968); *Vision and Aftermath: 4 Expressionist War Plays*, London, Calder & Boyars (1968).
11. SCHOENBERG, Arnold: 'New Music, My Music' in *Style and Idea: Selected Writings*, transl. Leo Black, ed. Leonard Stein, Faber (1975), p. 105.
12. LAMBERT, Constant: *Music Ho! A Study of Music in Decline*, London, Faber (1934), p. 32.
13. SCHOENBERG, Arnold: 'On Revient Toujours', in SCHOENBERG, op. cit., p. 109.
14. SCHOENBERG, Arnold: 'New Music, My Music', in SCHOENBERG, op. cit., p. 104.
15. POUSSEUR, Henri: op. cit., p. 97.
16. STRAVINSKY, Igor: Foreword to *Die Reihe 2: Anton Webern*, London, Universal Edition (1960), p. vii.
17. See *Die Reihe, Nos 1-8*, London, Universal Edition (1955-1962).
18. BACKUS, John: '*Die Reihe:* A Scientific Evaluation', *Perspectives of New Music*, Vol 1, No 1, Fall 1962, pp. 160-71.
19. BOULEZ, Pierre: 'Alea', transl. David Noakes and Paul Jacobs, *Perspectives of New Music*, Vol 3 No 1, Fall-Winter 1964, pp. 42-53.
20. MELLERS, Wilfrid: *Caliban Reborn: Renewal in Twentieth-Century Music*, London, Gollancz (1968), pp. 106-7.

It is a characteristic of tonal-harmonic music that it requires a high degree of subordination of the individual elements of the music to the total effect. Not only is the progress of each individual voice required to conform to the progression of chords, but also each individual note or chord is meaningless in itself, gaining significance only within the context of the total design, much as the authoritarian or totalitarian state requires the subordination of the interests of its individual citizens to its purposes. It is therefore interesting to see in the music of those British colonies which become the United States of America a disintegration of tonal functional harmony taking place long before such a process became detectable in Europe, and it is not too fanciful to view this as one expression of the ideal of individual liberty on which the United States was founded, an ideal which, however meagrely realized or even betrayed during the course of its history, has never quite disappeared.

The colonists who arrived in New England in the early seventeenth century had left behind the last days of a golden age of English musical culture. Many were, in the words of the first Governor of the New England colonies, 'very expert in music', and although the Pilgrims and Puritans favoured sacred over secular music, they had no objection to secular instrumental music, and even dance, as long as decorum was preserved. However, the Mayflower and her successors had little room for any but the most essential cargo, and only the smallest and hardiest musical instruments could be accommodated – certainly nothing so bulky and liable to damage as a virginal or organ. So far as is known, the early colonists could and did enjoy only music that was simple and functional, that is, social music and worship music. As far as the former is concerned, we do know that there were instruments around, though what they played is unclear – possibly from English collections like those of Thomas Ravenscroft, and later John Playford. Secular song was not unknown, not only in the Anglo-Celtic ballads which belonged to the ancient oral rather than to the literate tradition, and which in America proved extremely durable, but also songs from the various collections which had crossed the Atlantic with them. Worship music, on the other hand, meant almost exclusively the singing of the psalms in metrical translation, a practice which was not unknown in England even in the Established Church. This may seem a limited repertoire, but there are after all a hundred and fifty psalms, many of which are very long, and their emotional range is very wide. The version favoured by the early colonists was that of Henry Ainsworth, who used a variety of poetic metres and provided no less than thirty-nine different tunes, which were printed at the back of the book in the form of single lines of melody. Dissatisfaction was, however, early expressed by the Puritan divines, who alleged that faithfulness to the literal word of God was too often sacrificed to literary grace, and in 1640 a new metrical translation was made by a committee and published – the first book to be printed in the New England colony.

The translations were made into only six metrical schemes, mostly in four-line stanzas, so that the same tune could be used for several psalms, and the number of tunes that needed to be learnt was kept to a minimum. The new psalm book was adopted, after much disputation, throughout the New England colonies by the end of the seventeenth century; under the name of *Bay Psalm Book* it ran through innumerable editions over the next century. It was not until the ninth edition, of 1698, that tunes were provided – a mere thirteen – to which the psalms could be sung.

Irving Lowens makes a valuable comment on the American culture of this period:

> The story of the arts in seventeenth century New England is the tale of a people trying to plant in the New World the very vines whose fruit they had enjoyed in the Old, while, at the same time, it is the chronicle of the subconscious development of a totally different civilization. The seventeenth-century history of the *Bay Psalm Book* is a case in point, for although the psalm-tunes may superficially appear nothing more than a parochial utilization of certain music sung in the mother country, a mysterious qualitative change took place when they were sung on different soil. Here, they proved to be the seed from which a new, uniquely American music was later to flower.[1]

The first flowers did not appear until late in the eighteenth century, but even within the psalm-singing tradition some very interesting departures from European practice were very soon to appear. There was an inevitable decline in musical literacy after the first generation of the Pilgrims, brought about by the wilderness conditions in which they found themselves; psalm-singing was transformed from a written to a mainly oral tradition, and despite the efforts of the divines and the 'educated' musicians to instil what they called 'regular singing' (singing, that is, at that neat brisk jogtrot which every church organist still today likes to hear from his congregation), the folk persisted in planting their own fingerprint on the singing of the psalms. It is fascinating to see, at the very beginning of America's cultural history, the kind of clash between native and imported European tradition which was to recur again and again.

Because it was a folk and an oral tradition and frowned upon by educated people, we have only unsympathetic accounts of what was happening; the people, as usual, had no spokesman. Here is the Reverend Cotton Mather, writing in 1721: 'It has been found ... in some of our congregations that in length of time their singing has degenerated into an *odd noise,* that has more of what we want a name for, than any Regular Singing in it.'[2] And, in the same year, one Thomas Walter: 'I have observed in many places, one man is upon this note, while another is on the note before him, which produces something as hideous and disorderly as is beyond expression bad.'[3]

We can infer from these and other contemporary accounts that what was happening was that the people, singing unaccompanied as was usual, had evolved their own style, slowing up the putative beat almost to immobility (though probably each carrying within himself his own beat), gradually sinking in pitch and then perhaps jumping up an octave or a fifth to regain his own natural compass. Then, within each enormously prolonged note (as written), each would proceed to ornament each note with 'turnings and flourishings', grace notes and arabesques, with arbitrary alterations of melody and time. It must have been an astonishing noise; one would wish to have had a tape recorder in Plymouth, Mass., in the 1690s. And, at least in the country areas, there seemed little that the cultivated musicians could do to prevent it; the people sang in their own way as long as the singing remained unaccompanied and there were not enough trained musicians around to confine their musical devotions to the written note.

This continual clash between those who want to regulate and those who do not want to be regulated recurs time and again throughout America's history. Thoreau, for example, writing a hundred and thirty years after Cotton Mather, set the matter eloquently: 'Why should we be in such desperate haste to succeed, and in such desperate enterprises? If a man does not keep pace with his companions, perhaps it is because he hears a different drummer. Let him step to the music which he hears, however measured and far away. It is not important that he should mature as soon as an apple-tree or an oak. If the condition of things which we were made for is not yet, what were any reality which we can substitute?'[4]

The validity of this way of singing, reviled and ridiculed as it was by the cultivated musicians of two centuries, was affirmed by the town bandmaster of Danbury, Connecticut, George Ives, and his son Charles. The persistence of the tradition of spontaneous hymn-singing can be appreciated when we realize that what Charles writes of below must have been taking place in the 1880s: 'I remember when I was a boy — at the outdoor Camp Meeting services in Redding, all the farmers, their families and field hands for miles around used to come through the trees — when things like *Beulah Land, Woodworth, Nearer My God to Thee, The Shining Shore, Nettleton, In the Sweet Bye and Bye* and the like were sung by thousands of "let out" souls. The music notes and words on paper were about as much like what they "were" (at those moments) as the monogram on a man's necktie may be like his face. Father, who led the singing, sometimes with his cornet or his voice, sometimes with both voice and arms, sometimes in the quieter hymns with a French horn or violin, would always encourage the people to sing in their own way. Most of them knew the words and music (theirs) by heart, and sang it that way. If they threw the poet and the composer around a bit, so much the better for the poetry and the music. There was power and exultation in these great conclaves of sound from humanity.'[5]

The proponents of 'regular singing' were not slow to take action against what they regarded as the corruption of hymn singing. Innumerable books were published with the intention of schooling singers, and, more important, the institution of singing schools grew up. These were generally run by itinerant musicians, often doubling as peddlers of quack medicines or the like, who would settle in a village or town for a few weeks, announce their intention of instructing those who wished it in regular singing, and conduct classes for all comers in the evenings. This institution prospered for reasons which probably had as much to do with social as with purely musical factors, and became an important part of the life of the New England colonies, right down the eastern seaboard. It was these travelling singing masters who built up a musical community that gave rise in the late eighteenth century to the first group of native American composers.

The group who became known as the First New England School were humble men, who called themselves 'tunesmiths' rather than composers, since they regarded themselves as artisans whose function, like that of the blacksmith or wheelwright, was to serve the community. As H. Wiley Hitchcock says:

> This was a music completely in tune with the society for which it was written. These journeymen composers had a secure and respected function in Colonial and Federal-era life in general; viewed historically from a point two hundred years later, theirs was a sort of golden age of musical participation in which teachers, composers, singers and populace in general worked together fruitfully. If ever there was a truly popular music, the music of the New Englanders was popular; it arose from the deep, old traditions of early America; it was accessible to all and enjoyed by all; it was a plain-spoken music for plain people, and assessed on its own terms it was a stylistically homogeneous music of great integrity.[6]

These were down-to-earth men, then, and they had down-to-earth names; among them were Justin Morgan, Supply Belcher, Timothy Swan, and, the best known and most articulate member of the group, William Billings of Boston. Born in 1746, he was a tanner by trade; quite self-taught in music (though doubtless tutored in a singing school), he abandoned his trade and hung a shingle outside his house which read, simply, 'Billings – Songs'. He was apparently a remarkable man; a contemporary description says he was 'a singular man of moderate size, short of one leg, with one eye, without any address, with an uncommon negligence of person. Still he spake and thought as one above the common abilities.'[7] He published a number of collections of songs, hymn tunes and anthems, usually prefacing them with pungently expressed opinions, which give the flavour not only of the man but of the confident young society in which he lived in an intimate relationship which must be the envy of many a contemporary composer. For example:

> Perhaps it may be expected that I should say something concerning rules for composition; to those I answer that Nature is the best

dictator, for not all the hard, dry, studied rules that ever was prescribed, will not enable any person to form an air ... It must be Nature, Nature who must lay the foundation, Nature must inspire the thought ... For my own part, as I don't think myself confined to any rules of composition, laid down by any that went before me, neither should I think (were I to pretend to lay down rules) that any one who came after me were in any ways obligated to adhere to them, any further than they should think proper; so in fact I think it best for every composer to be his own carver.[7]

Brave words! But Billings has more for us:

Perhaps some may think I mean and intend to throw Art entirely out of the question. I answer, by no means, for the more art is displayed, the more Nature is decorated. And in some sorts of composition there is dry study required, and art very requisite. For instance, in a fuge, where the parts come in after each other with the same notes, but even here, art is subservient to genius, for fancy goes first and strikes out the work roughly, and art comes after and polishes it over.[7]

Billings was fourteen years younger than Haydn, ten years older than Mozart, but his music inhabits another world than that of European classicism. In some ways it seems to hark back to an earlier European style; it is modal rather than tonal, with a folkish flavour, deriving perhaps from the Anglo-Celtic folk tradition. It is to all intents and purposes non-harmonic; certainly tonal functional harmony plays no part in its repertory of expressive means. Any conflict between the needs of chord progression and the shape of an individual melodic line is invariably resolved in favour of the latter, even if this produces a harmonic clash, so that astounding dissonances unknown in contemporary European music are used freely and often without any feeling of need for resolution. Open and parallel fifths, both proscribed by European rules, are heard here so frequently that it is clear that the sound was positively enjoyed by these composers and their congregations. To harmonically attuned ears the music may sound tonally monotonous, the more so as modulation, apart from the occasional perfunctory movement to the dominant, is virtually non-existent, but to feel this is to miss the point of the music, which is concerned with other matters, and pursues its concerns in a remarkably stylish and consistent way. The music is mainly for unaccompanied chorus – at least, no accompaniment is provided, although wind and even string instruments might join in doubling the vocal parts should they happen to be available. Keyboard instruments were rare and played no part in the world of these composers — which may have been a contributing factor to the absence of harmonic device in their works, obliging them to think in terms of lines rather than of chords (the role of the keyboard, with its power of bringing complex textures under the control of a single individual, in the development of tonal harmony has already been remarked on).

A typical New England anthem consists of a number of short sections cunningly put together, with chordal sections alternating with sections in simple imitative counterpoint ('fuging') and remarkable manipulation of textural effect in which the whole group may be set against one, two or three voices, as well as contrasts of tempo, dynamics and vocal timbre, all used as structural rather than as decorative elements. That the first western non-harmonic music since the Renaissance should have been composed in a society founded on the ideal of individual liberty (Billings was an active supporter of the Colonial cause and wrote not only its principal rallying-song, *Chester,* but also an eloquent *Lament Over Boston* on the occasion of the burning of the city by the British) by a musician who believed that 'every composer should be his own carver' and that 'nature must inspire the thought' should come as no surprise to the reader who has thus far followed the argument of this book.

Billings, like his colleagues, was very concerned for the manner of performance; many of his ideas would have shocked his European contemporaries, and even today show a very cavalier attitude to the demands of traditional tonal-harmonic music, especially the importance it assigns to the real bass. He liked, for example, to have male and female voices on each part, producing an octave, and occasionally a double-octave, doubling — a kind of organ sonority in six or eight parts. His ear was very idiosyncratic, but it is clear that he knew the kind of sound he wanted:

> Suppose a company of forty people; twenty of them should sing the bass, and the other twenty should be divided according to the discretion of the company into the upper parts. Six or seven voices should sing the ground bass, which sung together with the upper parts, is most majestic, and so exceeding grand as to cause the floor to tremble, as I myself have often experienced ... Much caution should also be used in singing a solo (*sic*); in my opinion 2 or 3 at most are enough to sing it well. It should be sung soft as an echo, in

order to keep the hearers in agreeable suspense till all the parts join together in a full chorus, as sweet and strong as possible.[7]

It was also apparently not unusual for these composers to place the various parts at some distance from one another, making use of the spatial separation between them — attesting further to a concern for the individual part which was virtually unknown in the European music of the time.

Here, then, was the stuff of a new, democratic tradition in music, strong, confident, firmly rooted in the life of the people, and accessible to them, which could match the aspirations of Jeffersonian democracy. Yet it vanished without trace for almost two hundred years, swamped by the movement towards gentility and European-style 'correctness' which took place under the leadership of musicians such as Lowell Mason in the early years of the nineteenth century. To Mason, who, appropriately enough, was also the first to bring to music the methods of that typically American institution, Big Business (which was just getting under way in the early nineteenth century), music was principally a commodity. He published an enormous quantity of music, hymns, church music generally, children's instructional manuals and songbooks, secular songs, some of them his own compositions (*From Greenland's Icy Mountain* is his) but mostly taken from the work of lesser European composers and the lesser works of greater, often rearranged to take out their most striking features, leaving a bland and bloodless mixture, not unlike the products of present-day American television, and for much the same reasons. Mason grasped the fact that if music was to be treated as a commodity then clearly it had to appeal to the widest number of people and antagonize the fewest. Good quality, yes — but not so original as to disturb or frighten off a potential customer. (This blandness is still to be found today in many American collections of music for high school orchestras, bands and the like.) In any case the raw but richly alive works of the New England tunesmiths clearly would not do.

It is not too fanciful to see in this betrayal of the ideals of the early composers a parallel of the betrayal of the idea of the rights of man which began to take place in the early nineteenth century as industrialism got under way. America in the nineteenth century produced writers of real greatness who preserved an aggressive stance of independence — Melville, Twain, Whitman, Emerson, for example, and above all Thoreau, while American art music produced only Louis Moreau Gottschalk and Stephen Collins Foster, both interesting figures but scarcely of comparable stature. Could not this be because music, for the very reason that it is less precise in its outward meanings, less conscious of exactly what it is saying, gives even deeper expression than literature to the subconscious motivations of a culture? In any case, the history of nineteenth century American art music is a dismal affair; one after another, young composers crossed the Atlantic, to Dresden, to Leipzig, Vienna or Weimar, rarely to Paris, coming back with music which was no more than a pale imitation of German romanticism. As David Wooldridge in his recent biography of Charles Ives remarks, the vision of the New England tunesmiths 'went forfeit to the competent ... Only music malingered dismally, generation over generation of American composers making the pilgrimage to Europe like dowagers to a spa, to fetch back the continuing seed of a foreign culture for the continuing delight of old ladies.'⁸

It was not, however, the Europeanized American composers who dominated the art-music scene; indeed, they were hard put to it to get a hearing at all. It was European, and especially German, music, its apparatus and standard repertoire − a state of affairs which largely continues even today with the large and socially accepted concert organizations. And precisely because this music had, and has, no organic relationship with indigenous American culture it proved sterile, without roots; it is perhaps for this reason that, while in Europe those who find in themselves no point of contact with classical music (in the popular sense of the word) are content to ignore it and go their own way, in America it seems to arouse positive hostility. A standard plot for the Hollywood musicals of my youth concerned the confrontation between 'longhair' musicians and the 'regular kids', as portrayed by the young Mickey Rooney, Judy Garland, Bonita Granville and Jane Withers, who wanted to 'Hey kids, let's put on a show!' There is malice, too, in the Marx Brothers' hilarious destruction of a performance of *Il Trovatore* in *A Night at the Opera*, and in the cutting loose of the floating platform in *At the Circus* allowing the symphony orchestra under the baton of the outrageously caricatured Italian conductor to float out to sea still energetically playing Wagner − an architypal image if ever there was one. But we must be clear; it was not music that the average American disliked, then as now. His culture was full of it, from minstrel shows to southern hymnody, jazz, cowboy songs, vaudeville, 'burleycue' and military marches — all vigorous growths, all indigenously and characteristically American and all popular in the widest sense. It was specifically European art music that was and is rejected by the vast majority.

The triumph of the European tonal-harmonic tradition in the nineteenth century among Americans who considered themselves to be cultured went parallel to that of the post-Renaissance scientific world view, and its cognates the Protestant ethic, capitalism and industrialism. Only for those who lived outside the mainstream of American life did the older traditions survive. We have seen how the tradition of communal hymn singing in the old style persisted in rural areas into the late years of the nineteenth century; even today in the backwoods areas of Kentucky and the Carolinas one comes across thriving groups who sing the old hymns in the old way, using shape-note notation and 'fasola' syllables which date back to the days of the eighteenth-century song schools. The survival of modal Anglo-Celtic folksong among the remote rural populations of the Appalachian mountain region is well known; indeed, British folk-song collectors such as Cecil Sharp and Maud Karpeles found in the nineteen-twenties that these areas were an altogether richer source of British folk song than anywhere in England.

By far the largest group which until recently has been excluded from the mainstream of American economic, political and cultural life is the Negro population. We have already observed that the collision between the African and the European, notably Anglo-Celtic, traditions, has proved one of the most fruitful in the entire history of music, and although this is not the place for an examination of that collision and its fruits, we may perhaps make some observations on the music and its relation to Negro society.

First, the blues. In its classic form this consists, verbally, of stanzas of two lines of rhyming verse, with the first line repeated, so that the second when it comes forms a kind of punchline. The words are characterized by an unsentimental melancholy tinged with an ironic humour, frequently connected with deprivation of love, such as:

> *I'm gonna buy me a bulldog, watch you while I sleep*
> *(I said)   I'm gonna buy me a bulldog, watch you while I sleep,*
> *Just to keep those men from making their early mornin' creep'*

Often the imagery is explicitly sexual:

> *My baby got a little engine, call it my Ford machine,*
> *(I say)*   *My baby got a little engine, call it my Ford machine,*
> *If your generator ain't bad, baby, you must be buying bad*
> *gasoline.*

and is surprisingly little concerned with topics concerning racial discrimination or economic deprivation.

Musically the classic blues consists of twelve bars of music on a very simple and conventional sequence of I-IV-I-V-(IV)-I chords, alternating two sung bars with two bars of instrumental improvisation. Although it would thus seem to be based firmly on European harmonic progressions, the music preserves, as do black singers towards white American society, a very ambiguous relationship towards tonal harmony. Leaving aside the fact that the progression is an unvarying one which can therefore play no part in the actual expressive means, since what is expected, harmonically speaking, always arrives, we find that the favoured accompanying instrument, at least in country blues, is the guitar, an instrument which lends itself, especially when played with a sawn-off bottleneck, to bold pitch distortions, and is commonly used that way. We find, too, that the seventh degree of the major scale is frequently flattened, undermining the V-I progression, and that the third degree of the scale is commonly placed somewhere between the major and the minor third thus weakening if not destroying the distinction between major and minor scale so basic to the emotional expressiveness of tonal-harmonic music. The more sophisticated urban blues tends to use the piano, whose pitches are fixed on the tempered scale; the 'neutral' third is simulated by playing major and minor third simultaneously (a feature which it shares with jazz) giving the characteristic sound to piano blues and its offshoots, barrelhouse and boogie-woogie, both of which use the blues harmonic framework. In any case, the tremendous proliferation of styles, of melodies and types of texture which can be heard over that simple, conventional bass, shows that the interest of the music lies elsewhere than in harmony.

Many of the features are undoubtedly related to survivals of African music (the tenaciousness and persistence of African cultural elements in black people through generations of degradation and deliberate disruption is one of the cultural miracles of modern times) but that is not the present point; in the blues we see once again how the attitude to tonal harmony is a clear indicator of the ambiguity of its singers' position within and their attitude towards white society.

Blues was, and remains, an essentially oral tradition, with strong and close links with the society from which it arose. The blues singer, like his society, was, with a very few exceptions, and those only recently, poor. He was often itinerant, travelling large distances throughout the South, not infrequently blind, led, Tiresias-like, by a boy, and, like Tiresias, often treated by his people as a seer who 'saw' more than the sighted. As in many oral traditions, the material comes largely from a common stock, not only of musical phrases but also of verbal expressions and images such as 'I woke up this mornin' ...' or 'Just a poor boy, long ways from home', or 'Laughin' just to keep from cryin' '. This common stock of phrases, which was often shared by poor white, no less than black, musicians, is a universal characteristic of oral poetry (one thinks of Homer's stock of phrases such as 'the wine-dark sea' or 'bright-eyed Athene') and is a great aid to communality of expression. Everyone can play; the modestly talented singer can fall back on the common stock and by selection and permutation can make something which expresses how he feels, while the greatly gifted artist can take the common stock, building on it and creating something new and uniquely expressive, giving voice to feelings that all his hearers can recognize in themselves, thus remaining always in touch with the community as a whole and comprehensible to them.

These blues singers were − and still largely are − the seers and prophets of the black community. There is much cross-fertilization between blues and gospel music; Charles Keil points out that many black blues singers go on to become preachers in later life: 'The word "ritual" seems more appropriate than "performance" when the audience is committed rather than appreciative. And from this it follows that perhaps blues singing is more a belief role than a creative role − more priestly than artistic ... Bluesmen and preachers both provide models and orientations; both give public expression to privately held emotions; both promote catharsis; both increase feelings of solidarity, boost morale and strengthen the consensus.'[9]

Blues began, and has remained, very much a people's art. It preserves in its techniques similarly ambiguous attitudes to the European tonal-harmonic tradition to those of the community that gave it birth towards white American society. Jazz, on the other hand, is in its origins and its history much closer to white music and to white society. As Gunther Schuller points out,[10] the legend of the illiterate jazz musician in New Orleans in the early years of the century is not in general substantiated by the statements of musicians who were around at the time; many were highly trained in the western concert tradition with a wide knowledge of the various kinds of western concert music that New Orleans presented so richly. Many influences went into the shaping of jazz; Wilfrid Mellers, writing about Jelly Roll Morton's *Didn't He Ramble* sums them up thus:

> The military march becomes a rag, the hymn becomes a blues and a Latin-American dance-song brings in hints of French or Italian opera and maybe a whiff of Europeanized plantation music in the manner of Stephen Foster also. This melting-pot of a piece gives us an idea of the variety of music that shook New Orleans in the first decades of this century. Parade bands in the streets were so numerous that they were apt to bump into one another. Party bands in the streets and squares might be playing Negro rags or Latin-American tangos or French quadrilles or German waltzes.[11]

Jazz shows in its techniques that it is closer to white music. In fact the first jazz musicians to gain popular attention, especially those we know from the record companies, were white (King Oliver, Louis Armstrong, Bessie Smith and their black contemporaries were initially relegated to the 'race records' category). From its earliest days until, in the music of Ornette Coleman, John Coltrane and Albert Ayler, it abandoned contact altogether with the idea of the fundamental bass, at about the same time as the post-Webernian revolution in European art music, it has maintained the harmonic progression to a greater or lesser degree as one of its expressive devices. Throughout its history it has maintained a flirtation with European art music (the word is apt; it is the sheer *playfulness* of jazz that is one of its most enduring features, giving it a personal quality and almost physical presence that the other lacks), and the closeness of its contact with white society at any time can be assessed from the importance of the harmonic element in the music. The swing era, for example, was characterized by complex harmony in elaborate arrangements played from written scores; it was at the time a largely white and perfectly 'respectable' art in the eyes of the middle-American majority. The revolt against the over-smooth banalities of swing in the late forties which became known as bebop, in its origins an entirely black movement, diminished the importance of harmony to a point where its role was associative rather than explicit (much of it was blues-derived), while rhythm regained the central position it had lost. Bop was also, quite explicitly, a music of black social revolt, so it is understandable not only that tonal harmony was the first casualty but also that at the time white people mainly detested it (today, of course, bop is history and thus safe to like).

It is a commonplace that much of the vitality of jazz comes from the tension between the African and the European elements which it incorporates. It is interesting, therefore, to see that the moment when it rejected tonality altogether in favour of a modal or even atonal heterophony in the music of Coleman, Coltrane, Ayler and others was the point at which it stopped being a popular art and became virtually another branch of art music appealing to a public of *cognoscenti* rather than to a community. Blues, on the other hand, remains a communal art, and it was blues rather than jazz that became, along with country and western music, the main source of the other major non-harmonic (although still tonal) music of our time, rock'n'roll, and its successors in the sixties and seventies. These will be discussed more fully in the next chapter.

I stated earlier that American culture is full of music, a line of thought that brings us directly to Charles Edward Ives, the one composer who brings together all the threads of specifically American music and links them with the European tradition. He had a wide knowledge of European music and a comfortable mastery of its techniques, yet his relationship to it was highly ambivalent and his commitment was first and foremost to America. I have already remarked on his experience of the outdoor camp meetings at which his father led the singing, and there is a memorable passage in his *Memos* telling how his father rebuked a smart young Boston musician for ridiculing the out-of-tune hymn singing of an old stonemason: 'Watch him closely and reverently, look into his eyes and hear the music of the ages. Don't pay too much attention to the sounds — for if you do you may miss the music. You won't get a wild, heroic ride to heaven on pretty little sounds.'[12]

The view of Ives· as a cranky amateur who stumbled almost unawares on some of the most revolutionary musical discoveries of the century is now, one hopes, well and truly dead. He was a sophisticated, cultured musician with a powerful mind and an incredibly alert ear, and was very clear about what it was he was doing, as can be seen from his *Essays Before a Sonata*[13] and the more recently published *Memos*. The reason why his music makes so little appeal to so many European academic composers and critics is that it celebrates, not some beautiful, orderly ideal world but the *real* world, contradictory, untidy, even chaotic as it is. He accepts and glories in the multiplicity of human experience, and the asymmetry and unexpectedness of the music is not the result of incompetence or naivety but arises naturally from his personality, from his belief in the freedom and autonomy of the individual, and above all in the unity that underlies all the variety of nature. There are those who, like David Wooldridge in his biography, and John Cage, blame Ives for abandoning the full-time profession of music and going into business. Cage writes: 'I don't so much admire the way Ives treated his music socially (separating it from his insurance business); it made his life too safe economically and it is in living dangerously economically that one shows bravery socially.'[14] Wooldridge and Cage reveal what is in fact an inappropriately romantic view of the position of a composer in society which would no doubt have been quickly dismissed by William Billings and his colleagues. Ives's life in business is an expression of his faith in the unity of life; it was a gesture towards life and against fragmentation and the isolation of the artist. The rightness of his course is shown by the fact that his inspiration dried up as soon as he retired from business.

In considering both his beliefs and his techniques, the idea of Ives held by many Europeans, even among those who are sympathetic to his music, as a great original who sprang from nowhere, dissolves when we become aware of the nature of the American musical tradition, outside that of the Europeanized art music of the nineteenth century. At the same time, he had been thoroughly grounded in the European tradition both by his father (whose own musical training had included the working of Bach chorales and the transcription of opera scenes from Gluck and Mozart as well as of baroque masses, and whose small-town orchestra was capable of turning in excellent performances of Rossini, Mendelssohn, Verdi, Meyerbeer and even Mozart) and by the conventional but expert Horatio Parker at Yale. But his attitude towards the great masters of that tradition remained equivocal; on the one hand he could assert with confidence that 'Bach, Beethoven and Brahms are the strongest and greatest in all art, and nothing since is stronger than their strongest and greatest', while at other times he could voice interesting doubts, speaking of 'a vague feeling that even the best music we know – Beethoven, Bach and Brahms – was too cooped up – more so than nature intended it to be – not only in its chord systems and relations, lines, etc, but also in its time, or rather its rhythms and spaces – blows or not blows – all up and down even little compartments, over and over (prime numbers and their multiples) all so even and nice – producing some sense of weakness, even in the great.' And again: 'I remember feeling towards Beethoven that he's a great man – but Oh for just one big strong chord not tied to any key'.[15]

His relationship with the indigenous music of the United States, on the other hand, was much more positive. His awareness of the continuity of the outdoor camp meetings with the psalm singing of the early colonists is as obvious as his love of the music. There is little in his compositions that actually suggests the quality of such meetings in a literal way, although the marvellous choral outburst at the end of the *Thanksgiving* movement of the *Holidays Symphony* comes near to it. But this wild, highly individualistic quality runs through all of his music. The *Second String Quartet* is in fact based on it; the four instruments are all characterized (the second violin is cast as Rollo, the type of prissy milksop musician whom Ives so despised), while the three movements are entitled: *Four Men Have a Discussion, Arguments and Fight,* and *They Climb a Mountain and Contemplate.* Other examples are to be found in the early scherzo, *Over the Pavements,* a representation of the different independent walking rhythms that could be heard in a busy street before the advent of the internal combustion engine.

In most of Ives's work, as in that of the New England tunesmiths, the needs of the individual voice or part take precedence over the neatness or consistency of the over-all effect (one is reminded of Whitman's bold 'Do I contradict myself? Very well, I contradict myself!'). It is this fact that accounts for the notorious dissonance of his work, as well as for its rhythmic complexity. In allowing each voice to go its own way he was expressing his version of the ideal of individual freedom, but we should notice that while the relationships between the voices are complex in the extreme, often allowing no room for the stately, logical chord progressions of tonal functional harmony, they are not chaotic; Ives has them under control. There are accounts from those who knew him well of his ability to keep a number of rhythmic patterns going simultaneously, and he was well able to play his own music on the piano. His ideal of liberty remained firmly within the law, although the law was to be subtle and flexible to allow for the greatest degree of variety of individual interaction. He could be tolerant when it came to performances of his own music; provided that the music was attempted with sincerity and simplicity of purpose, he did not mind too much if it did not come out exactly as he wrote it – hence his famous comment on an early well-intentioned but botched performance of *Three Places in New England* – 'Just like a town meeting – every man for himself. Wonderful how it came out!' One wonders, in fact, whether he would have liked some of today's recorded performances by the same kind of superstar conductor and instrumentalist as those who once pronounced the music unplayable, so smoothly and perfectly co-ordinated; in their very technical proficiency they are regressing towards the mean of European music, and the quality of adventure which he treasured is lacking from the experience.

In the multiplicity of his sources, from Beethoven to American folk tunes, gospel hymnody and ragtime, in the protean variety of his musical styles, from straightforward tonal harmony (regarded by him as only one of an infinite number of expressive means) to polytonality, polyrhythm and polymetre, proto-serial music, spatial music, Ives introduced something completely new into western music, which has become an increasingly important factor in it, especially to those Americans who succeeded him. In European music we obtain a hint of this all-embracing quality only in the work of Mahler, and in his famous remark, made to Sibelius, that 'A symphony must be like the world; it must contain everything!' In the music of Ives, in fact, the work of art becomes not just an expression of nature or of an attitude to nature; it becomes a part of nature, flowing along in the flux of time as much as a rock or a tree. Like a natural object it contains not one but many meanings; the extraction of meaning requires more work on the part of the hearer, but the music allows the hearer to enter in and find his own meaning, rather than have it presented to him ready-made, depending on the aspects of it on which we concentrate our attention. This, for example, is what he says of the pieces which he calls *Tone Roads*:

The *Tone Roads* are roads leading right and left – 'F.E. Hartwell & Co., Gents' Furnishings' – just starting an afternoon's sport. If horses and wagons can go sometimes on different roads (hill road, muddy road, straight, hilly hard road) at the same time, and get to Main Street eventually – why can't different instruments on different staffs? The wagons and people and roads are all in the same township – same mud, breathing the same air, same temperature, going to the same place, speaking the same language (sometimes) – but not all going on the same road, all going their own way, each trip different to each driver, different people, different cuds, not all chewing in the key of C – that is, not all in the same

key – or same number of steps per mile ... Why can't each one, if
he feels like trying to go, go along the staff-highways of music, each
hearing the other's 'trip' making its own sound-way, in the same
township of fundamental sounds – yet different, when you think of
where George is now, down in the swamp, while you are on Tallcot
Mountain – then the sun sets and all are on Main Street.[16]

And elsewhere in the *Memos* he discusses the structure of a piece
and comments, 'This may not be a nice way to write music, but it's
one way! – and who knows the only real nice way?'[16]

In his multiplicity Ives draws together many threads of
American music and brings them to the surface from where they
had lain, submerged and neglected, for more than a century. He
celebrates the fact that what people play or sing is not necessarily
the same as what they *think* they are playing and singing, and
acknowledges their right to sing or play as they wish; indeed, given
the right attitude in the listener, the result can be just as beautiful as
more accurate or more formally disciplined music making.

Ives seems never to have seriously considered studying in
Europe; those who did go to Europe either before or after him
came back imbued with European attitudes, no matter how
'American' they believed themselves to be. The music of Aaron
Copland, Virgil Thomson, Roy Harris, even of Elliott Carter and
Milton Babbitt, remains European-style concert music with an
American accent, not unlike the nationalist concert music of such
nineteenth-century composers as Smetana, Dvorak, Greig, whose
national accents (this is not to deny their many virtues or even
genius) remain mere dialects of the prevailing European polyglot.
Of the generation following Ives, only Henry Cowell showed
anything of Ives's bent for uninhibited experimentation with sound,
free from harmonic preconceptions. Cowell's early pieces for piano,
using tone-clusters (a term which was in fact invented by him) and
plucked and rubbed strings may have been naïf (some were
published while he was still in his teens) but their spirit was the
same as had animated the eighteenth-century tunesmiths, and is
directed towards liberating the inner nature of the sounds
themselves. If his later work falls back into the European concert-
music manner, albeit with an exotic seasoning, he had opened up
some important new resources, and, as editor of the journal *New
Music,* he became, in the words of John Cage, 'the open sesame for
new music in America ... From him, as from an efficient telephone
booth, you could always get not only the address and telephone

number of anyone working in a lively way with music, but you could also get an unbiased introduction from him as to what anyone was doing. He was not attached (as Varèse also was not attached) to what seemed to many the important question: Whether to follow Schoenberg or Stravinsky.'[17] The last is an important point; to be aware of the essential irrelevance of both Schoenberg and Stravinsky (obscured by the fact that both composers were resident in the United States, Schoenberg since 1934 and Stravinsky since the 1940s) to the growth of a genuinely American tradition was a state which Cage himself reached only in later life.

It is in fact in the music and the writings of Cage that the tendencies we have been observing over the three-hundred-and-fifty-year history of American music finally become explicit. His first confrontation with European concepts of harmony seems to have occurred when he was studying with Schoenberg, that most committedly European of all twentieth-century composers. He tells the story as if he were unaware of its significance, a fact that testifies to the depth, albeit perhaps unconscious, of his feeling. When he had been with Schoenberg for five years the master said that to write music one must have a feeling for harmony. 'I told him,' says Cage, 'that I had no feeling for harmony. He then said that I would always encounter an obstacle, that it would be as though I came to a wall through which I could not pass. I said, "In that case I will devote my life to beating my head against that wall." '[18] Schoenberg, from his own point of view and that of the European tradition was of course right, but in fact Cage has felt no such neccessity; going ahead as if western concepts of harmony and the associated ideas of linear time and climax had never existed, he has found in rhythm the organizing principle for which harmony served in traditional western music. 'Sounds, including noises, it seemed to me, had four characteristics (pitch, loudness, timbre and duration) while silence had only one (duration). I therefore devised a rhythmic structure based on the duration, not of notes, but of spaces in time ... It is analogous to Indian *Tala* (rhythmic method) but it has the Western characteristic of a beginning and an ending.'[19] The first sentence here seems to take Cage close to the position of Webern in the thirties; the last two emphasize how far from that position he actually was.

A piece by Cage, in fact, rarely develops, rarely works towards any kind of climax or apotheosis, but deals in what is known in Indian aesthetic theory as 'permanent emotion' (one ancient work of theory lists these as Heroic, Erotic, Wondrous, Mirthful, Odious, Fearful, Angry and Sorrowful) — a single emotional state which persists through the piece. The music may thus be boring to some; once it has made its point, many feel, there seems little purpose in continuing it. Virgil Thomson, for example, says, 'The Cage works have some intrinsic interest and much charm, but after a few minutes very little urgency. They do not seem to be designed for holding the attention and generally speaking they do not hold it.'[20] This is the verdict of a western composer accustomed to the concept of music as drama, but it may also be a just criticism; it could be, as used to be said of Berlioz, that Cage just has not enough talent for his genius.

He has taken the denial of the European spirit even further than the simple rejection of harmony, and has attempted to eliminate as completely as possible the imposition of the composer's will upon the sounds, finding justification for this in his studies of Zen Buddhism. His renunciation of harmony 'and its effect of fusing sounds in a fixed relationship', his desire to allow sounds simply to 'be themselves', to refrain from imposing any outside order on them, is clearly anarchistic (we remind ourselves that the world 'anarchism' is not a synonym for 'chaos' but indicates rather a state in which men *need* no externally imposed laws), a metaphor for a potential society which few Europeans have so far dared to imagine. His refusal to impose his will on the sounds has led him to his well-known use of chance operations, by the throwing of dice, the consultation of the Chinese *Book of Changes,* the *I-Ching,* or, more recently, the use of computers; he tries 'to arrange my composing means so that I won't have any knowledge of what might happen ... I like to think that I'm outside the circle of a known universe and dealing with things I literally don't know anything about.'[21] Boulez' criticism, made from his *echt*-European viewpoint, that such procedures merely cover 'weaknesses in the compositional methods involved',[22] is regarded by Cage as irrelevant, since if compositional methods are designed to assist the composer to submit the sound materials to his will, the absence of any desire to do so renders all such methods superfluous.

The use of chance operations has a further consequence: that one accepts the validity of whatever sound chance turns up, without making any kind of value judgement on it. 'Value judgements are destructive to our proper business, which is curiosity and awareness. How are you going to use this situation if you are there? That is the question,'[23] he says, and quotes the

Hindu aphorism, 'Imitate the sands of the Ganges who are not pleased by perfume and who are not disgusted by filth.' And again: 'Why do you waste your time and mine by trying to get value judgements? Don't you know that when you get a value judgement that's all you have?'[24]

It is true that the European habit of placing value judgements on everything pervades our thinking to a degree that we hardly realize. Our minds are full of hierarchies; among composers, for example, we are accustomed to think of Bach and Beethoven, perhaps of Mozart (the hierarchy differs in detail between individuals but the main outlines are clear), with Brahms and Haydn perhaps a little below them, and so on down through Tchaikowsky, Schumann, Delibes, to Chaminade and Ketèlby to the lady next door who makes up little songs. This habit of thought is a cognate of the value placed on the art object rather than the creative process, since once a value is placed on the art object the natural question is, what value? Part of the reasoning behind Cage's frequent refusal to fix his works in final form, behind his use of chance and indeterminacy, is the desire to preserve as much of the art process as is possible for the performer and even the listener; 'Art instead of being an object made by one person is a process set in motion by a group of people. Art's socialized. It isn't someone saying something but people doing things, giving everyone (including those involved) the opportunity to have experiences they would not otherwise have had.'[25] So, at least in many later works, he provides the structure leaving the performer to fill in the actual material in his own way. So, too, the apparent chaos of vast multi-media works such as *HPSCHD* is intended to allow the listener to put his own meaning on the piece, rather than to present him with a ready-made meaning. He makes an interesting antitheses between 'emerging' and 'entering in'; 'Everybody,' he says, 'hears the same thing if it emerges. Everybody hears what he alone hears if he enters in.'[26] Again, to an interviewer who claimed to hear a sense of logic and cohesion in one of his indeterminate pieces, he replied, sharply, 'This logic was not put there by me, but was the result of chance operations. The thought that it is logical grows up in you.'[27]

With Cage, then, it would appear as if the emancipation from the drama, tension and domination of the will of European music is complete. And yet a doubt remains; the simple refusal to make any kind of value judgement, the unquestioning acceptance of any sound that happens along (which obliges us, it must be said, to accept at times some pretty excruciating sounds), is based on perhaps too facile an interpretation of Zen doctrines of art. Alan Watts points out, 'Even in painting, the work of art is considered not as representing nature but as being itself a work of nature.' So far so good, but he goes on, 'This does not mean that the art forms of Zen are left to mere chance … The point is rather that for Zen there is no duality, no conflict between the natural element of chance and the human element of control. The constructive powers of the human mind are no more artificial than the formative action of plants or bees, so that from the standpoint of Zen it is no contradiction to say that artistic technique is discipline in spontaneity and spontaneity in discipline.'[28] Not even his worst enemies would accuse Cage of lack of discipline; nevertheless, to deny the reality of value is simply to continue the discourse on value on the same level as it has been conducted since the time of Aristotle. What is needed is a new concept of value that transcends western hierarchical thinking, and this Cage, for all the magnitude of his achievement, for all the new freedom he has brought into ways of musical thinking, has not succeeded in establishing.

Since Cage, however, tonal harmony has no longer been a concern to those American musicians whose thinking does not follow that of Europe. American music no longer needs to protest its independence; that can now be taken for granted as American musicians compose their own models of the potential society that owe little to European precedents. I must emphasize again that this chapter makes no claim to being a comprehensive survey of American music, but simply attempts to offer an interpretation of certain aspects of that music in the light of the ideas presented in the earlier chapters, and in particular in the light of the ideal of individual liberty upon which the Republic was founded. With this in mind, let us consider only four of those musicians whose work is making the American scene today so much more lively than its European counterpart. The language may have changed, but the vision of the potential society remains as pervasive as ever.

The principal concern of these musicians seems to be the projection of sounds into time, the loving exploration of the inner nature of sounds, in a world where the structures which contain the sounds are relatively unimportant − a complete reversal, in fact, of the classical European aesthetic of music. The antithesis is summed up neatly in an exchange, reported by the pianist John Tilbury, which is supposed to have taken place between Morton Feldman and Stockhausen:

Karlheinz Stockhausen: Morton, I know you have no system, but what's your secret?

Morton Feldman: Leave the sounds alone, Karlheinz, don't push them around.

Karlheinz Stockhausen: Not even just a little bit?[29]

Feldman, who acknowledges Cage as having given him 'early permissions to have confidence in my instincts', takes sounds, as it were, and holds them up for our pleasure and admiration. The sounds he presents to us are generally quiet and unobtrusive, changing gently, creating stillness and peacefulness. The temporal order of the sounds scarcely matters, so that conventional concepts of musical time have no meaning; one feels that if it were possible to project the entire piece simultaneously Feldman would do so.

La Monte Young is concerned also in the exploration of the inner nature of sounds. He recalls from childhood his fascination with the sound of the wind in telephone wires and says, 'I noticed about 1956 that I seemed more interested in listening to chords than in listening to melodies. In other words, I was more interested in concurrency or simultaneity than in sequence.'[30] The result of this concern was, for example, *Composition 1960 No 7*, which consists of the instruction 'B and F sharp. To be held for a long time,' and the very long composition *The Tortoise, His Dreams and Journeys*, in which 'Young and three associates chant an open chord of intrinsically infinite duration, amplified to the point of aural pain. Public performances usually consist of two sessions, each nearly two hours in length, within a darkened room illuminated only by projections of pattern-art.'[31] Young's music, then, has little to do with listening in the traditional western sense, and much with absorption in the timeless rituals of Buddhism and Lamaism. The extreme length of time each sound lasts is vital to the awareness of each nuance of its nature; just as the ethologist must sit and wait for a long time for the living community to reveal itself, so Young's music can be regarded as a kind of ethology of sound, as an observation of sounds when they are allowed to be themselves, not fashioned into shapes determined by human will.

Steve Reich, for long an associate and friend of Young, is also an observer of the behaviour of sounds, but sounds not stationary but gradually changing from within, following their own natural evolution. His compositions are, as he himself says, literally processes, which happen extremely gradually, much as a plant unfolds. One often fails to perceive the process happening, but only becomes aware that a change has taken place. Reich compares such processes to 'pulling back a swing, releasing it, and observing it gradually come to rest; turning over an hour glass and watching the sand slowly run through to the bottom; placing your feet in the sand by the ocean's edge and watching, feeling and listening to the waves gradually bury them.'[32] Such processes, though fascinating to the mind that is prepared to sit and let them happen, are essentially undramatic; so is Reich's music, which might be dismissed as monotonous by minds attuned to the violent and dramatic contrasts of classical music. A piece tends to consist of an extremely small amount of material, both rhythmic and melodic, played by several performers (or, in the earlier pieces, on several tape recorders) who are slightly out of phase with one another, so that material is constantly being revealed in new, gradually changing relationships with itself; fascinating and beautiful new melodic and rhythmic patterns are constantly being created. The music is not difficult to play in terms of the actual notes, which tend to be simple repetitions of melodic patterns, but the task of playing the same pattern as one's neighbour at a slightly different but perfectly controlled speed requires intense discipline and months of rehearsal for each piece. Reich has collected around him a group of musicians who have developed the kind of social rather than individual virtuosity which is perhaps the most important fruit of his period of study under a master drummer in Ghana. The nature of the processes at work is always perfectly clear to the listener; unlike tonal-harmonic or serial music it keeps no secrets. As Reich says, in the same article, 'We all listen to the process together since it's quite audible, and one of the reasons why it's quite audible is because it's happening extremely gradually. The use of hidden structural devices has never appealed to me. Even when all the cards are on the table and everyone hears what is happening in a musical process there are still enough mysteries to satisfy all. These mysteries are the impersonal, unintended, psycho-acoustic by-products of the intended process. These might include sub-melodies heard within repeated melodic patterns, stereophonic effects due to listener location, slight irregularities in performance, harmonics, difference tones, etc.'[32]

Reich's largest and most ambitious work to date is *Drumming,* a work for tuned tomtoms, glockenspiels and marimbas, with singers, whistlers and piccolo to outline the melodic patterns that are implied as the highly disciplined performers move in and out of phase with one another; it was for me a musical experience of great beauty and joy when it was first performed in London in 1972. Reich's gift is the ability to set up situations in which, as the sounds unfold according to the rules of their own evolution, they make continuously beautiful and interesting patterns without the apparent intervention of the composer's will. There is an openness and a complex simplicity about this exploration of sounds that parallels the workings of nature herself.

The music of Terry Riley, a Californian and friend of both Young and Reich, takes place in a similar area of musical sound; it first struck a wide public at least, in this country with *In C,* where some fifty short melodic fragments, all diatonic on the scale of C, are played by as many instrumentalists as desired; each player plays each fragment as many times as he wishes before moving on to the next, the performance being held together rhythmically by a rapidly repeated high C on the piano. The result is an extremely pleasing music, not unlike Reich's in sound, but governed more by the whims of the performers than by the internal logic of the sounds; it is a less rigorous, more engaging, perhaps finally less satisfying music than Reich's. Later works have included tape loops and feedback systems, sometimes with delays built in; the sound is relaxed and slow-changing, and takes the listener again far into the awareness of the sounds themselves.

In these and other ways the ideas of Cage have been taken forward, ways which in the purely musical results are perhaps more sympathetic to the uncommitted ear than those of Cage himself. There has always been a strong didactic, even dogmatic, streak in Cage; one sometimes has the impression that certain pieces were composed more to prove a point than from any genuine aesthetic impulse in any traditionally comprehensible sense of the word, and having heard the piece, one frequently has no real desire to hear it again; the point has been made, the idea got across, and there seems no need to repeat the experience.

There is perhaps a parallel here with the modern movement in American painting, discussed wittily in a recent magazine article by Tom Wolfe, who sees it not as the consequence of an aesthetic impulse but as a response to a theory of art, usually propounded by a critic. He says, 'Frankly, these days, without a theory to go with it I can't *see* a painting',[33] and suggests, tongue only half in cheek, that when the final great retrospective exhibition of American art 1945-75 is presented at the Museum of Modern Art in the year 2000 the exhibits will consist of blow-ups of the writings of critics with, by way of illustration, tiny reproductions of the paintings themselves. Cage does not always avoid the trap of the piece written to illustrate a point about perception, sound, silence or society. If music is to be alive, however, Art, to parody Billings, must go first and strike out the work, then Theory comes after and polishes it over.

For this reason, it could be that despite the power of Cage's ideas to shock and disturb our preconceptions, a much more seminal figure will in time prove to be Harry Partch, who, born in 1901, was vouchsafed a mere four lines in a recently published history of music in the United States; his death at the end of 1974 passed almost unnoticed in the musical, not to say the general, press. If we compare Cage with the African and Balinese musicians discussed in Chapter 2, it will be clear that he remains, for all his invaluable study of non-European ways, very much tied to western urban culture, and that his discourse is still carried on within the conditions of the western concert tradition. It is Partch, more than any other twentieth-century western musician, who represents a real challenge to that tradition, a challenge which stems not from the 'Tomorrow's World' optimism of Cage, who is still, it seems, hung up on the engaging technological lunacy of Buckminster Fuller and the behaviourist nightmares of B.F. Skinner, but from the old, universal and forever new ways of ritual theatre. 'The work that I have been doing these many years,' says Partch, 'parallels much in the attitudes and actions of primitive man. He found sound-magic in the common materials around him. He then proceeded to make the vehicle, the instrument, as visually beautiful as he could. Finally, he evolved the sound-magic and the visual beauty in his everyday words and experiences, his ritual and drama, in order to lend greater meaning to his life. This is my trinity: sound-magic, visual beauty, experience-ritual.'[34]

Partch, in fact, may be the first musician of the west to have transcended the limitations of its concert tradition – or at least to have pointed a way in which this can be done. He is unique, not only in the thoroughness and explicitness of his rejection of European classical music, a rejection more complete than that of Cage or indeed of anyone since Billings and the New England tunesmiths, but also in the fact that he has succeeded in erecting a living alternative to it, growing not out of theory (though well supported by theory, coming *after* the creative fact) but out of 'an acoustical ardour and a conceptual fervour'[35] – out of the fundamental creative impulse. In a single robustly-written chapter in his book *Genesis of a Music,* he surveys the whole of western music from Terpander in 700 BC to the present and finds it wanting in what he calls corporeality, that quality of being 'vital to a time and a place, a here and now',[35] of being 'emotionally tactile'. To him, the overwhelming majority of western musical compositions, including almost all of the post-Renaissance tradition (he has an interesting list of honorable exceptions which includes the Florentine Camerata and Monteverdi, Berlioz, Mussorgski, the Mahler of *Das Lied von der Erde,* Debussy's *Pelléas et Mélisande,* the *Pierrot Lunaire* of Schoenberg − but nothing else by him − and Satie) is irretrievably lost in abstraction, in the denial of the physical being of man. In its place 'We are reduced to specialisms − a theatre of dialogue, for example, and a concert of music without drama − basic mutilations of ancient concept. My music is visual − it is corporeal, aural *and* visual ...'[36] The development of polyphony, of tonal harmony, and of the large abstract forms based on them, he sees as a distortion of the essential reality of music, which is the making of magic; and the principal bearer of that magic, as he sees it, is the human voice bringing the word.

So his music is composed around the human voice and the word − which of course means the theatre. His works are almost exclusively large music dramas, a theatre of mime, of farce and dance, of shouting and vocalizing, relating clearly to the great traditional dramas of Japan, of Ancient Greece, of Java and Bali − wherever in fact men have not forgotten how to act out ritually the myths that sustain their lives. Were this all, Partch would have little claim to uniqueness; many western musicians have looked in this direction for fresh inspiration. But he has gone further. Wishing to transcend the, to him, wholly artificial and unacceptable tempered scale, with its twelve equal out-of-tune intervals to the octave, he developed a different scale based on just intonation with natural acoustic intervals, comprising no less than forty-three tones to the octave, all of whose intervals are derived from the perfect fifth and perfect third, permitting not only an enriched concept of harmony owing little to European tonal-harmonic music but also a tremendously enriched source of melody which can approach the subtlety of speech inflection. As Peter Yates says:

> With a scale of intervals so finely divided, one is able to speak to exact pitches as easily as to sing. The artificiality of recitative is done away with ... Instead there is by the use of the forty-three-tone scale a continuous field of melodic and harmonic relationship

among the degree of spoken, intoned, chanted, sung, melismatic and shouted vocal utterance, a tonal spectrum filling the gap between the vocal coloration of opera and the spoken drama. Spoken drama can be taken over by the instruments and translated back into change and song.[37]

But how can spoken melody of forty-three tones to the octave — feasible for sensitive singers — be taken over by instruments, when all the instruments of the western tradition are built to a specification of only twelve? This was the problem Partch faced and solved with the simplicity of genius; he invented and built his own instruments. Over a period of more than forty years he designed and built nearly thirty new instruments, with an eye no less for visual than an ear for aural beauty, not to mention a considerable verbal flair in naming them. He has been responsible for inventing possibly more new instruments than Adolph Sax, yet he described himself modestly as 'not an instrument builder but a philosophical music-man seduced into carpentry.'[35] The instruments are mainly plucked and plectrum stringed instruments, often with the strings arranged three-dimensionally, as well as variations of the marimba and xylophone, with adaptations of more conventional instruments such as harmonium and viola (he was later to find wind players who could realize his scale on their instruments), and, apart from the beauty and expressiveness of their sounds, they represent as important a conceptual challenge as does the music itself. In the first place, they are hand-built by the composer to his own purposes, not mass-produced to a conventional specification; there is in existence only one set of instruments, and if one wants to hear Partch's music and see his dramas one has to go to them. Secondly, the instruments are as important a part of the musico-dramatic work as the actors; Partch specified that they be placed in full view of the spectators as part of the set, and that the musicians playing them take a full part in the dramatic action.

And, further, the construction of the instruments is regarded, not as a necessary task to be carried out before the real job of music making can be got on with, but as an essential part of the musical process, just as with any African musician; *his* music requires *his* instruments. While many of the instruments, built in that most beautiful of all materials, wood, are triumphs of the woodworker's skill, being beautiful and dramatic in appearance as well as sound, others equally are triumphs of bricolage, being made from old shell cases ('Better to have them here than shredding young boys' skins on the battlefield'[38]), light bulbs, Pyrex gas jars, hub caps and other cast-offs of technological society, materials available to anyone with the imagination to perceive their possibilities. Partch was not anti-technology; years of working with his own hands made him too wise to fall into that trap. His attitude towards the instruments of music resembles that of Robert Persig towards the art of motorcycle maintenance: He says

> Musicians who are generally awkward with common tools, nevertheless expect faultless perfection from their instruments. These are mechanical contrivances, however, and it would be salutary if musicians developed the elementary skills needed to maintain them. In particular, the elementary skill of tuning is of supreme importance to musicianship, and a deeper understanding would certainly ensue if it were developed .... The instruments do not maintain themselves, especially under the wear and tear and sometimes violent treatment (which I myself stipulate) of daily playing. And not a small part of the element of good condition is the visual; the instruments must be kept *looking well*, since they are almost always on stage as part of the set.[39]

In Partch's music, writings, and above all in his instruments, we see a vision of a communal musical art, and of a technology made human by the element of commitment, of care. Here the composer – or any other maker – is not merely the producer of a commodity for others to consume but the leader and pacemaker in the common activity. From the music of Partch, western music could learn to take a large step towards rejoining the musical community of the human race.

He was fond of quoting some lines written by a child:

> *Once upon a time*
> *There was a little boy*
> *And he went outside.*[40]

This childlike (not to be confused with childish) ability to 'go outside' has been a recurring feature of American music, indeed of American culture, since the earliest days, and it remains no less a feature, despite recent disasters and betrayals, of the contemporary scene. This is not to deny that there flows, and has always flowed, a strong counter-current in the direction of Europe and of conformity to European rules, a music of academic formalism as strict as or stricter than anything practised in Europe. That this is so should not be surprising; America has always been a country of extremes of conformism and non-conformism. Of the latter group no-one, not even Cage, has shown such integrity, such humour, such staying power, and such sheer, beautiful musicality as has Partch, such ability to 'go outside' (where, as far as the American and European musical establishments are concerned he still largely remains), and, naturally and unselfconsciously, to propose new relationships in society as in music, to work untrammelled by 'all the hard, dry, studied rules that ever was prescribed'. If American music contains within it the possibility of becoming a force for the regeneration of western music in its society, a state which, however long heralded on both sides of the Atlantic, and however wished for, is still to come about, the music and the simple, complex, eloquent and loving personality of Harry Partch will prove an important factor in bringing about such an event.

Chapter 6: Bibliography

1. LOWENS, Irving: *Music and Musicians in Early America,* New York, Norton (1964), p. 37.
2. Quoted in CHASE, Gilbert: America's Music, 2nd edn., New York, McGraw Hill (1966), pp. 23-4.
3. ibid.
4. THOREAU, Henry David: *Walden, or Life in the Woods* (1854), Everyman Edition (n.d.), p. 287.
5. IVES, Charles E., *Memos,* ed. John Kirkpatrick, London, Calder & Boyars (1973), p. 132.
6. HITCHCOCK, H. Wiley: *Music in the United States: A Historical Introduction,* 2nd edn., New York, Prentice-Hall (1974), p. 20.
7. Quoted in CHASE, Gilbert: op. cit., pp. 129-30.
8. WOOLDRIDGE, David: *From the Steeples and Mountains: A Study of Charles Ives,* New York, Knopf (1974), p. 6.
9. KEIL, Charles: *Urban Blues,* Chicago, University of Chicago Press (1966), p. 164.
10. SCHULLER, Gunther: *Early Jazz,* New York, Oxford University Press (1968), p. 56ff.
11. MELLERS, Wilfrid: *Music in a New Found Land: Themes and Developments in the History of American Music,* London, Barrie & Rockliff (1964), p. 283.
12. IVES, Charles E.: op. cit., p. 132.
13. IVES, Charles E.: *Essays Before a Sonata and Other Writings,* ed. Howard Boatwright, London, Calder & Boyars (1969).
14. CAGE, John: 'Two Statements on Ives' in *A Year From Monday,* London, Calder and Boyars (1968), p. 40.

15. IVES, Charles E.: *Memos,* ed. John Kirkpatrick, London, Calder & Boyars (1973), pp. 100, 135, 44.

16. IVES, Charles E.: ibid., pp. 63-4.

17. CAGE, John: *Silence,* The Wesleyan University Press (1961), Calder and Boyars, London, p. 71.

18. CAGE, John: op. cit., p. 261.

19. CAGE, John: 'On Earlier Pieces' in KOSTELANETZ, Richard (ed.): *John Cage,* London, Allen Lane The Penguin Press (1971), p. 127.

20. THOMSON, Virgil: *Twentieth-Century Composers 1: American Composers Since 1910,* London, Weidenfeld & Nicholson (1970), p. 76.

21. CAGE, John; op. cit., p. 146.

22. BOULEZ, Pierre: 'Alea', transl. David Noakes and Paul Jacobs, *Perspectives of New Music,* Vol 3 No 1, Fall-Winter 1964, pp 42-53.

23. Quoted in KOSTELANETZ, Richard: op. cit., p. 196.

24. Quoted in KOSTELANETZ, Richard: ibid., p. 21.

25. CAGE, John: *A Year from Monday,* London, Calder & Boyars (1968), p. 151.

26. CAGE, John: ibid., p. 39.

27. CAGE, John: Sleeve note to recording of *Fontana Mix,* Turnabout TV 34046S.

28. WATTS, Alan: *The Way of Zen,* Harmondsworth, Pelican Books (1962), p. 193.

29. TILBURY, John: Untitled article in *Ark,* No 45, Winter 1969, p. 43.

30. YOUNG, LaMonte and ZARZEELA, Marion: *Selected Writings,* Munich, Heiner Friedrich (1969), n.p.

31. KOSTELANETZ, Richard, in YOUNG, LaMonte and ZARZEELA, Marion; ibid., n.p.

32. REICH, Steve: *Writings About Music,* London, Universal Edition (1974), pp. 9-10.

33. WOLFE, Tom: 'The Painted Word', *Harper's and Queen,* February 1976, pp. 70-96.

34. PARTCH, Harry: *Genesis of a Music,* 2nd edn., New York, Da Capo Press (1974), p. viii.

35. Quoted in COTT, Jonathan: 'Partch: The Forgotten Visionary', *Rolling Stone,* April 11 1974, p. 20.

36. PARTCH, Harry: Recorded comment on record accompanying *Delusion of the Fury,* Columbia MS 30576.

37. YATES, Peter: *Twentieth Century Music,* London, Allen & Unwin (1968), p. 297.

38. Quoted in COTT, Jonathan, op. cit., p. 20.

39. PARTCH, Harry: op. cit., p. 196.

40. Quoted in PARTCH, Harry: op. cit., p. xiii.

The revolution which has taken place in the technical means of music during the twentieth century may seem to point to a revolution in the conceptual life of western man, yet this revolution obstinately refuses to take place; we remain as tied as ever to the scientific world view. We have examined the kind of thinking that is prefigured by the musical revolution, but that thinking remains latent, a virtuality rather than an actuality, and the majority of those who call themselves music lovers want nothing to do with it. The time-lag for the assimilation of new music grows longer; works of Schoenberg and Webern, for example, written before the first world war, are only now beginning to find tentative acceptance with some audiences. On the other hand, when the work of a composer does become appreciated by a sizeable public it is usually an indication that it has become assimilated into the main stream of middle-class culture, in other words, that it has ceased to disturb. The composer's ideas, however directly antagonistic they may once have been to the values and beliefs of its audience, however passionately and eloquently they may have been expressed, become sterilized. There seems no alternative to this situation; either an artist is unappreciated, in which case he speaks to the empty air, or at most to a group of intimates, or else he becomes a classic, and loses the power to disturb.

It is instructive to watch the process occur; the transition from dangerous outsider to tame entertainer and the darling of the superstar performers can take place almost overnight. It happened to Mahler, as far as the British public was concerned, in the early sixties, and to Stravinsky perhaps a little later; that Schoenberg might make the transition at all would have been unthinkable fifteen years ago, when it seemed that he was fated to remain forever more argued about than performed and listened to, to remain a 'composer's composer', yet there are signs that this is about to take place, at least with some of his works. Schoenberg himself, in fact, predicted it when he said that 'The second half of this century will spoil by over-estimation whatever the first half by under-estimation left unspoilt.' It can be taken as a sign that the transition has taken place with any work when audiences cease arguing over it and begin comparing performances or, even better, recordings; the work can at this stage be said to have been rendered innocuous, to have ended its task of challenging our sensibilities. It has become a classic.

Once a work has made the transition to classic it can never, however, we may try, revive its power to disturb our sensibilities. It may continue to delight us, to move us, to astonish us even, but it can never provoke us. This is the reason for our puzzlement at the outrage of even intelligent critics on the first appearance of some of the greatest masterpieces of the western tradition, at Weber, for example, a greater musician than perhaps we realize and certainly no fool, saying of Beethoven's *Seventh Symphony* that its composer was 'now ripe for the madhouse', or at Saint-Saëns, saying that he found 'no trace of a musical idea' in the *Prélude à l'Après-midi d'un Faune,* or a critic in the London Times who found Chopin's *F minor Concerto* 'dry and unattractive' — we just cannot comprehend what could have made them react so. It is possible to multiply such examples indefinitely, not to have easy fun at the expense of critics (who, to be sure, might have enough humility, or at least common sense, to refrain from the categorical damning of what they do not understand), but rather to emphasize the fact that our safe and reassuring concert classics were once dangerous and disturbing. Anton Ehrenzweig has remarked how the music of Brahms, which in his youth sounded 'acid and brittle, and lacking in smooth finish; his intricate and widely-spaced polyphony produced a hollow sound that failed to support the thin flow of the melody,' and which he loved for its masculinity, for its expression of Brahms' 'forbidding and lonely personality', lost those qualities for him in later life. 'As time went by the hard edges of the music were smoothed down. Today there is a luscious velvetiness, an almost erotic warmth about his melody that makes the same music almost too rich and sweet a fare ... I myself can quite clearly remember the harsh and hollow sound of the Brahms of my youth, but I cannot, however hard I try, associate this memory with the sweet, lush sonority which meets me when I listen to the same music in the concert-hall today.'[1]

My own experience of Sibelius is similar; as a student I admired and loved his music for its remote, forbidding, uncompromising quality, but when I listen to the same works (even sometimes on the same recordings) today I hear a music that is lush, over-romantic, even on occasion self-indulgent. In the same way I am finding that the wild polyrhythmic, polytonal extravagances of Ives are beginning to take on a more comfortable quality; the music no longer jolts me out of my seat, no longer disconcerts me with its unexpected juxtapositions, but begins to sound reasonable and even normal.

Some music survives this transition to the status of classic, some does not. To Ehrenzweig, Brahms, despite the much regretted loss of the power to disturb, clearly did survive; for me Sibelius has not, but Ives has. It is on thousands of small individual decisions, taken mostly unawares, by thousands of hearers, perhaps over a very long period of time (the fact that Ives has to me become a classic while others are hearing his music for the first time reflects nothing more than the accident of my having had access to the record library of the American Embassy in London in the early sixties) that the survival of a composer's oeuvre depends. There is probably a 'critical mass' of appreciative listeners — a number of listeners for whom the composer's music retains sufficient attraction to make it worth while for publishers, record companies and impresarios to present his works — below which a composer fails to survive as a living force, and no amount of advocacy by interested individuals or even organizations will reverse the process, at least for a generation, more probably for ever. Ehrenzweig remarks also on the factors which kept Beethoven's last quartets virtually unperformed for almost a century, keeping them intact, like a fly in amber, and preserving their power to disturb almost to the present day; my own generation, growing up in the forties in a remote colonial society (the geographical factor, too, is important) was probably the last that found them difficult to understand and therefore disturbing. Today they are repertory pieces and pose no more problems than the once-alarming *Fifth Symphony*.

The majority of concert-goers and buyers of classical records are unaware of and uninterested in this phenomenon, which Ehrenzweig calls secondary rationalization, since for them the function of music is not to disturb but to reassure. It is understandable that a classic should be reassuring, since it is precisely these classics that formed our modes of musical perception in the first place, and each hearing of a classic serves to confirm us ever more firmly in those modes. The music is cut off even more effectively from any disturbing function by being placed firmly in a time, and often a place, set aside from everyday life, becoming thus an antidote to, rather than an exploration of, our lives, a relaxation after our struggles to maintain ourselves in what seems an uncaring or even hostile society. In addition, the majority of those who regard themselves as music lovers are essentially passive in their attitude; music exists as something quite apart from themselves, to be listened to, in concert hall, opera house or on records, but that is all. They have no part to play in the creative act, but content themselves with the contemplation of the finished musical work as it is presented to them, the work itself having an abstract existence apart from themselves as listeners, indeed even apart from the performer to whose performance they are listening. The parallel between this abstract view of the musical work and the abstract view of knowledge held in our culture is clear; both are thought to exist 'Out There', independently of the listener and of the knower, and both are thought to be essentially unchanged whether or not any individual, as it were, plugs himself in to them (where 'Out There' is remains a mystery).

In parallel with the abdication of any creative role for the listener has gone the greater and greater professionalization of music. Composers and performers alike strive for, and many reach, more and more dizzy heights of technical proficiency; an increasing number of competitions for young pianists, instrumentalists, singers and conductors produces crops of young hopefuls armed with technical equipment that would make Liszt or Paganini blench, who, despite the fact that occasionally one or two actually show signs of real musicality, in their understandable pursuit of the social and financial rewards of fame, in most cases do much to destroy the musicality of the ordinary person. The virtuoso composer and the virtuoso performer are seen by the ordinary person as inhabiting a world of money and glamour from which he is forever excluded (recent revelations of the astronomical fees demanded and obtained by superstar performers would seem to make nonsense of protestations of disinterested devotion to art), a world which, encouraged by the writings of sycophantic journalists and critics, he might be excused for mistaking for the true sphere of the activity of music. A great and widening gulf stretches between the amateur and the professional and by the time a child reaches adolescence, at the latest, it is usually clear (though not always, alas, to the child or his fond parents) on which side of the gulf he is to spend his life. It is no wonder that the average amateur performer is unwilling to appear in public, knowing that whatever he can do has been done before, with infinitely more expertise, by professionals.

'Middle-class audiences consume Brecht and Beckett like a new breakfast cereal.' Thus Ed Berman summarizes neatly the dilemma of the artist today within our society. As has already been remarked, the artist has been forced into the position, like the rest of society, of producer of a commodity for others to consume; the world of art is full not only of producers with something to sell, but of middlemen, whose function is to promote and sell the art products and in turn make a living from them. Impresarios, publishers, art dealers, agents, A & R men, film distributors, all live off the product that the artist produces (this is not to say they are parasites; indeed, they perform a valuable function as retailers of the art product) and all are concerned with the selling of a commodity. The techniques of advertising and marketing thus become relevant to the propagation of art, techniques which date back, perhaps not inappropriately, at least, to Luther, whose famous plea 'Why should the Devil have all the best tunes?' reveals an awareness of the importance of good publicity. Advertisements appear in the musical press for the work of this or that composer (inserted of course usually by his publisher) while articles in those same journals tend to use – discreetly of course and perhaps not consciously – some of the techniques of advertising, praising the composer at the expense of rivals. In this situation, with so many products – and a performance can be a product no less than can a composition – vying for the attention of the public, the critic functions rather like *Which?* magazine, advising us to pay attention here but not there; the wide range of critical opinion on any artist merely reflects the fact that objective testing of a pianist is more difficult than of a washing machine or a package tour. For the would-be purchaser in the field of music, all that is at risk is the price of a concert ticket or an LP record, plus the outlay of an evening, but for the would-be vendor an unfavourable critical verdict can destroy a career. Nevertheless, it is clear that most critics feel a primary responsibility to the consumer, which, given the mercantile nature of our society and the fact that music is in the main a buyer's market, is scarcely surprising.

It is a sad but undeniable fact that a 'serious' composer working in our society today is addressing a smaller proportion of the population than in any other period in the history of western music; not only is the audience for concert music a minority within the general population, but the contemporary composer is able to engage the attention of only a small minority of that minority. This situation is often blamed on the lack of enterprise of concert promoters and record companies, and they must certainly bear some share of responsibility, if only in so far as they must make a profit from the music; but they are victims of the larger situation like the musicians themselves.

It has often been said that the differences between capitalist western Europe and America on the one hand and the allegedly communist Soviet Union and its satellite states on the other are less profound than they appear. Certainly it is clear that Soviet culture is as committed as the most capitalist society to the art object in preference to the art process, as can be seen not only from the astonishing stone-for-stone rebuilding of imperial Leningrad after its destruction in the second world war, but even more clearly in the status of music in the Soviet Union. In the first place, its concert life, with its orchestras, opera and ballet companies, famous conductors and soloists, all of whom are able (when the political climate is favourable) to move effortlessly into the western glamour circuit, is virtually indistinguishable from that of the west. Even the doctrine of Socialist Realism rests, ironically, on exactly the same view of music as commodity as that which inspired Lowell Mason to turn it into big business in America; in both cases, even if for different reasons, it becomes desirable to make the commodity available, in the best possible quality, to as many of the population as possible. The egalitarian societies of nineteenth-century America, chillingly described by de Tocqueville, and of post-revolutionary Russia both attempted (unsuccessfully) to discourage the formation of cultural elites by the enforced production of music that was comprehensible to all. Given the premise that art is a commodity and somehow beneficial, the desire to make it as widely available as possible is a not unworthy ideal, and we should not be too incensed when a Marshal Zhdanov tries to enforce it upon the musicians of the Soviet Union. They, after all, live otherwise highly pampered lives, like pedigree cattle that must be given the best fodder in order to produce the richest milk. The mistake lies in a basic misunderstanding of the nature and function of art, and this they hold in common with the rest of the industrialized, scientized world, whose ideology of production transcends the less important issue of who owns the means of production. The Soviets, like ourselves, have given their society over to the production of commodities, and it is a notable fact that wherever western consumer values go, western classical music follows quickly, as can be seen most vividly in Japan.

It is ironic that the dictatorship of the proletariat should be the one society that has remained most faithful to those most 'bourgeois' types of music making, the forms and gestures of late Romantic music, especially the programme symphony. The symphonies of Shostakovich, for example, however ingeniously 'revolutionary' their programmes, do not conceal the fact that they merely re-enact the same psychodrama that preoccupied composers throughout the later period of the symphonic tradition, that is to say from Beethoven onwards. They consist in essence of a progression from doubt and turbulence to triumph and apotheosis, with lyrical and dance-like interludes, and whether one disguises this as the progress of a Soviet composer towards maturity, as in the *Fifth*, or as a survey of the year 1917 (St Petersburg in turmoil, Lenin relaxing before the campaign, the bombardment by the *Aurora* and the final triumph of the people) as in the *Twelfth*, it remains the same programme. This is the more surprising in that it was a Russian composer, Tchaikowsky, who finally perceived with the simplicity of genius that a symphony did not have to have a happy ending, and in his *Sixth Symphony* portrayed the destruction of his hero and his dissolution into the depths from which he had come.

It is thus clear that, notwithstanding the enormous changes that have occurred in western music in this century, and despite the visions of a new society that these changes evoke, there has been no fundamental alteration in its attitudes and assumptions, any more than there have been in the societies that gave it birth. Art remains a commodity whose production remains in the hands of experts, which we purchase when we feel the need of it, and in whose making we have no more hand than we have in the manufacture of our breakfast cereal. We can perceive now that a true regeneration of western music, and western society, can come only when we can restore the power of creation to each individual in our society.

Let us consider for a moment the training of a western 'classical' musician. I have already described how musicians are trained in Bali and in black Africa; McPhee and Tracey give almost identical vignettes of fathers taking their small sons on their lap, putting the xylophone beaters into their hands and guiding them to the keys, not in rehearsal, but during a performance. Can one imagine a violinist in a western symphony orchestra doing the same? In both the non-Western societies, as in many others, the education of children to music pursues an effortless course; the young musician plays his instrument from the very start. Of course he works hard, not to gain mastery over his instrument (in fact the very idea of mastery is alien to a musician who regards his instrument as a loved colleague in the creative work) but to increase the fluency, expressiveness and naturalness of his playing, and this he does, not through technical exercises but through constant playing and exposure to musical experience within the framework of his society.

In our culture there is an unspoken assumption made when a child starts to learn an instrument that he must practise hard, do his scales and exercises, and some day, perhaps, he will be able to play it. It is difficult to see, if one considers this proposition, just what being able to play the instrument really means. If he is a pianist, does it mean playing like Rubinstein? or like a diploma candidate? or like myself, who plays for his own pleasure and that of indulgent friends? (One is reminded of the immortal Haydn, falling ill in his sixties and praying for recovery, as he was 'just learning how to compose'.) The training of the professional musician, as we know, is an arduous business, and in much of it there is little pleasure; I have heard a famous pianist say that she thought her musicality had been almost killed by the thousands of technical studies, figurations and exercises to which she had been obliged to submit in order to perfect her technique. How often does one hear a successful musician referred to as the 'product' of a certain school or college? The product is produced, standards of production are maintained, again without much care as to the nature of the process by which it is obtained.

As with performers, so with composers. It nowadays seems almost impossible to consider oneself a composer without years-long study, with preferably a university doctorate and study under at least two or three famous names, to which may be added a knowledge of phonology, electronics, psycholinguistics, number distribution and oriental philosophy. On a lower level of musical skill, something of tonal functional harmony in the manner of Bach, Haydn and Brahms, and counterpoint in the manner of Palestrina and Bach (or at least their lesser contemporaries) are essential before one is to be taken seriously as a student of music at all — certainly before one is to be thought of as capable of generating a single musical idea of one's own. Satie's 'licence to engage in the practice of composition' once more comes to mind.

The logical conclusion of this model of musical skill has been reached in the recent establishment in Paris of an *Institute for Research and Acoustic/Musical Co-ordination* (IRCAM), presided over by Pierre Boulez, whose appropriately underground home is to be built on the site of the late central market, *Les Halles*. The founding fathers of this Institute appear so bedazzled by the scientific model of knowledge that they have allowed their concept of music to be taken over completely by it; from now on, it seems, no-one is to be deemed fit to make music until he has completed a scientific study of psycho-acoustics, computerized analysis of sound, the structure of language and the mechanisms of the human brain. Following this model, the compositions resulting from the Paris research will presumably be published in learned journals, with resumés available for those who are too busy to attend to the whole, and will require teams of expert listeners to unravel the thoughts of these teams of composers. To be fair, something not unlike this has been occurring for some years, in the pages of journals like *Die Reihe* and *Perspectives of New Music,* but the work of the new French institute will apparently venture far beyond even the dreams of the Darmstadters or of Milton Babbitt and his colleagues at Princeton.

One could dismiss this ivory tower of culture as the aberration of musical minds were it not that the Institute is contributing still further to the current alienation of man from his own creativity, with the assistance of some of the most famous names in western music. As in the final days of so many earlier cultures and traditions, we see some of the finest minds of a generation (after all, Boulez and Berio are both major composers) wasting their creative energy in exercises which can prove only counter-productive in the business of survival. It is a phenomenon that resembles those strange and extravagant but useless and even fatal ornaments on animals and plants in an evolutionary line that is heading for extinction: the dinosaur with enormous spines and protuberances on its armour, the sabre-tooth tiger with canine teeth so long as to destroy their function. How like these is this *Institute for Research and Acoustic/Musical Co-ordination,* in which the ardent spirit of enquiry which animated Monteverdi and Haydn, brimming with optimism and the spell of the brave new world, has weighed itself down with the intellectual paraphernalia of outdated scientific notions that have nothing to do with the practice of music.

We are forced once again to contemplate the melancholy fact that notwithstanding the achievements of Debussy, Schoenberg, Stravinsky, Webern, Ives, Cage, Partch and many others, the experience of music in the western art tradition remains essentially unchanged. It remains as cut off, not only from that vaguely-defined group known as 'the people' but even from its immediate audience, as any music since the Renaissance. It is still composed by highly trained and remote specialists, played by professional musicians in concert halls and other spaces set aside for the purpose, at times set apart from our everyday lives. The musicians may wear rollneck sweaters instead of evening dress (which may point rather more to a raising of the social status of the rollneck sweater than to any genuine spirit of informality), the spaces may be converted engine sheds, but the essential experience has not changed. The professional players remain as uninvolved as ever in what they are playing, the audience still (despite certain tricks by the composer to simulate involvement) remains apart from the real process of creation, and the musical work remains an object for pure abstract contemplation whether it is a Beethoven symphony or a piece for prepared piano by John Cage. The audience remains essentially the same, drawn from the same social groups as those who greeted the doings of the *Davidsbündler,* or fought the battles over *Tannhäuser* or *Pelléas* (whether Debussy's or Schoenberg's — or indeed Maeterlinck's). The race against built-in obsolescence is still on in both music and technology, and the quest for new sources of energy, both physical and mental, becomes more urgent every year. This situation is likely to persist as long as the art object remains the principal object of interest, as long as ordinary people are cut off from the creative process and left with nothing but the finished object to admire.

There was a time, in the sixties, when it looked as if the situation was about to be broken up, by a new and revolutionary popular music of unprecedented and unexpected power. The so-called rock revolution began in fact back in the mid-fifties, and was based firmly on the discontent of the younger generation who were in revolt against the values of their elders; naturally they espoused new musical values, and equally naturally these values were a negation of everything in the musical world their elders inhabited — the virtual elimination of harmony, or at least its reduction to the few conventional progressions of the blues, an emphasis on the beat, a tendency towards modality and pentatonicism, new types of voice production owing much to sophisticated use of amplification, and a simplification of instrumental technique. Those who commented scornfully that these days any kid who could bash out a couple of chords on a guitar could become a pop star were right, but they were missing the fact not only that the simplicity of this music was its principal strength but also that it was drawing on new kinds of technical sophistication that were unknown to the conservatoire-trained musician. It parallels in many ways the work of the New England tunesmiths, in that harmony is relatively insignificant and importance is given to timbre, tone colour, volume and texture, as well as to a new — and very old — kind of modal melody freed from the restraints of classical chord progressions. Each singer or group is recognizable as much from their characteristic 'sound' as from what they actually sing or play, and they manipulate tone colour, aided by new electronic techniques, with a virtuosity that owes nothing to either the classical or the Tin Pan Alley tradition. One thinks, for example, of the voice of Elvis Presley, which has been described thus: 'As an expressive vehicle it shifts from high to low notes, it groans, it slurs, and it produces breathless changes of rhythm. To many listeners Presley's voice may have seemed crude, but its folk immediacy resided in this crudeness.'[2]

There followed rapidly an extraordinary musical eruption based on the percussive sound of the electric guitar, the rock-'n'-roll beat and blues harmony. The story of rock has been much told, and its association with the hippie movement and the revolutionary youth movements of the sixties is well known, with its love-ins, rock festivals, and the spirit of Woodstock. It seemed a tremendous and liberating rush of fresh air, a new art of community in which anyone could participate. And yet, even in the euphoria of 'Woodstock Nation' it was clear that commercial interests were strongly represented, and it seems likely that even that great festival of peace, music and love was, in one critic's words, 'an environment created by a couple of hip entrepreneurs to consolidate the cultural revolution and ... extract the money of its troops.'[3] And somewhere the whole movement of liberation from the Protestant Ethic, with which this movement was so intimately associated, went wrong; not only did the forces of the establishment hit back, hard, as at Chicago and Kent State University, but the movement itself became soured. Haight-Ashbury, in San Francisco, changed in less than a year from a centre of liberated youth to a sink of drugs, crime and disintegration. There was the Rolling Stones' free concert at Altamont, California in December 1969, only a few months after Woodstock, where Hell's Angels, hired and fed beer by the Stones to keep order, ran amok, killed four people and injured many more. Jimi Hendrix and Janis Joplin, Brian Jones and Jim Morrison, cult figures of the movement, died in their prime within a short period of each other; the Beatles broke up among bitter recriminations and a succession of charges and counter-charges over money and management.

And yet, at Woodstock and numerous other festivals all over the western world, in spite of the commercial interests which very soon came to dominate the world of rock music, something did take place; there *was* a new kind of experience that had nothing to do with the world of the concert hall or opera house, or even of the dance hall, the jazz club or the discothèque. Let us consider for a moment the nature of the experience as it seemed to one ageing member of that crowd of perhaps six hundred thousand who attended what proved to be the last of the great British three-day festivals, at Freshwater on the Isle of Wight, in July 1970. In the first place, music was only a part of the experience, albeit the most important part. It was not quite continuous; it would start each day around midday and finish a little after sun-up on the following morning, leaving a few hours for the huge arena to be cleaned up (after a fashion), and running repairs carried out on the amplification equipment, ready for the next marathon session. Now it is quite clearly impossible for anyone to listen to music, in the way that one listens to a symphony, for close on twenty hours non-stop; the same thing happened here as happens during all-night Balinese *wayang* performances. One listens with attention, one's attention wanders, one even drops off to sleep from time to time, to be awoken perhaps by a new and riveting sound; I remember vividly the beginning of an electrifying performance by The Who, which began around 3 am. The music, such of it as one heard, was mainly marvellous, but it was not just a musical occasion. At the risk of sounding credulous and cliché-ridden one must say that the social experience was even more remarkable. For those three days on the Isle of Wight there came into at least partial existence the potential society which lies otherwise beyond our grasp; young people released from the stresses and restrictions of their everyday life were engaging in the celebration of a common myth, a common life-style, which, even if it did not yet exist, they were able to conjure into existence for a while. Faces were relaxed and beautiful; I have never seen so many beautiful young people. There were bonfires, ancient expression of communality, burning through the nights; the passing of time, other than the indubitable natural facts of day and night, went more or less unnoticed. For a brief moment in western society, music became, not merely an intellectual, aesthetic or even emotional experience, but the centre of a communal ritual which subsumed all the other experiences and showed how partial and incomplete they in fact are. It was no doubt all an illusion; to the performers it was just another, albeit major, gig for which they were being paid by entrepreneurs whose principal interest in the event was to make money, but it seemed real enough at the time. It represented to me the closest that some people in our society have come to achieving that kind of communality which we have noted in other musical cultures, and of which ours is in desperate need.

It may appear as if the new popular music has been effortlessly absorbed into the main stream of western culture and its revolt neutralized. Its performers are professionals selling the public a product, as much as the straightest of 'straight' symphony orchestra players (the latter in fact appear in the backing of many a hit record), backed by an infrastructure of advertising and marketing which, not surprisingly considering the vastly larger sums of money involved, dwarfs that for 'classical' music; the ordinary listener can play no part in the creative process. Recordings have, of course, a great deal to do with this situation; much of the music can exist only on record or tape, for much the same reasons as *Stagecoach* or *The Towering Inferno* could exist only on film, and a record is ineluctably a product for sale, the only degree of choice that one has in relation to it being either to play or not to play it. Much money is invested in every disc; the sophisticated equipment needed for today's forty-eight or sixty-four-track recording as well as the expenditure of highly skilled time in editing and mixing tapes and making masters costs as much as that needed for a small film, not to mention the design and making of the sleeve (in itself a minor art form) without which no record would sell.

But this is only half the truth, or rather concerns only half the scene. The ephemeral popular music heard on pop radio stations and in discos can be said to be an unashamedly commercial product, made to sell and make money. This does not mean that even this market is necessarily totally corrupt or that because of this the music cannot be of good quality. Despite such dismal non-events as the Eurovision Song Contest, which disgusts even most pop musicians, the pop field can, and often does, throw up music that is exciting and beautiful, even though it is frankly designed to appeal to the largest possible number and to be quite ephemeral. There is vitality there, and a casual technical mastery which was not learned in any school of music.

We should remember, too, that it is in this field that the Beatles, The Rolling Stones, Bob Dylan, The Grateful Dead and many other leading groups and individual performers from the early sixties onwards lived and moved and had their being; if they transcended its limitations it was not through rejection of the terms and techniques of popular music but rather through their expansion and consolidation — as can be heard by comparing The Beatles' early *Please Please Me* or *Love Me Do* with *Sergeant Pepper's Lonely Hearts Club Band*, in itself a remarkable accession of sophistication to have occurred in a new style within less than five years. This mainly modal, non-harmonic music based on the sound of electric guitars and percussion — which we can conveniently if not really accurately call rock — exists on a continuous spectrum from the most frivolous and commercially-motivated to the most complex and intense, making possible its continuing vitality as the various kinds feed ideas to one another, a situation which the contemporary 'serious' composer, lacking any comparable power base in a popular style, might find enviable.

The music that exists at the more popular end of the scale is more or less inescapable, but that of the other end is virtually unknown to the ordinary classical music lover, who hardly notices the flyposted concert and record notices on condemned buildings and building-site hoardings on his way to his symphony concert; in fact, at least in Britain, unless he makes a special effort he is unlikely to hear it at all, since it receives little airplay on the radio, apart from late-night programmes on commercial stations. (Americans, with their better grasp of the function of radio in the TV age, fare better in this respect.) It is a deeply serious, though not at all intellectual, music, composed and played by musicians to whom it is not only a means of personal expression but a whole lifestyle; they live, eat and sleep the music to an extent rarely. matched by their 'classical' counterparts. Their music assimilates influences from blues, jazz, black gospel music, country music, from Anglo-Celtic folksong and, more, recently, from black West Indian music, especially reggae and dub, into a form of musical expression which, as we have seen, has moved further towards that of the rest of the human race than perhaps any since the Renaissance, and may even in a sense be said to negate the spirit of Renaissance man.

As in non-western musics, there is virtuosity here, but it is cultivated, not for its own sake in scales, exercises and studies, but in pursuit of a deeper, more intense, more individual expression; one remembers indelibly Jimi Hendrix's breathtaking control of electronic feedback in his tortured and torturing version of *The Star-Spangled Banner* at Woodstock, the airy, graceful and rhythmically fascinating non-harmonic guitar polyphony of The

Grateful Dead's *Dark Star*, whose twenty-minute span is based on an unchanging dominant discord of A, the pounding, buzzing, feedback-distorted sound of Velvet Underground, the vivid, surrealist imagery, both verbal and musical, of *Sergeant Pepper,* among many musical experiences of power, beauty and casual virtuosity.

The vision of the potential society evoked by this music was, as I have said, directly related to that of the youth and liberation movements of the sixties, which in fact tried to bring that vision to realization. Today the vision has faded and the rock music of the seventies has accordingly lost much of its immediacy and power, and contents itself mainly with purely aesthetic experimentation, much of it admittedly fascinating and beautiful, for the benefit of a knowledgeable audience. But the music of the sixties remains on record; as with jazz in its early days, a music born out of the intimate contact between an artist and his instrument, without the interference of notation, has been preserved, and it is, ironically, those very commercial interests which contributed much to the emasculation of the music that have been responsible for its preservation. One wonders what later generations will make of it all.

The gramophone record is in fact a very mixed blessing. Certainly its significance has taken a long time to be understood, and even now, especially among classical music enthusiasts, it is regarded as merely a vehicle for the bringing of 'good' music from the concert hall to the living room. It is not my purpose here to consider the changes that it has brought about in both the performance of music and in the way it is heard; I want only to remark on its status as package par excellence, and its tendency to emphasize the product status of the music engraved upon it. Not only do record reviews, both in print and on radio, discuss records from precisely this point of view (consider for example the BBC's regular feature *Building a Library,* in which all the available versions of a particular classic work are compared; the reviewer is generally very emphatic in his verdict on the various recordings considered as value for money), but also the idea becomes subtly implanted, not necessarily deliberately, that in owning a record one somehow owns a piece of the work itself — as one can hear in listening to conversations between gramophiles. The record also has the undesirable effect, especially in many modern works where a degree of choice is left to the performer, and in improvised music, of fixing one particular version to the exclusion of all other possibilities, frustrating the express intentions of the composer and performer.

There is today, however, a small but growing number of musicians who are attempting to restore lost communality to western music, to restore the importance of the creative process over that of the glossy finished product; perhaps the most visible of these attempts lies in a return to the improvisatory roots of music. Improvisation has always, of course, played an essential part in jazz, and although it had been traditionally carried out over a framework of harmonic progressions generally derived from popular tunes, much room had been left for the creativity of the individual performer; the existence of standardized riffs and melodic progressions, a common stock of material, made it possible for only moderately talented individuals to make something they could call their own, while the exceptionally gifted could build new ideas from it. When jazz cut itself off from the harmonic bass and chord progressions, it sometimes became difficult to define what it was in the music that made it jazz at all: only a certain cast to the melodic invention and the use of bass and rhythm sections (both hanging, as it were, in space and free of both the rhythms and the harmonic progressions of earlier jazz) remind the hearer of the music's origins. Some recent jazz performances, for example those of the pianist Cecil Taylor, lack even this backing; the music's demonic energy is almost the only remaining sign of jazz in any traditional sense of the word. The new jazz, since Charlie Parker, is characterized also by the exploitation of new instrumental sounds, of squeaks, grunts and slides which are not merely ornamental to a basically diatonic melodic line but are integral to the conception of the music.

It is therefore natural that jazzmen should have been among the leading spirits of a new attempt to revitalize our musical culture, to remove it from the grip of what is seen as a repressive musical-political establishment, through a return to improvisation, especially group improvisation. But the impetus has come not from jazz only; many musicians trained in the conservatoire tradition have found themselves deeply dissatisfied with playing only from a score and indeed with making musical scores for others to play from. It is already implicit in Cage's idea that sounds, simply as sounds, are to be enjoyed for their own sakes; why then bother with elaborately organized sound structures, but simply go along with the sounds, without any preconceived plan, wherever they take you? Many younger composers, whether or not they accepted (or were even familiar with) Cage's ideas, thought so. And of course, some of the world's great musical cultures, notably that of India, are founded on improvisation, albeit within a strict framework.

Improvisation differs from composed and written-down music in two important ways. The first is that the finished art object barely exists; the music is an activity, a process, which at no stage can be said to be a completed work of art. As Cornelius Cardew said of the AMM group, of which he was for a time a member, 'We are *searching* for sounds and for the responses that attach to them, rather than thinking them up, preparing them and producing them. The search is conducted through the medium of sound and the musician himself is at the heart of the experiment'.[4] The second difference may perhaps be best put by a metaphor. Western composed music resembles an account of a journey of exploration that has been taken by the composer, who comes back, as it were, from 'Out There', and tells us something, as best he can, of what it was like. The journey may have been a long, arduous and fascinating one, and we may be excited, moved, even amused, by it, but we cannot enter fully into the experience with him because the experience was over and he was safely home before we came to hear of it. (The small but significant number of artists who go mad testifies to the perilousness of the journey; but in that case we get to know no more of it than we learn of the last days of Franklin, Kingsford Smith, Fawcett or other explorers who failed to return from their journeys.)

In improvising, on the other hand, the musician takes us with him on his journey of exploration; we negotiate with him every twist and turn, every precipice and danger. We may not know how long the trip is going to be, or even necessarily where we are going. It may be that we shall not enter any new territory at all, or even if we do, that it will prove just a dismal swamp that no-one will wish to revisit, but every now and then we obtain glimpses of glittering new lands, are dazzled by the sight of beauty and meaning which is all the more astonishing for being unexpected. Composed music is like a travel book, which we can open and read at will, but it remains essentially an account of a journey which soon becomes familiar; we may read it with repeated pleasure but without any expectation of seeing anything new other than perhaps some previously unnoticed detail.

In short, composed music is the account of the journey of exploration, which might well have been momentous, but is over before we learn of it, while improvisation is the journey itself, which is likely to make small discoveries rather than large, or even no discoveries at all, but in which everything that *is* found can be of interest or value. It is, unfortunately for its audience appeal in our culture, for that reason a chancy business, and audiences in the main want security and certainty. The average concert or opera performance is a strictly predictable affair; at least in professional music making, there is little chance that the performance will go seriously wrong, little risk that the listener will not hear what he came to hear. It is understandable that an audience that pays for admission to a performance should want to get what it pays for; as with any product offered for sale, certain standards of quality are expected and that is precisely what an improvising musician cannot guarantee. Improvisation, therefore, tends to wither under the mercantile conditions of modern concert life.

It is interesting in this regard to see how the western 'classical' audience, while seeking the security of predictable musical quality, nevertheless guards against the boredom induced by situations of total certainty. Audiences to western classical music may not possess the refined discrimination of pitch or rhythm of, say, Indian or African hearers, but they have cultivated an incredibly fine ear for subtle differences between performers and performances of the same score. The range of vocal quality subsumed, for example, under the heading 'soprano' is small indeed compared even to that between two singers of similar vocal range in jazz; the difference in tone between two instrumentalists playing the same passage, the number of possible durations implied by a printed crotchet in allegro tempo, the number of possible ways of playing a given written phrase, are all minute when compared to such differences in other cultures. It is these, and many other such extremely fine discriminations, which make the difference between one performance of a score and another, and which keep interest in our well-worn classics alive for the musical cognoscenti of our culture.

But the improvising musician senses, however inarticulately, that success has meaning only when there is possibility of failure. The succession of competent performances differing only in minute details such as one finds in any of the great concert halls of the western world produces, perhaps inevitably where the audience is paying for quality and wants to get it, a blandness of diet which is not unlike that offered by any large supermarket. One would expect, therefore, to find improvisation flourishing only in highly communal groups where the musicians are known personally to their hearers, and the hearers are willing to go along with them in their adventures, however small or however venturesome.

It need not surprise us to find that those western musicians who are abandoning the written score and giving themselves over to improvised music (or, as many prefer to call it, free music), and especially group improvisation, tend to play either just for themselves or for relatively small groups of highly committed listeners, and do not expect to make much money from their performances. As suggested earlier, they are largely, but by no means exclusively, jazz musicians who tend to form a kind of sub-community within the community of musicians, who come together rather as friends than as professional colleagues, and play for long hours together, in many cases more for the feeling of communality than for the actual sounds — although these are frequently of great beauty. Groups who play together for any length of time find a group style and an empathy. They place little importance on technical prowess for its own sake; one plays as well as one can, and works harder at developing group awareness and empathy than at individual virtuosity. As Cardew says, 'Training is substituted for rehearsal, and a certain moral discipline is an essential part of this training'[5], and he lists the virtues an improvising musician can develop (or, rather, those virtues a musician can develop through improvisation) as simplicity, integrity, selflessness, forbearance, preparedness (or awareness), identification with nature and acceptance of death.

In an article in *Time Out* John Lewis surveyed the various groups playing free music in London in 1972; he concluded,

> For most people in free music groups the activity is serious and even vital to the well-being of the participants. It can be joyous and invigorating nonetheless. But it is not principally entertainment. So those people who want to make a living through their playing have a hard path to follow. They are dependent on finding an audience willing to listen to them without any need for compromises. A few groups are managing to do so, and the audiences for workshops are growing in number. It is a genuine musical alternative to the establishment jazz, rock and straight scenes.[6]

The movement towards improvisation has even thrown up its own periodicals; in London, *Microphone* and *Musics* (now both, sadly, defunct) have provided a lively forum for improvising musicians. The format of these magazines reflects the ethos of improvisation; they are thin, cheap, typewritten and mimeographed, hard to read, poorly laid out, while the text consists largely of theological arguments between musicians who are in very broad general agreement. But they are also stimulating, with occasional flashes of insight and enlightening statements of position; above all, they are groping towards the formulation of the essential questions of western music and western society, and do not fail to perceive the intimate connection between the two. As with the music itself, one has to be prepared to cope with boredom and even irritation, which is made worthwhile by the streaks of gold in the ore. As with improvisation one accepts it all, gratefully, as clear signs of a communal feeling and an emotional liveliness which is lacking in our more widely accepted concert life.

Improvising musicians are represented on a number of small record labels, although the position of improvisation vis-à-vis recording is anomalous. It is clear that an improvisation is an ephemeral thing; the music dies as soon as it is made and cannot be recalled. This character changes once it is recorded, not only through the fixing of something that was not intended to be fixed, but also because it becomes once again an object like any composed music, fixed in time and space. As Cardew says, 'Documents such as tape recordings of improvisations are essentially empty, as they preserve chiefly the form that something took and give at best an indistinct hint as to the feeling and cannot convey any sense of time and place.' But he adds, 'News has to travel somehow, and tape is probably in the last analysis just as adequate as hearsay, and certainly just as accurate.'[7]

The forms taken by improvised music are very various, ranging from completely free improvisation depending simply on the inspiration of the moment guided by the empathy between the players (this, unless the players practice most assiduously the virtues listed by Cardew, generally degenerates into a shapeless free-for-all with everyone making as much noise as he can in order even to hear himself) through improvisation guided by a previously decided over-all plan, to the use of visual patterns or verbal instructions whose purpose is to stimulate the imagination of the players. There is more skill than might be imagined in the making of such patterns or such instructions in order to provide the right amount of stimulus without limiting unduly the players' freedom of action; it is no less a social than a purely musical skill. But whatever its external form the aim is generally clear: to restore lost communality to western music, to take it out of the hegemony of virtuosi of both the concert platform and the composer's studio, to encourage the participation of all members of the community at whatever level of competence they happen to be. The composer is generally thought of as at best obsolete; many musicians even regard the existence of a single person who gives instructions to others as politically undesirable, and a model, at one extreme, of colonialism.

Clearly, the ethic of improvisation, with its freedom from the constraints of harmony and counterpoint as well as from the necessity for high development of instrumental skill and the written-out score, is in fact politically very closely allied to anarchism, in the true rather than the popular-press sense. A situation in which all individuals can be relied on, without force of rules, to contribute freely to the common good can probably be realized, musically no less than socially, only among small groups of people who know, understand and respect one another. It is nevertheless a noble ideal; having myself engaged in group improvisation over a period of time I can testify to its power to liberate aspects of one's musicality and sense of musical responsibility in a way that no other musical activity can achieve. I have been lucky enough to encounter musical experiences of power and beauty of an altogether different kind from that of either listening to, performing or even creating composed music; the degree of involvement is of a quite different kind, as one might expect from the exploration of one another's musical personalities in a loving way (remembering that groups of improvising musicians, no less than close-knit families, frequently quarrel). Cardew does not exaggerate in describing the experience as erotic; it is small wonder that recordings and broadcasts can give no more than a pale misty image of the experience of improvised music, even with the finest and most intimately close-knit groups of performers.

But the experience of improvisation, valid and valuable as it is, can be only partial. Like anarchism, like the flight from technology, it represents, not a transcending of, but a retreat from, the western experience which is our inheritance and which we cannot, however we may try, throw off. Improvisation is, and should be, an essential element of the experience of all musicians, indeed perhaps of everyone, but it can give only a partial cure to the malaise of our musical culture. I believe that a more comprehensive answer can be found, to which the ethic of improvisation can contribute, no less than can our experience of other musics (seen within their total social setting and not just as a source of novel technical devices) as well as our observations on the nature of western classical music and of the revolt against the domination of the scientific world view as revealed in the music of our century.

There is one further ingredient in this mix of ideas, which I have so far touched on only in passing: the processes of education. The melancholy experiences of the last two decades have permanently scotched the optimistic forecasts of enthusiasts who believed that the answer to the problems of our society lay within the schools. However, the mood of hopelessness engendered in so many educationalists today by this overwhelming and universal evidence of failure is as unjustified as the earlier over-optimism, since the reasons for failure lie not within the idea of education itself but within the practice of education as it is more or less universally conceived throughout western culture, a practice which rests on a fundamental misconception — one might almost say a fantasy — of the nature of knowledge and of the ways in which learning occurs. From the matters discussed so far in this book, we can begin to seek a new perspective on education and the assumptions upon which it based, a new set of tentative answers which are potentially fruitful because they attach to new questions. Before going on to consider these questions, let us look at the education of children as at present practised within our society, in much the same manner as we examined, in Chapter 1, the practice of music. I intend to suggest that another approach is not only possible but also essential if we are to find a way out of the impasse which afflicts our society and our music no less than our system of education.

Chapter 7: Bibliography

1. EHRENZWEIG, Anton: *The Hidden Order of Art,* London, Weidenfeld & Nicholson (1967), Paladin (1970), p. 87.
2. BELZ, Carl: *The Story of Rock,* 2nd edn., New York, Oxford University Press (1972), p. 42.
3. KOPKIND, Andrew, quoted in BELZ, Carl; ibid., p. 211.
4. CARDEW, Cornelius: 'Towards an Ethic of Improvisation', *Treatise Handbook,* London, Edition Peters (1971), p. xviii.
5. CARDEW, Cornelius: ibid., p. xvii.
6. LEWIS, John: 'So What do you want from Music — Security?', *Time Out,* December 14 1972, pp. 38-40.
7. CARDEW, Cornelius: op. cit., p. xvii.

The point at which the twin concepts, the producer-consumer relationship and knowledge as essentially outside of and independent of the knower, come together most significantly is in the field of education, or rather, to use Ivan Illich's valuable distinction, in schooling, since schooling and education are by no means synonymous; contrary to popular supposition, one does not need to go to school to become educated, and, conversely, going to school does not necessarily give one an education, as thousands of frustrated pupils and ex-pupils can testify. As Illich points out, not only is schooling essentially a commodity which a community buys on behalf of its younger members (and even the richest societies are beginning to find the price higher than they can afford), but also the purveyors of the commodity find themselves in a monopoly situation; its recipients have no choice but to accept what is offered. Just as any other monopolistic purveyor will try to disguise the lack of real choice of product by offering a number of different-sounding brand names, so the western system of schooling offers different brands which are in all essentials the same product. In Britain these brands go under the names of public school, independent school, preparatory school, comprehensive, grammar and secondary modern school, but what is offered is always the same: packaged knowledge which the pupil is expected to consume but which it is not expected he can create for himself. Each package is called a course, and each has a catalogue of contents known as the syllabus, and, like parcels labelled 'Not to be opened till Christmas Day', the packages may be opened only in classrooms in the presence of a teacher, and then only when the pupil has first shown that he has consumed the contents of other, simpler, packages.

Illich's criticisms cover a wider area than solely education; he is concerned that all social services are undergoing the same processes. Health becomes the province exclusively of doctors, community care that of social workers and so on, and he rightly comments on the way in which the professionalization of these services is undermining the ability of the individual to help himself or his neighbour (these comments, thus starkly put, may seem to come from the lunatic Right, but Illich's concern is with the revival of community responsibility, or what he calls conviviality). Illich is also more cautious than many of his enthusiastic deschooling followers on the schools' monopoly of education:

> The rash and uncritical disestablishment of school could lead to a free-for-all in the production and consumption of more vulgar learning, acquired for immediate utility or eventual prestige. The discrediting of school-produced, complex curricular packages would be an empty victory if there were no simultaneous disavowal of the very idea that knowledge is more valuable because it comes in certified packages and is acquired from a mythological knowledge-stock controlled by professional guardians. I believe that only actual participation constitutes socially valuable learning, a participation by the learner in every stage of the learning process, including not only a free choice of what is to be learned and how it is to be learned but also a free determination by each learner of his own reason for living and learning – the part that his knowledge is to play in his life.[1]

The effects of professionalized and monopolistic schooling can be seen no less on the worried faced of grammar-school sixth formers than in the truancy statistics, and 'bright' and 'dull' pupils alike leave school, at whatever age, convinced that effective knowledge comes from the school and only from the school and that examination and certification are essential elements in the gaining of that knowledge. The only difference in this regard between the 'bright' and the 'dull' is that the former believes himself capable of obtaining that knowledge while the latter has been convinced that he cannot; while one is a success in school and the other a failure they are united by the fact that neither has the vocabulary (that is, the conceptual equipment) to question the assumptions and criteria upon which he is labelled. (That this remains true even into the upper echelons of the teaching profession is borne out by a recent rebuke offered by the Chief Examiner of a British public examinations board to those who criticise the examination system; they should remember, he said, that they owed the fact that they were in an interesting or well-paid job to that very system. The closed circle remains intact!)

The experienced reader will at this point begin to realize that he is entering familiar territory, that of not only Illich but of such eloquent critics of present concepts of education as Paul Goodman,

Everett Reimer, Jules Henry, Edwin Mason, Postman and Weingartner, and many others;[2] and the experienced reader will be perfectly correct. But it is my intention here, not to restate what has been said before very much better than I could say it, but rather to re-interpret the criticisms offered by these writers in the light of our investigations into the nature and function of music in this and other societies, and of the nature of the concept of knowledge revealed by those investigations. Let us examine first some of the assumptions which underlie the system of schooling to which nearly all the youth of the industrialized world are subjected today, and then look more closely at music education as at present practised, and see how these assumptions relate to the general world view of western man.

The idea of knowledge as an independent entity, that is, as existing outside the knower and regardless of whether anyone knows it or not, pervades our entire system of schooling from beginning to end. We have seen always how such a notion was essential before western science could begin its task of colonizing the physical universe; we now see that it determines the whole nature of the schooling process. Just as, in science, the experiential factor is ignored, so in schooling; the teacher is obliged to transmit to his pupils as much as he can of this abstract body of information, regardless of the quality of the experience which in so doing he inflicts on the pupil. This is not to say that teachers are not in the main thoroughly humane people who would not wantonly inflict unpleasant experiences on their pupils; it is simply that when obliged to choose between the quality of their pupils' present experience and the assimilation by those pupils of information which is believed to be necessary for their future benefit (ie their success in examinations), they will inevitably choose the latter, indeed, they have no option but to do so. The general dreariness of most school environments — especially in secondary schools and to a great extent in further and higher education, at least outside the privileged sector of fashionable universities — is eloquent testimony to the lack of concern for experience in the pursuit of abstract knowledge. No child, at least after his first few years at school (though one must pay tribute to many primary schools for their valiant attempts to undo this situation), actually *expects* school to be an enjoyable experience; if it proves so, he regards it, rightly, as a lucky bonus. He is made aware that what he is being subjected to is in his own best interest, for the sake of some vaguely-defined future advantage which for most remains perpetually out of reach.

Our culture's will-o'-the-wisp promise of future satisfaction in return for sacrifice of present pleasure becomes imprinted very early in children's minds, and yet another generation is conditioned to the industrial philosophy. One wonders how long that philosophy would survive if school were to afford an opportunity to all for the creation as well as the consumption of knowledge, becoming in itself a satisfying experience.

It has been often pointed out that the very physical structure of the orthodox classroom, which so resembles that of the orthodox concert hall, with its rows of desks facing the blackboard and the teacher, making interaction possible only between teacher and pupil, never between pupil and pupil, makes clear, before a word has been uttered, the direction from which knowledge is to come (knowledge passed from pupil to pupil goes often under the name of 'cheating'). Textbooks, blackboards and the majority of what has become known as educational technology all serve to confirm the pupils as consumers of knowledge, as do examinations, to which, acknowledged or not, the learning activity is directed. The physical isolation of the school, and of the classroom within the school, likewise reveals in metaphoric form the remoteness of most of what is expected to be learnt from the real lives of the pupils.

I have already commented on the fragmentation of life in western society; school produces its own brand of fragmentation in the form of subjects, and in the fragmentation of the pupil's day as he is moved passively from one room to another to absorb forty- or fifty-minute chunks, one after the other, of 'branches of knowledge'. It is of course clear that everybody knows many things, and that some agreed subdivision of this knowledge is useful in order to make manageable the processes of interaction. But the conventional 'subjects' represent only one possible way of slicing up reality, and others can exist which are at right angles, or indeed at any angle, to these. A man may study a city, for example, and the subjects history, geography, seismology, heraldry, music, architecture, nutrition and dozens of others may be subsumed indissolubly into the single subject, which is bounded only by a man's passion for knowledge. Nature in any case does not favour clear-cut categories; there is no clear differentiation between a tree and a shrub, a growth of hairs on a chin and a beard. These differences exist in our minds only, as convenient subdivisions. The school, however, like our society as a whole, bases its practice on the assumption that these convenient subdivisions are inherent in the structure of external reality, an assumption which disregards the fact that their boundaries are constantly changing and remain obstinately unclear when one tries to align them precisely. Even music as a subject, which we imagine we can delineate clearly, has a very different significance, as we have seen, in Bali or black Africa from that which it has in modern Europe; we have seen how the word 'music' does not exist at all in Swahili, so all-embracing is the concept. A medieval schoolman would define it differently from a modern western composer, and we are seeing how the concept of music, not merely western art music but music as an activity in society, is changing rapidly in our culture today. Again, new subjects keep appearing, either overlapping the areas of previously existing subjects or by slicing external reality at a new angle; who, a hundred years ago, would have thought of phenomenology or semiology (even though phenomena and signs have always been with us), or such hybrids as molecular biology, psycholinguistics, ethnomusicology, rock musicals or mixed-media happenings?

This uncertainty, this fuzziness at the edges and changeability occurs because, while the objects of our knowledge are outside us, our knowledge of them is within us; knowledge cannot thus exist without a knower, and may in fact be said to be a relationship between the knower and the known. The divisions of knowledge are likewise within us, which is why, given the nature of the human mind, their edges remain blurred. And it is precisely on the fuzzy edges of those convenient sub-divisions which we call subjects that the most interesting and rewarding speculations are liable to take place, speculations which are specifically barred by the rigid enforcement of subject boundaries in our educational endeavours. Who would have thought, for example, to associate the findings of a long sea voyage with an eighteenth-century clergyman's speculations on population (read, according to Darwin, 'for amusement') to produce a theory of the mechanism of organic evolution? Or who would have imagined that the attempt of a group of Florentine amateurs to reconstruct the performance of ancient Greek drama would have produced, when brought into collision with late sixteenth-century musical style, an art form that was to dominate European musical life for three centuries?

The outward and visible sign of the subject is the syllabus, a table of contents which lays down what the student is required to learn and on what he is to be examined. At least, that is what the syllabus purports to do; in practice it equally effectively cuts him off from learning, since everything lying outside the syllabus is not examinable and therefore not worth teaching. The syllabus narrows the student's vision of knowledge and cuts him off from precisely those fuzzy areas at the edges of subjects that are the most interesting and rewarding — if, in fact, he is allowed to become aware of their very existence. When one considers a school, college or university and the resources of skill, knowledge and experience it contains (itself only a tiny fraction of the community's store of skill and knowledge which is waiting to be drawn upon) one greatly regrets that only a tiny, arbitrarily chosen, sector is accessible to any individual student; the rest, if he is aware at all of its existence, is put out of his reach by the demands of the syllabus and of examinations.

A response to this problem that is gaining popularity is the construction of what are called interdisciplinary courses, comprising segments taken from one subject and portions taken from another to form a new syllabus. But a new syllabus simply defines a new subject, and the student finds himself once more frozen into a single posture that is not his own, different from the old perhaps but just as rigid. It is the freedom to make one's own connections, one's own subject, which coincides with one's own interests and needs, that is still missing. I have sometimes day-dreamed that the institution in which I work, with its splendid variety of skills from professional cookery to librarianship, from music to Latin American politics, from photography to English as a foreign language, might be thrown open to students with the single instruction: 'Here we are — use us.' But, alas, who would examine? and how could we grade? and what body would issue a certificate of proficiency with a first-class, a second or a third-class pass? and in what would the certificate be awarded? The vision is clearly unrealizable within the present dispensation, and it fades; but it will not be banished ....

A further undesirable feature of syllabuses is inertia; it is practically impossible to construct a syllabus which has built-in allowance for advances in knowledge, if such occur, or for artistic development, or, most crippling of all, for the growing experience of the teacher. The last point relates vitally to the thinking behind the construction of a syllabus; its purpose is to standardize the learning which takes place between one classroom and the next, one institution and the next, one set of pupils and the next, one teacher and the next, in fact to eliminate as far as is possible the essentially human elements from the situation. It renders the teacher interchangeable with any other teacher, provided that he has the necessary abstract information at his disposal, and the pupils with all other pupils. It makes teachers and pupils as interchangeable as the workers on the production line, or indeed as the parts of the products they assemble.

The syllabus is organized on the basis of logical, linear progression, one item of information proceeding from the preceding, in a manner which is in fact quite unrelated to the way in which we really learn. How we learn naturally if left to ourselves is much more like a network or the assembly of a jigsaw puzzle than any straight-line succession. When I first arrived in London I began, like any good colonial, in Earl's Court, the bedsitter centre of the metropolis. On my first morning in the city I took the Underground to Piccadilly Circus, explored the area a little, returning to base by bus. The two separate areas which I had now explored were linked by the overground journey, aided by a street map (that is, by personal exploration aided by received information), so that my mental map of London at that stage consisted of two areas linked by a line. A subsequent trip to Hampstead by tube added a new element, which did not link with the existing areas until I made a second expedition, this time in the car of an acquaintance. Thus, little by little, my mental map of London was constructed. It took in fact several years before all the major areas were placeable on that map, and some even now are a little vague. But the map was built up by my own journeys, in an order which might appear random but was in fact intimately linked with my pattern of friendship, work and entertainment, the essential logic of my experience. And further, the knowledge came into existence as and when I needed it, not when somebody else thought I was ready for it.

Continuing the geographical metaphor, we might describe a syllabus as the guided tour of an area, while the curriculum, that is, the total of all that a pupil is expected to learn in his progress through school, is the guided tour of an entire terrain, through which experts are appointed to guide the pupils in groups. The trouble with experts, of course, is that each looks at the world with eyes that are blinded to anything but his own speciality; each in approaching the terrain seeks out those features that interest him and ignores the rest. Rivers, savannahs, gorges, deserts he looks at with eyes that see nothing but the possibility of a payoff. He cannot allow his attention to be seduced by what is beautiful, dramatic or awe-inspiring; what does not relate directly to his quest is left out of consideration. Here again is clear evidence that knowledge is a function of the knower no less than the known, since although the terrain has a real existence what this expert knows of it will differ from that of experts in other fields, who will look at the terrain for other things — cattlemen, perhaps, miners looking for metals, planners looking for somewhere to put down a new city. Each will see the landscape only through the partial vision of his own expertise, each will look at the landscape for what can be got out of it. None will see the terrain as a whole.

The curriculum specifies the nature of the guided tour and decides which experts will act as guides. The pupils are herded around, shown the oil wells, the cattle country, the cities, regardless of whether or not they are interested; they are moved on relentlessly with the rest of the party regardless of whether they have assimilated the information or whether they might wish to linger over some feature that catches their attention or imagination. They may even have some features pointed out to them as beautiful — if there is time after dealing with more important matters — but are never allowed to find their own way around it and discover their own beauties or their own possible paydirt. All are led along the same track in the same direction, the path becoming in the process so well worn that it seems as if it had been put there by God. None are allowed to stray into interesting-looking areas off the track, and at the end of the tour all are required to give evidence that they have seen the same things at the same time from the same point of view.

But however carefully planned the tour, no matter how expertly devised by the best and latest research, it is impossible that it can prove a source of useable experience for everyone. Each life has its own logic, its own fund of experiences and analogies, and no amount of outside direction can substitute for the inner logic of that experience. A guided tour, as any experienced traveller knows, is no way to discover the best means of survival in a strange country, and to improve the organization of the tour is merely to make the traveller even less able to look after himself. This is true even with subjects which concern themselves, as does mathematics, with logical relations. David Hawkins put the matter in less metaphorical terms:

> Learning does not have any close or intimate connection with logical organization. The order in which children come to understand a logical pattern is not by following that logical order from the beginning ... We all agree that there is a body of connective ideas and propositions we call mathematics. Nobody

has ever written it all down but it's all there; all the logical connections that exist among all the ideas in the area we agree to call mathematics. There isn't any linear order among them. They're connected in a very complex sort of network and you can make your way through them along thousands of paths, depending on your momentary readiness, your understanding, your fund of analogies and your interests. You can get into it in many different ways. The obvious thing from the point of view of teaching is to say, well, we want to find that way which is optimal for a particular child at a particular time. We don't know how to do this, we're not omniscient, but one of the very practical ways of getting on with it is to give the child himself free choice.[3]

Finally, a syllabus assumes the existence of some kind of absolute standard of merit, external to any pupil, by which his attainment is to be measured. We are not quite sure what this standard is supposed to be, any more than we can define standards of musical greatness, but our education is conducted on the assumption that it does exist. The British system of public examinations, as well as those of universities and other institutions, recognizes not only the possibility of passing or failing but also the existence of anything up to half a dozen possible grades of passing. There is much worried talk today about falling standards; it might be more realistic to concern ourselves with the relation of those standards we set to the real world of the pupil. The idea of standards is of course a natural consequence of the abstract concept of knowledge which we have met at every turn in our investigation and which lies behind the construction of a syllabus; they are a measure of the degree of assimilation of that knowledge by the pupil. The teacher is thought to possess the knowledge, while the pupil needs it and must accede to the teacher's (or rather, the teaching institution's) terms if he is to obtain it; it is never envisaged that he might be capable of obtaining it for himself, much less of generating it. The transaction is thus a one-way affair; it is one-dimensional also, since the relation between teacher and pupil is expected to be confined to this transaction of abstract knowledge. The pupil has no right to any knowledge of the teacher or of his life outside the school gate. That this one-dimensional quality frequently proves impossible to sustain, especially in small communities, is a tribute to the power of the human urge towards full-scale relationship, but the coy and knowing looks that greet a young teacher when sighted in the street by his pupils with a friend of the opposite sex testifies to the fact that such knowledge is essentially clandestine and outside the relationships which are supposed to exist between teacher and pupil. Teachers, as far as the system is concerned, are not supposed to have private lives, or even emotions, any display of which is regarded, rightly in the context, as a display of weakness. Conversely, most teachers know little and care less about their pupils' out-of-school lives, unless there are features of those lives which are militating against the schooling process; the admirable minority who do actively care are generally obliged to do so without any support which the school can provide. The rigidly intellectual level upon which school is supposed to be conducted is yet another sign of the fragmentation of life in our society. In so far as any attention is paid to the emotions in schools, they are treated as at worst dangerous, at best a nuisance, but in any case to be kept under control.

In that excellent and witty book *Teaching as a Subversive Activity*[4] the authors have some dry fun with the metaphors which teachers use (not perhaps always consciously) to characterize their function; there is the 'Lamplighter', who wishes to bring light into dark minds, the 'Gardener', who wants to cultivate their minds and make them grow, the 'Personnel Manager', who wants to make them busy and efficient, the 'Muscle Builder', the 'Potter', the 'Dietician', the 'Bucket Filler' and the 'Builder'. All these metaphors have one thing in common, that they derive from the abstract, the scientific, model of knowledge, and they thus assume young minds to be so much passive material, to be worked on, fed, filled, shaped and made to grow. The metaphors may vary but the basic assumption remains the same; the pupils are the object-other of the scientific experiment, to be operated on. The whole nature, indeed the very existence, of the educational research industry hinges on this assumption, since if these young minds *are* so much passive material it follows that we need to understand them, exactly as we need to understand the atom or the chromosome (and by the same methods) the more effectively to work on them. The problem, and the approach to its solution, is essentially the same in all these cases. Most educational research and the methods derived from it treat children's minds exactly thus, and as object-other a child is not expected to have any comprehension of the processes wrought upon him (the jargon in which most research and teaching method is couched will in any case cut him off from understanding). He is expected to submit passively and trustingly to that which is being done for him, or to him, and to believe that it is all in his own eventual best interests. This, I think, is the basis of Illich's mistrust of 'school-based, complex curricular packages'. That we persist in the development of such curricula, no matter how impeccably backed by educational research or how assisted by costly educational technology, in the face of their manifest failure to assist any but those who are probably perfectly capable of helping themselves, is a striking tribute to the power of the scientific model of knowledge, and of the relation between teacher and taught, to bemuse us; but it only parallels the ways in which social and pyschological scientists persist in their efforts to understand the nature of the human mind by totally unsuitable means, in the face of their failure to produce any insights of use in our personal, social or political lives.

The basic flaw in the abstract model of knowledge, knowledge, that is, which is divorced from experience, is that, do what we will, pupils, like all other humans, *will* continue to experience, and we cannot stop them; it seems ridiculously obvious, but we must acknowledge that if they do not experience one thing they will experience something else. We cannot stop the processes of experience, and yet the school seems expressly designed to do so. In a school pupils are taken away from their experience of the world (which even at the age of five is considerable) and experience instead only the hermetic world of the classroom and playground. If they are successful in school they may even learn a great deal about the world, but, successful or not, their experience of it is seriously impaired; we have produced a generation who know more about the world, and experience it less, than perhaps any generation in human history.

'We have produced ...' How many times do we not hear of successful (or indeed of unsuccessful) adults as being 'products' of a certain school or other institution? The word is revealing, and lets drop the real processes at work in school. A child (or indeed a student in the older age groups) is regarded, like a substance in a chemical laboratory, like iron ore in a foundry, like sheet steel in a car factory, as so much raw material to be worked on and made something of. The purpose of schooling, as of the blast furnace or the assembly line, as even of the painter's studio or the composer's desk, is the production of a commodity, something that will be as valuable as possible. The product of schooling is expected to come fully to life only after the production process is complete; if a good product he will be able to sell himself as high up the market as it will bear. The product of an English public school, of Oxbridge or the Ivy League will fetch as high a price proportionately as a Rolls-Royce or a Cadillac.

It is not surprising to find that education in music takes on the nature of both western music and western education, and that both the latter assume the nature of western society. Here, as in general education, the concept of the product is dominant. If music is, as we have seen, a product, the musician is in the paradoxical position of being not only the purveyor of that product but also, as one who has passed through a type of schooling, as himself a product. The number of young products of music schools seeking the attention of the public becomes every year larger, while the concern for standards, as in industry, becomes more pressing. It is probably true, as is frequently asserted, that performance standards are becoming higher; at least, technical standards are becoming more and more exacting, and the young virtuoso comes on the market with a set of technical equipment that would make the great performers of the past gasp. The concern for the product, as usual, means that little attention is given to the process, and we find that the training of these young lions becomes ever more arduous; scales, exercises, *solfège* and studies dominate the life of the aspiring virtuoso to the point that it is a miracle that any love of music survives at all. In fact, if those young hopefuls who take part in competitions are any guide, musicality is often killed by the demands for ever greater technical proficiency; many young instrumentalists and singers would be far better musicians were they less obsessed with technical matters. Here again we have much to learn from other musical cultures.

In Britain complaints of falling standards of industrial production can be set beside reminders of how much higher standards of production in music are than formerly, such reminders being generally accompanied by warnings of the barbarian takeover that will occur if we relax our vigilance for a moment. We read, for example, in the London *Daily Telegraph* and quoted with obvious approval in the journal *Composer*, Yehudi Menuhin's assessment of the position: 'There is no gainsaying Britain's leading position in the quality, style and sheer mass of music, not only in London ... But however encouraging this picture is, we cannot afford any complacency, for we are fighting a battle against crass materialism which is choking us with rubbish ... We are fortunate indeed to live in a country in which the guardians of the law and the custodians of our hearts and minds can still be joined in dedicated and disciplined service to human and exacting standards.'⁵ In the same article he refers to a battle 'against the mindless, against the stultifying encroachment by and plottings of those groups who would reduce us in dignity, stature and self-determination', although how we can maintain our dignity, stature and self-determination by submitting our hearts and minds to some undefined group of custodians is not altogether clear. Leaving aside reflections on 'crass materialism' in the light of recent revelations of the exorbitant fees demanded by and paid to superstar conductors and soloists, there are some astonishing assumptions, obviously unexamined (one *hopes* they are unexamined), contained in that statement, especially in view of the fact that the famous violinist has founded a school devoted to the production of young musicians; but his pronouncement is no more than typical of the opinions of many well-known performing artists, and simply reveals the extent to which he is bewitched by the idea of music as product. His remarks might be those of the chairman of the board of any industrial concern at the annual shareholders' meeting.

Apart from the before-noted evil effects of the excessive professionalization of music, this situation might be tolerable if it applied only to the training of the professional musician, but the training of professionals is unfortunately taken to a very large extent as the model for music in education generally, including that of the vast majority who have no intention of making music a career. It is a sad fact that a sizeable minority, if not a majority, of specialist teachers of music in schools are musicians who tried, and failed, to establish themselves as professional performers, and that they tend to regard the professional training they themselves received in university or conservatoire as a model for their task in school; it is doubly unfortunate, to say no worse, that this model is reinforced in many teacher-training establishments (themselves staffed largely by failed professionals), thus completing the vicious circle which excludes the majority of children from any significant musical experience in school.

We have encountered two societies in which the training of musicians takes place within actual musical situations, where, as McPhee puts it, 'learning is a pleasure from the very start', but it seems that our society is too concerned with the production of a good (i.e. efficient) end-product to concern itself with the quality of experience of those who are being made into musicians. With the situation as it is in our society, it seems that the aspiring professional has no option but to submit to long years of drudgery in order to attain the dizzying heights of technical proficiency which the professional needs if he is to obtain a hearing, and which places such a great and ever-growing gulf between the amateur and the professional, but it should be understood that those school pupils who wish to do so are in a very small minority; their needs, as at present understood, are in direct opposition to the needs of those to whom music is just part of a general education. The conflict produces in the teacher a basic uncertainty of aim. As far as the former are concerned, the aim is clear, and appears to be confirmed by the entry requirements of universities and conservatoires; it is to produce performers of the music of the western classical tradition (mainly that of the eighteenth and nineteenth centuries) and to instil into them as much as possible of the history and compositional conventions of that tradition. This the teacher will willingly do for those who are prepared to submit to what they have been assured (and, to be sure, the rest of their school experience appears to confirm this) is the necessary drudgery. To the less ambitious, or those whose musical interests lie elsewhere (a completely unmusical child is an extreme rarity), school music traditionally has little to offer; they tend to undergo a kind of caricature of professional training, being told *about* music rather than being involved in its creation, or, mostly, even re-creation. Lacking confidence in his ability to give the class as a whole anything of value, the teacher is frequently obliged to confine his classroom activities to those which experience has shown involve fewest disciplinary problems – which for the most part means the passing of snippets of information about music and 'the great' composers, some attempt to teach traditional notation (despite the fact that most would have no use for it even if they could read and write it), the playing of records of a remarkably stereotyped repertoire of eighteenth, nineteenth, and the 'safer' kind of twentieth century music, and singing. The teacher often considers himself lucky if, as often happens, class music ceases after the age of about fourteen, and he is left free to concentrate on the small minority who are willing and able to accept what he has to offer. The attempt to salvage from this situation the more obviously (or conventionally) gifted by removing them to special schools is no solution; to take children away from day-to-day contact with the infinite variability of the human race and place them in an educational monoculture where their only contact is with contemporaries of similar background and interests is to deprive them of an essential dimension of the experience of growing up – a price far too high to pay for additional musical expertise and even some unquestionable career advantages.

In music, as in other areas of education dominated by the idea of making a product, there exists an elaborate system of quality control, designed to assess the process of manufacture at all stages. In Britain and those parts of the world which were Europeanized under its influence, Trinity College, London, and the Associated Board of the Royal Schools of Music, both established by our industrious Victorian forebears, have assumed this responsibility. Twice a year, from Manchester to Singapore to Port of Spain to Dar-es-Salaam to Wellington, young musicians are lined up before learned gentlemen specially sent from London to have their progress measured; sons and daughters of master drummers, maybe, or of steel-pan virtuosi, are all checked for uniformity of growth, and to make sure all are growing in the same direction, on piano, violin and a limited number of approved western instruments. The six- or seven-year-old who can play a couple of childish pieces is awarded Grade I, while his elder brothers and sisters are struggling through Grade V, VII or VIII, or even, at the end of adolescence, a diploma, the four magic letters to put after one's name. All are stamped with the British standard of quality, all of a similar kind, tested and approved, with irritating idiosyncracies removed as far as is humanly possible. It does not matter if the children's musical experience is limited to a tiny repertoire of established classics and a few of the more vacuous examples of modern British music as is demanded by the syllabus for each grade, or if the individuality to which we pay such ardent lipservice is crushed into a uniform mould of boring competence from which only the strongest escape; the product, as can be seen from Menuhin's approving words, is of the highest quality.

This network of 'practical' testing is paralleled by one in tests of 'theory', that is, notational conventions and basic compositional concepts of the western classical tradition (though what could be more *practical* than the composition of music is hard to imagine), which are examined in parallel with the performance tests, but the 'theoretical' work climaxes, as far as British children are concerned, with the *General Certificate of Education,* at 'Ordinary' and 'Advanced' level (it is, ironically, often necessary for pupils to abandon their instrumental tuition and their practice in order to get through these examinations). These measure the pupil's skill in traditional techniques, most notably in tonal functional harmony and harmonically conceived counterpoint, his ability to perceive pitch relationships within the tempered scale and his knowledge of the accepted canon of musical works of the classical tradition. We have seen that it is in the nature of syllabuses and of examinations to demand a standardized type of abstract knowledge, and these music examinations once more ensure that a standard product comes from the schools. True, some uneasiness has of late been felt about this demand for standardization, and attempts are made from time to time to 'loosen up' or 'broaden' the syllabus to make possible more individuality. These attempts, however well-meaning, are doomed to failure, or at best to very modest success; since examinations are by their very nature tools of standardization, to permit any considerable manifestation of individuality would destroy strict comparability and thus undermine the very function which they are designed to serve. Would-be purchasers would no longer feel able to accept the examination certificate as a stamp of approved quality.

Standardization of teaching, it may be, is no more than a sign of the standardization of musical practice throughout the world of western music (as I write this the BBC is broadcasting a concert from Stuttgart, in which the BBC Northern Symphony Orchestra, taken there at presumably great expense, is playing a concert consisting of Beethoven's *Egmont Overture* and *Emperor Concerto,* and Tchaikowsky's *Fourth Symphony,* and it occurs to me to wonder, since there are undoubtedly in Stuttgart orchestras perfectly capable of playing these well-known works, why they have gone to so much trouble). It is instructive to consider by contrast the training of musicians in blues and jazz, those musical arts which in our century have resisted assimilation into the conventional world of western aesthetics more than others. If one asks how jazz musicians were trained in the heroic early decades of this century, one finds, quite simply, that they were not — not at least in any formal sense as jazz musicians. There were some, of whom Duke Ellington was perhaps the most shining example, who had solid training in the classical tradition and simply found their own way into jazz; Fletcher Henderson, the first successful big-band leader and arranger, was a chemistry graduate in the days when Negroes could not gain entrance to the professions; Louis Armstrong learned cornet in the band of the reform school where he passed much of his adolescence; Jelly Roll Morton trained as a classical pianist and was thoroughly familiar with the various musics that were to be heard in New Orleans at the turn of the century; Bix Beiderbecke learnt cornet in his high school band. Jazz musicians came from a wide variety of musical as well as social backgrounds; each learnt the rudiments of his instrument in one way or another, and from then on he was on his own, left like an African musician to develop his own manner of playing. He did not practise jazz scales, arpeggios or studies, or do written exercises involving blue notes and syncopations. This does not mean that there was not a great deal of practice or hard work involved in developing his technique; but the musician learnt to play the figurations, the riffs, to develop the tone colour and the mannerisms that he felt useful to his own expressive purpose and to ignore what he did not need. There was a great deal of imitation of admired musicians, heard either in the flesh or on records, and generally the jazz musician would grow up within a community of like-minded musicians. This informal, ad hoc training left room for a great variety of tone production and of pitch and rhythmic sense, for individual inventiveness and for improvisatory skill. Musicians who felt in sympathy with one another would form groups, which over the years would form and re-form, appear and disappear, changing their sound and their repertoire as players came and went. Even written-down arrangements did not, at their best, cramp the style of players too much, since, as with Duke Ellington and his arranger Billy Strayhorn, the arrangements were built around the capabilities, the individual sounds and the favourite procedures of the musicians who were in the band at the time (the personnel of Ellington's band remained in fact remarkably stable over the years). The fact that there are now, in this country no less than in the United States, formal courses of training for jazz musicians may signal the end of jazz as a living force; an art that is truly living resists the codification, the establishment of canons of taste and of practice, that schools by their nature impose.

I do not suggest that 'classical' musicians should necessarily adopt the training methods of these jazz musicians, any more than that they should adopt those of Balinese or African players; nonetheless, it is important that we be aware that other methods of musical training, both formal and informal, do exist that have equal validity with those of the classical tradition of western music (schools of music in the modern sense are in any case a nineteenth-century invention), and that we should recognize that our own methods of training musicians do sacrifice elements of the essential musicality of man in pursuit of the ideals of individual virtuosity and standardization of technique. It could be that we have something to learn from other cultures. Virtuosity, it must be understood, does exist in other musical cultures (hear Louis

Armstrong and Jimi Hendrix!), but it is a by-product of the pursuit of music; it is only in traditional western culture that it is an end in itself, and we should be aware of the price we pay for it, especially in terms of musical communality, in terms of the ability of all to take an active part, not just as listener or even as one who realizes the ideas of others, but in the creative process itself. It is the same communality that Wagner celebrated and mourned in *Die Meistersinger*, the same that we have sacrificed in our pursuit of technological progress, of abstract knowledge and of power over nature and over one another.

We can understand what it was that Erik Satie was ridiculing as he waved his certificate in counterpoint before his friends and declared he now had a licence to compose music. Satie, like all great clowns, was a deeply serious and perceptive man, and in this one offhand joke he put his finger on a deep malaise of western art – indeed of western society; it was not just the narrow-mindedness of an academic establishment but the pursuit by our society of the products (things) rather than the processes (experiences) of life and the restrictions and standardization imposed in that pursuit. We fail, too, to see that from the moment the beginner first puts his fingers on the piano keyboard, takes up a crayon to scribble or draw a stick figure, or begins to knead a piece of clay, he is exploring both himself and the nature of the material world, exploring it not to dominate it but to live more fully in it. Indeed, one can go back further; the infant babbling 'dad-dad-dad-dad' in his cot is exploring both music and his own dawning powers of speech, since there is as yet no differentiation between the two. It is the process of exploration, not its product, that is precious; a child perhaps knows this better than his proud parents when, having spent painstaking hours making a picture he will be quite indifferent when they exhibit it in a place of honour. For him the work has served its purpose, and the product can be discarded.

An interesting consequence of this misunderstanding lies in the question, frequently raised, as to whether musicians raised in one culture can ever learn to play the music of another. Ravi Shankar, for instance, doubts whether any westerner can learn to play classical Indian music – at least until he has submitted himself to a *guru* for many years, served him faithfully and immersed himself in Indian philosophy, religion and art. Such a question, of course, need not have been asked before western and eastern musicians became aware of each other, and Ravi Shankar's answer makes certain western-style assumptions about the nature and purpose of the act of performing music; his prescription is only a version of the western recipe for 'producing' a performer, and begs the question of when one can be said to be able to play an instrument. If, however, we assume that the act of playing the sitar, like that of playing any other instrument, is one of exploration, then from the moment we take the instrument in hand we are beginning that exploration, not only of the instrument and the culture that gave it birth but also of ourselves, and carrying out a mode of self-exploration which is different from any that can be done on a western instrument. We shall of course learn these things only if we approach the enterprise in a spirit of humility, to learn the nature of the instrument and submit to it, but one will learn more of Indian culture through playing the sitar in this way than one will of the sitar through the study of Indian culture. Ravi Shankar is, of course, right in his caution against those musicians who treat the instrument as only another species of guitar and as a few technical problems to be solved; to work on such crude assumptions is to imprison the player even more firmly, despite any exotic sounds he may produce, in the conventions of western music. To begin playing an instrument is to set out on a voyage of exploration that has no end, and thus no goal; we need not think of future virtuosity but only of present experience.

I spoke earlier of the terrible ubiquity of masterpieces, those products of the creative process that we value more than the process itself, and which we keep in existence often at the cost of so much time and effort that might be better spent on creation. It is not only the masterpieces themselves that inhibit creation (though one might question the wisdom of thrusting upon the young a number of musical works that could by no stretch of the imagination provide them with a model) but also the fact that teaching is dominated by the values and the technical conventions of the past. This surely is what was in the mind of the English pianist John Tilbury when he wrote that 'The college of music has only one monstrous department — the history of music department.'[6] The musical techniques taught in school and music college alike are mainly those of the classical era in western music, techniques that have been used by few serious composers for fifty years or more. One can see perhaps some limited use for this, in that those who wish to perform the music of the past may be helped by some understanding of the processes going on within that music; the trouble is, that, unlike jazz, blues and rock musicians, who follow the oldest and most enduring way of learning one's craft — the imitation of a master or an admired figure — most teaching in the classical techniques is carried out through the medium of textbooks, and textbooks have an uncanny way of taking on a pseudo-life of their own, thrusting the work of those masters on which they are ostensibly based into the background. One of the best-known and most widely used textbooks of tonal harmony used in British schools, for example, contains throughout its 110 page length not so much as a mention of a single great practitioner of the art, or any reference to the practice of a 'real' composer — all the music examples are made up (I hesitate to use the word 'composed') by the author, and are in the style of hymn tunes. My own recollection of beginning the formal study of harmony at the age of twenty-two, having been playing the piano since seven, is that the study of four-part hymn tune harmonization did not seem to have much to do with my understanding of the Haydn sonatas (with which I was just beginning a love affair that has lasted undimmed for nearly thirty years), and that what I was learning was mostly to put a name to processes that I already understood well — or as well as a performer might need to know them — but could not name. It would seem to a detached observer that the best way to understand the beautifully lucid harmonic processes of a Haydn sonata was to study the Haydn sonata, not some cloud-cuckoo-land of music that never existed outside the pages of *Hymns Ancient and Modern*. In any case, the majority of students who complete secondary schooling in music do not acquire, by either this means or that other standby of music examiners, pastiche composition, enough harmonic technique to be of use in the understanding of a Beethoven sonata, let alone a Wagner opera. And as far as young composers are concerned, any African musician (any at least who has not been subjected to the ministrations of the Royal Schools of Music) would tell us emphatically that the best way to acquire the techniques of composition is to start using them.

If the last sentence reads oddly it is a measure of the way in which we have been conditioned to think: first acquire your techniques and then use them — as if it is possible to know in advance which techniques will be needed. What I have been trying to show is that, whether in performance or composition, this view of artistic education does violence to the facts of both art and learning. Techniques and creative purposes grow together by mutual stimulation; not only could Beethoven not have had the technique to compose the *Heilige Danksgesang* at the age of twenty – he could not even have imagined it. An artist (and we are all, at least potentially, artists, even if few have aspirations to making it a profession) knows what techniques he is going to need only by using them; no-one else can tell him. This is not to say that no-one can teach him anything, but it does mean that he must be left free to decide what it is he needs (I repeat, *needs*) to learn. It is probable that most people will in fact want to learn very similar things, but the freedom to decide for oneself makes the vital difference between a living experience of learning and drudgery.

One contemporary manifestation of the idea that it is necessary to know about it before one can do it, as well as of the notion that knowledge lies outside and independently of the knower, is the development of programmed learning systems. These, whether in the form of machines or of ingeniously devised books, begin with simple concepts and tasks, leading the pupil in carefully planned steps to more complex operations, testing him at every stage and returning him to previous material if he cannot answer the questions correctly. I do not propose questioning their effectiveness on their own terms (although they do appear to be of use mainly in training people to mechanical tasks which no-one in his right mind would voluntarily undertake); it is those terms themselves that are questionable. The machines and books are strictly logical devices, but it is an objectified logic which denies the logic of the individual experience that is at the heart of learning. They are, to revert to an earlier metaphor, merely devices for speeding up the guided tour, and their ultimate valuelessness for true learning becomes clear when they are applied to programmes of artistic creation. An account of a classic misunderstanding of the nature of both artistic experience and of learning appeared a few years ago in the journal *Music in Education.* Under the heading *Teaching Music by Computer,* the article tells of an experimental programme being tried out by Systems Development Corporation of Santa Monica, California, in conjunction with the Wurlitzer Corporation (strange how much educational technology is developed by those who just might have something to sell): 'The new computerized music experiment will have a class of youngsters simultaneously playing electric pianos connected to a computer. The classroom is silent. (*This is a music lesson*!) Through headphones each child hears only his own playing and the instructions or musical notes generated by the computer. Different combinations of musical notes (*who decides what is a musical note*?) are generated in response to each student's activities ... Each child can control his own programme to a degree (*it is good to know we can be creative – to a degree*) making fascinating after fascinating discovery in music of his own choosing.'[7] One can picture the happy scene of silent music making, row upon row of children, like battery chickens, each on his own electronic umbilicus, denied the fundamental joy of music, which is a communal pleasure if it is a pleasure at all, and can only shake one's head and say, with Lear, 'O that way madness lies.' We should, however, at the same time notice that it is no more than a mechanized, and possibly, on its own terms, more efficient, version of something that happens daily in classrooms.

The situation that provoked John Tilbury's comment has a certain inevitability when one considers this aspect of musical education. For if we are required to *know* about music before we can *do* it, and if knowledge is a matter of certainties that exist outside us, then we are in the nature of things confined to learning about that music upon which it is possible to speak with anything like certainty: the music of the past, upon which the verdict of posterity has been delivered, and which can hold no surprises. The music of the present is too diverse, too changeable, its values too uncertain, for it to be possible to present it in anything like the neat encapsulated form that is essential before one can design a syllabus or set and mark an examination. It is only the procedures and conventions of the past that can be transmitted with any degree of objectivity and any possibility of reliable evaluation. Thus it is that educational conventions and current musical tastes work to reinforce each other, keeping pupils effectively isolated from the world of music as it is in the present, turbulent, exciting, disturbing, possibly as decadent as some maintain that it is, full of good music and bad music but mostly, as in any other period of history, of music of no particular merit or demerit, but also alive and developing and allowing space for the individual to respond directly, not mediated through the judgement of generations. It is rare to find a teacher of music who has much acquaintance with the music of our own time, rarer still if one includes rock, jazz and other popular forms; his own training, for the reasons given, will have afforded him little opportunity of meeting it, and once his training is completed there is little incentive (or, to be fair, time) for him to do so. Every now and then music syllabuses take a heave forward, with a great gesture of up-to-dateness, but always only into those areas which have recently been abandoned by living musical composition; thus, with twelve-tone composition, at least in its classic form, now a matter of history, it becomes possible to codify its rules and practices and introduce, as has recently occurred, a work of Webern written nearly forty years ago into the syllabus of the British *General Certificate of Education* at Advanced level. One deplores this time-lag, but it is inherent in the nature of syllabuses and ultimately in the scientific model of knowledge.

I must make it clear that I in no way seek to blame teachers of music for this state of affairs; the situation is one which concerns our entire culture, its concept of knowledge, its attitude towards art and the consequent nature of its system of education. Teachers, no matter how well-meaning, are as much at the mercy of these assumptions as are their charges – and their employers – and it is not possible to make any radical changes in one element of the culture without making changes in the others. It has been the main argument of this book that society, musical culture and education are inextricably interdependent, and reflect back and forth from one to the other any changes. The leverage which education can exert on society has been shown by bitter experience to be small, and the leverage of music on education appears to be even smaller. Nonetheless it can provide a *point d'appui* on which to base those changes in fundamental attitudes, in the organization of our mental universe, which are necessary if our society is to be released from the oppressive grip of a world view which negates and devalues our experience. In new art one can see vaguely the lineaments of new attitudes, and it is these which we can, by the encouragement of the creativity of each individual, gradually give shape and reality in the minds of our pupils. In the next, final, chapter, I shall try to propose some directions in which we music teachers, and others, might try to move.

Chapter 8: Bibliography

1. ILLICH, Ivan: *After Deschooling, What?*, London, Writers' and Readers' Publishing Corporation (1974), p. 14.
2. See, for instance,
    GOODMAN, Paul: *Compulsory Miseducation,* New York, Horizon Books (1962), and Harmondsworth, Penguin Books (1971);
    REIMER, Everett: *School is Dead: An Essay in Alternatives in Education,* Harmondsworth, Penguin Books (1971);

HENRY, Jules: *Culture Against Man,* New York, Random House (1963) and Harmondsworth, Penguin Books (1972);

HENRY, Jules: *Essays in Education,* Harmondsworth, Penguin Books (1971);

MASON, Edwin: *Collaborative Learning,* London, Ward Lock Educational (1970);

POSTMAN, Neil and WEINGARTNER, Charles: *Teaching as a Subversive Activity,* New York, Delacorte Press (1969) and Harmondsworth, Penguin Books (1971).

3. HAWKINS, David: 'How to Plan for Spontaneity' in SILBERMAN, Charles E. (ed.): *The Open Classroom Reader,* New York, Vintage Books (1973) p. 501.

4. POSTMAN, Neil and WEINGARTNER, Charles: op. cit., p. 86.

5. MENUHIN, Yehudi: article in London *Daily Telegraph* colour supplement tenth anniversary number, quoted in *Composer* No 53, Winter 1974-5, p. 5.

6. TILBURY, John: untitled article in *Ark,* Winter 1969, p. 43.

7. HEGARTY, A.: 'Teaching Music by Computer', *Music in Education,* Vol 34 No 345, Sept/Oct 1970, p. 261.

I have said that art, education and society move in a kind of loosely
lockstepped three-legged race; each can change only very little
without involving corresponding changes in the other two. Of the
three, clearly, society as a whole exerts the most leverage but since
it is ideas that shape society none is completely without influence.
Daniel Bell: 'Ideas and cultural styles do not change history — at
least, not overnight. But they are a necessary prelude to change,
since a change in consciousness — in values and moral reasoning
(*he might have added 'styles of perception'*) is what moves men to
change their social arrangements and institutions.'[1] Teachers, as we
have seen, whether in school, college or university, have extremely
little room for manoeuvre in this respect, being obliged to work
within the framework of an organization which, despite its apparent
diversity, is in fact extremely unified in its purposes, its monopoly
control of the market and, especially, its devotion to the ethic of
production. The relation of this organization to society is clear: it
exists to serve society's needs (one could go further and say the
interests of the dominant sectors of society, since it obviously
serves large sections, even perhaps the majority, of society
extremely ill) and it is therefore kept on a very tight rein. Art, on the
other hand, exists in a very ambiguous relation to society, and is
generally considered to have only the most tenuous of effects upon
it; it is therefore indulged in its eccentricities like a child, and no-
one other than the conservative critic worries too much when it
veers from one extreme attitude to the other. (One can see this
perhaps most clearly in the situation of music on many university
campuses, where the most outrageous musical experiment is
tolerated, even welcomed — and rendered socially innocuous.) So in
the last fifty years or so we have seen artistic movements following
one another in dizzying succession without visible effect on the
fabric of our society. Although they may have had a more
profound effect than is recognized — art, as I hope I have shown,
exists in much closer relation to the fabric of society than is
imagined — the apparently complete revolution which has taken

place in western music in this century has in fact, as can be seen from a comparison with other musics, taken place still within the framework of an aesthetic and a set of institutions and conventions that have changed hardly at all since the end of the nineteenth century. The present-day proliferation of musical styles may, in fact, represent not a new movement but the last efflorescence of the post-Renaissance western tradition, rather like those strange and baroque forms of life that often appear at the end of an evolutionary line. I did, however, suggest that the beginnings of the post-revolutionary forms are already with us, not in majestic concert halls like the Royal Festival Hall or Philharmonic Hall but in draughty church halls and council-flat living rooms, in condemned houses inhabited only by squatters, and even for all we know in the barradas that fringe the great cities of South America, in the African slums of Johannesburg or the shanty towns of West Kingston. History suggests that it is equally possible that new dominant classes may emerge from these same places. These musics, unnoticed by the cultural establishment, receiving no subsidy from arts councils or foundations or support from wealthy patrons, are analogous to those rat-sized creatures, ancestors of the mammals, that scurried around the feet of the dinosaurs and were adaptable and sufficiently uncommitted to any single lifestyle to flourish when a slight shift in climate wiped out their larger and more impressive contemporaries, which were unable to adapt. We have already received hints of the changes in social and financial climate that could wipe out our symphony orchestras, concert halls and opera houses more easily and sooner than the ordinary music lover might imagine; Stockhausen showed his awareness of this in a 1971 interview in which he said, 'The system is dying. It's in its last agony right now, only the musicians themselves are not sufficiently aware of it .... What I'm trying to do ... is to produce models that herald the stage after destruction ... and that is going to be badly needed in the time of shocks and disasters that is to come.'[2] (I do not, however, believe that Stockhausen is capable, despite his diagnosis of the condition, of providing a cure.)

But if the revolution in music has not yet taken place, and cannot, as I believe, take place fully until the values of our culture change, we can nonetheless see in the music of our century the shape of a society to which it aspires, that 'potential society' of which Duvignaud speaks, 'which lies beyond our grasp.' It is now time to consider the features of this potential society that are thus outlined, vaguely perhaps, but sometimes with startling precision, as in a painting by Turner, in this music.

Modern music, as Boulez said, awoke with the flute of Debussy's Faun, but we should not on that account imagine that all the manifestations of modern music stem directly or even indirectly from Debussy, powerfully influential as he has been. Art, like dreams, is not bound by chronology, and we should not fall into the scientistic trap of equating things that happen *after* with things that happen *because of* a certain event. Ideas, unlike bacteria, are capable of spontaneous generation (a fact that academic psychologists seem to forget) and the simultaneous and independent appearance of ideas in many different minds within the same historical period merely testifies to the fact that their time has come. We have seen the emergence of a new attitude to the nature of sound itself in music as diverse as the fastidiously-constructed works of Webern, the languorous chords of Morton Feldman, the wails of the blues guitarist, the birdsongs and massive tamtam strokes of Messiaen, the electronic distortions of rock and the miraculous new instrumental sounds of Harry Partch, reaching its *reductio ad absurdum* in those pieces of John Cage in which any sound, including no sound at all, is acceptable, and the hours-long prolongation of a single sine tone by LaMonte Young. We have seen it in the abandonment of tonal functional harmony in music as diverse as that of Schoenberg (whose uneasy compromise between irreconcilable factors speaks with anguished clarity of the predicament of modern western man), of Stravinsky, of rock and modern jazz, of the total serialists and improvisors alike. We see the attempt to break out of the frame in which western art music has been contained, in works like Pousseur's *Votre Faust,* in which the audience is given the opportunity to determine the course of the story of the opera (it remains an opera), of Xenakis's *Terretektorh,* in which the orchestra sit among the audience (but remain professional players playing to an audience in a concert hall), Berio's *Passaggio*, in which members of the cast sit among the audience and purport to represent their attitudes (but remain members of the cast), of Stockhausen's *Piano Piece XI,* in which the performer decides, on the spur of the moment, which of a number of musical cells he is going to play next (but still plays from the composer's published score). That these, and other similar attempts, have been unable to restore lost communality to music is the fault not of composers but of the prevailing aesthetic, the prevailing relationship between composer, performer and audience, the prevailing position of composers in society, the prevailing position in society of music and the mechanisms and institutions that exist for presenting it. These pieces do point in the direction in which creators of music wish to move, however they may be prevented from moving in that direction. A composer needs an audience, and to gain that audience he is obliged, in our society, to work with professional musicians whose commitment to the music is probably less than total, to have his work performed in concert halls, to appeal to a corps of critics whose perceptions have mostly been formed by and remain tied to an aesthetic framework that has existed for the last three hundred years — and whose continued existence in fact testifies to the persistence of that framework. It is of importance, therefore, to examine the direction in which these, and other musicians of our time, are trying to go, and make the attempt to perceive the 'potential society' towards which they, albeit in many cases not fully consciously, are struggling.

What then is the nature of the potential society? First, it stands in a new relationship to nature, no longer in antithesis but recognizing the fact that the human race is a part of that vast and infinitely complex system with which our present culture can see itself only in a relationship that is essentially hostile or at best exploitative. In learning to live with nature, western man can learn to live with himself, and no longer split his life into fragments isolated from one another, can transcend the time of clocks and the tyranny of the future, and can enjoy the present for itself, developing the life of his senses uninhibitedly. Knowledge is freed from the urge to domination; the urge to know is placed in proper perspective, not as an impulsion overriding all others but as an aid to living, and dying, well in our world. The individual finds his proper relation to society, neither dominating nor being dominated by it, while society finds its proper role as the essential stage on which the individual life is acted out; a set of mutually enhancing functions between the individual and society is evolved. Hierarchical organizations are replaced by networks of co-operating individuals, in whose lives art becomes once more as essential an element as finding a living, in which, perhaps, art as we know it is replaced by ritual and a concept akin to the Balinese notion of 'doing things as well as possible'.

The relation between music and such a concept of society becomes overt in Terry Riley's *A Rainbow in Curved Air,* a work of by no means major importance, but one which is non-harmonic (it is based throughout its eighteen-minute length on a finally unresolved dominant discord of A) which contains no tension, no development, no drama, exists wholly in the present and does not demand concentrated, steady listening. The sleeve note to the recording of this piece contains no musicological information on either composer or work, but consists simply of a vision of the potential society: 'And then all wars ended .... The Pentagon was turned on its side and painted purple, yellow and green .... People swam in the sparkling rivers under blue skies streaked only with incense pouring from the new factories .... National flags were sewn together into brightly coloured circus tents under which politicians were allowed to perform harmless theatrical games / The concept of work was forgotten.'[3] This is a naïf (how naïf is shown by 'The energy from dismantled nuclear weapons provided free heat and light.'), albeit engaging, version of a vision which has tantalized western culture for centuries, but which has gained a new potency in our own time as revolt against the scientific world view develops. A society such as much contemporary music envisages does not (one might even say could not) exist, although many so-called primitive cultures stand much closer to it than we might imagine – certainly closer than does our own. Of course, too, for many who live in present-day western society such a life would be worse than death, those who, in this country for example, hail the advent of supersonic air transport as a great step forward in the welfare of the human race. To those who are convinced beyond all chance of change that man exists in inevitable conflict with nature and with others of his species and has no alternative but to fight continually with both in order to survive, who are convinced that western technological culture is the highest point yet in the continuing ascent of man, and that other beings in nature have no rights if their interests conflict with the needs, or even the wants, of western man, this book will have nothing to say, other than to furnish them with solid reasons for their predictable dislike of 'difficult' modern music. Nevertheless the presence of those ideas – less explicit and less naïf than Riley's – in the music of our century speaks clearly and eloquently of their presence within the matrix of our society, in however latent a form. It behoves those who wish to see an increase in what Illich calls conviviality in our culture to consider the possible effects of rethinking our education along artistic rather than scientistic lines. It has become ruefully commonplace among educationalists today that schooling can do little to improve the lot of children whose backgrounds are, to use the conventional euphemism, deprived. Even such massive injections of money and conventional resources as was carried out in the United States in the mid-sixties under the name of *Title One,* when over three billion dollars were spent on six million children, produced no discernable amelioration; in fact the children on whom the money was spent appeared to have become even further disadvantaged by comparison with their better-off contemporaries. All over the world, wherever western methods of schooling prevail, the result is the same; it seems now that even the very richest countries are unable to afford a system of schooling that will adequately educate all their young citizens. It seems, too, that the very concept of an adequate education is very much open to question, and it appears certain that the wider dissemination of advanced schooling has not been to make higher-level jobs widely available but instead to make the educational demands of lower-level jobs more stringent, as was demonstrated by Ivar Berg in his aptly titled book *The Great Training Robbery*;[4] one is reminded of a recent cartoon showing a butcher's shop where is displayed a sign 'Smart Grad Wanted'.

It could be that we are pushing ever harder and harder against a door, not understanding its nature, which is to open towards us effortlessly when we relax our pressure. I believe this to be true of a number of situations in our society; but nowhere is our unwillingness to let nature, especially human nature, alone to work out her own processes in her own time more apparent than in education. In the previous chapter I discussed schooling in general, as it is at present, concentrating later on musical education; I should like to reverse this order, showing how education in music could be changed and how this changed idea of education could become a model for the whole educative process. We can turn the relative unimportance of the arts in our society and in education, and the fact that we therefore enjoy wider tolerance in innovation, to our advantage, to introduce a joyful experience for the pupils *in the present*, thus beginning the subversion of the whole process of schooling, revealing to the pupils the quite simple fact that learning is not a preparation for life but a basic experience of life itself, and giving them confidence in their ability to learn whatever it is they wish to learn.

I must digress here briefly to discuss the matter of discipline. It is common today for various individuals and organizations, both within and outside the field of professional education, to deplore the lack of discipline in schools, and to use this to account for all kinds of atrocity stories from the beating up of teachers to football hooliganism to increasing illiteracy (as if more than a small proportion of the population have even been fully literate). The word 'discipline' has in fact acquired so many meanings that it becomes almost impossible to define or use it in any useful manner whatsoever. Two things, however, are clear: first, anyone who wants badly enough to do something will discipline himself to do it, and in fact will scarcely think in terms of discipline at all. And secondly, before anyone will accept the discipline necessary to undertake any task he will need not only to want to do it but also to have some feeling that he might be able to do it. It becomes necessary therefore, before any talk of discipline is raised, to convince pupils that they are capable of doing what they are asked to do, and second, to make sure that they have some desire to achieve the end, be it short-term or long-term, to which they are being asked to look. This is not a question of 'motivation' (a current in-term in educational circles) with its suggestion of manipulating the pupil's desires so that he will wish to learn what we wish to teach, but rather of making sure that what we wish to teach is what the pupil wishes to learn. Roy Campbell has encapsulated it neatly in a quatrain addressed to literary critics:

> You praise the firm restraint with which they write —
> I'm with you there, of course;
> They use the snaffle and the curb all right,
> But where's the bloody horse?[5]

If discipline is the snaffle and the curb, confidence and desire are the horse, and one is useless without the other, although one might argue that a horse without a curb is of more value than a curb without a horse; in any case, the horse comes first. Our schooling system, in emphasising the curb, destroys or diverts that confidence which is such a vital element of the urge to learn, to experiment and explore. One is sometimes tempted to conclude that the destruction of the exploratory urge runs in direct parallel with degree of success in school, and that conversely those who are most troublesome in school are those who are protesting most strongly (if unconsciously and possibly even self-destructively) against the assault on their creative urge and confidence. After all, even the most anarchistic and destructive classroom behaviour could be viewed as a kind of research — testing to destruction is a respectable scientific procedure, and some children are as expert in testing teachers to destruction as are behavioural scientists at destroying the inborn behaviour patterns of pigeons.

We can break out of this situation by a step which is in principle very simple: by acknowledging the inbuilt creative power of young minds, by harnessing and at the same time releasing it to find its own solutions, or, more fundamentally, to ask its own questions. The fundamental question, as Postman and Weingartner[6] point out, is, 'What's worth knowing?' — to which one might add, 'What's worth doing?' (although that is perhaps basically the same question); both are sufficient to keep any individual gainfully employed for several lifetimes. Scientific knowledge has an obvious place in such questions (though one would wish to see a science that was free from the enslaving urge to dominate) and artistic experience and skill will find once more its rightful place. As the creative act is at the centre of all artistic activity, so we place creative activity firmly at the centre of musical education, from which all other, more traditional activities radiate, fed by the work of creation and in turn feeding back into it: compositional skills, notation (as and *if* needed), listening, performing, study of the work of other musicians of many periods, styles and cultures.

In so doing, we need pay less attention to long-term aims, and let each moment be enjoyed for itself, each achievement generate its own enthusiasm, its own confidence, and let the skills develop as they are needed. We can accept the fact that much of the music made will be simply rearrangements of material already known to the young composers who will draw, like blues singers, like all participants in a living tradition, on a common stock of material. We can even accept that 'lowering of standards' of performance and other skills which is so dreaded by the musical cognoscenti, the abandonment, in other words, of the pursuit of virtuosity for its own sake (a virtuosity paralleling so strangely and yet so convincingly such pursuit of technological virtuosity beyond the bounds of any possible utility as supersonic aircraft and moonshots) in favour of the all-round development of musical experience as the prerogative of all, just as it is accessible to all in Africa and in Bali.

The schoolboy definition of music as 'Music is what musicians do' sums up the present situation in all but a minority of schools (the notorious finding of the British Schools Council *Enquiry One*,[7] that young school leavers place music bottom of the list of school subjects both for enjoyment and potential usefulness needs no further labouring by this time). How often have I entered a primary classroom run by a devoted and competent teacher, full of that buzz of activity that bespeaks a happy class, full too of paintings, sculptures, puppets, maps, poems, artefacts of all kinds — but no music. Why not? – 'I'm not a trained musician.' The untrained artist has elicited from his pupils art works of all kinds, the untrained writer has had them writing poems, projects, assorted writings, but the untrained musician has been convinced (and here teacher training institutions must bear much of the blame) that he can do nothing to help his children develop that musicality which is just as powerful as the other artistic impulses he has so generously released in his pupils. And how often in secondary schools does one find an unhappy musician faced with bored and rebellious groups who want nothing of what he has to give, nothing of the Mozart, Tchaikowsky or Brahms that he loves so well and is trying to propagate in these minds, whose frustrating and humiliating situation is made tolerable only by the thought of the school choir or orchestra practice after school. These situations are the result of the domination of music by experts and their insistence on *knowing about* before one is allowed to *do*.

Music is too important to be left to the musicians, and in recognizing this fact we strike a blow at the experts' domination, not only of our music but also of our very lives. If it is possible to control our own musical destiny, provide our own music rather than leaving it altogether to someone else to provide, then perhaps some of the other outside expertise that controls our lives can be brought under our control also. True, it might mean the sacrifice of some of the more complex amenities of modern life, but there is an increasing number of people who believe not only that this may not be a bad thing but even that if we do not relinquish them voluntarily we may well lose them through *force majeure*.

Ivan Illich in his least noticed but, I believe, most important book *Energy and Equity* points out that not only does a consumption of energy beyond a certain per capita amount introduce into a society built-in inequalities and injustices that are impossible to legislate out of existence, but also that some of the apparent gains in leisure and freedom are in fact illusory. He observes that the average American adult male devotes more than 1600 hours per year to his car, that is, not only in driving it but in paying for it and its maintenance and for the petrol it needs, while he travels on average 7500 miles per year, making a true average speed of less than five miles per hour – about the same as the average Mexican peasant.[8] Thoreau, over a hundred years ago, made the same point:

> One says to me, 'I wonder that you do not lay up money; you love to travel; you might take the cars and go to Fitchburg to-day and

see the country.' But I am wiser than that. I have learned that the swiftest traveller is he who goes afoot. I say to my friend, Suppose we try who will get there first. The distance is thirty miles; the fare ninety cents. That is almost a day's wages. I remember when wages were sixty cents a day on this very road. Well, I start now on foot, and get there before night; I have travelled at the rate by the week together. You will in the meantime have earned your fare, and arrive there some time tomorrow, or possibly this evening, if you are lucky enough to get a job in season. Instead of going to Fitchburg, you will be working here for the greater part of the day. And so, if the railroad reached you round the world, I think that I should keep ahead of you, and as for seeing the country and getting experience of that kind, I should have to cut your acquaintance altogether.

Such is the universal law, which no man can ever outwit, and with regard to the railroad even we may say it is as broad as it is long. To make a railroad round the world available to all mankind is equivalent to grading the whole surface of the planet. Men have an indistinct notion that if they keep up this activity of joint stocks and spades long enough all will at length ride somewhere, in next to no time, and for nothing; but though a crowd rushes to the depot, and the conductor shouts 'all aboard', when the smoke is blown away and the vapor condensed, it will be perceived that a few are riding but the rest are run over — and it can be called, and will be, 'A melancholy accident'. No doubt they can ride at last who have earned their fare, that is, if they survive so long, but they will probably have lost their elasticity and desire to travel by that time.[9]

So we might give up many of our technological toys and find ourselves not worse but better off, in command of our own lives once more and not in pawn to those experts who know more of our lives and our needs than we ourselves, and alone have the power to satisfy the needs they have created in us. Both Illich and Thoreau have perceived that, to use the latter's metaphor, both those who catch the train and those who are left behind suffer in different ways, the former through being harnessed to the necessity to earn the money for travel, the latter through being unable to do so and thus being cut off from natural human mobility by the greater distances created by high-speed transport. And all alike are placed in the power of those who have the coal, the oil, or, if our society adopts atomic energy as prime mover, uranium, for sale, as well as of those who decide where we are to travel to. We become, in fact, consumers rather than producers of mobility, and the product, arrival, has destroyed, as Thoreau suggests, the awareness of travel, the stages of the way; the incidental pleasures of way-stations and the assimilation of different landscapes through which we pass have been debased to the wait in the airport transit lounge, the glimpse of the Alps as we traverse them at thirty thousand feet and six hundred miles per hour.

To travel hopefully, said Stephenson, is better than to arrive, and indeed in many of the journeys of life there is no destination. At what stage of skill can one say, I can play the piano, I can paint a picture, I can build a shed, or maintain a motorcycle? There is only the constant exploration of physical space, of musical space, visual space and inner space, which we are carrying out from the moment when we first lay hands on the instruments, pick up a brush or a saw and hammer. To strive for virtuosity with the necessary single-mindedness is to miss the incidental pleasures and joys of a journey which is the more exciting because we do not know, or perhaps care, where it is we are going. The mind of the Chopi composer and his colleagues of the *ngodo*, or of the members of the gamelan, is on the present music, the present experience, the present creation, and once the possibilities of the present work have exhausted themselves they are content to let it go.

By allowing our pupils the opportunity to make music in the present tense, we can introduce into the school, through this largely unregarded (because for most people it is not directly related to the needs of earning a living) area of activity, a concept that can overthrow the future-oriented, instrumental ethos of the school, and the preoccupation with producing a product. For if we acknowledge the creative power of children in art, we must also recognize their ability to create other forms of knowledge (since art is a form of knowledge, but knowledge that is directly experienced rather than absorbed in the abstract), and to ask their own questions, which often cross the boundaries of our own treasured subjects and specialities.

It may be that in doing so we will sacrifice some of the virtuosity which we so admire in professional musicians, but we can remind ourselves that it is precisely this admiration for virtuosity for its own sake that cuts the majority off from true musical experience, just as it is our admiration for high-energy technology that cuts the majority off from most of its benefits; we shall gain more than we lose. But there can also be other consequences. The great dilemma of our musical culture today is the position of the composer, who is an isolated figure, cut off from the vast majority of the community, sending out his messages into the void and wondering if anyone is listening, condemned always to speak to an essentially passive audience, with whom the closest relationship he can achieve is that of producer to paying customers at a concert. He has not even the satisfaction of feeling that he is doing something that the community values; most composers have to fight hard even to have their music heard, and if a plague were to carry off every composer listed in John Vinton's *Twentieth Century Music Dictionary*[10] I very much doubt if the majority of the community would even notice their absence.

That this need not necessarily be so is clear from our cursory examination of other musical cultures, as well as that of eighteenth-century New England, where all are free to participate in the work of creation (not everyone wants to, but that is another matter) and the composer is a valued and necessary member of the community. From the point of view of individual virtuosity, speaking technologically these are all 'low-energy' cultures. The position of the 'professional', in so far as he exists at all, is that of leader, of pacemaker, of mentor, rather than of producer and his work is intimately bound up with the community of which he is so important a member. His work arises from and articulates the experience of the people, being rooted in it and yet spiritualizing it. As Bebey says, 'However transcendent the substance of African music may be, it is always expressed at human level. This is perhaps the most baffling paradox of all; the celestial music that is raised to the glory of the gods has its roots in the terrestrial realities of everyday life.'[11]

It *is* possible to restore the communality of music which we have lost in our pursuit of what are finally illusory ends, and the initiation of the process is within the power of every music teacher. Of course, full communality can be found only in a fully communal, or convivial society. As I remarked earlier, the arts, education and society move in a kind of loose lockstep with one another; of the three, art has apparently the least leverage, but it is in fact not without influence on the way people think, feel and perceive, matters which are finally of more importance than what they know, or think they know. The arts, and music in particular, can put us in mind of that potential society which does not yet exist; the power of art to disturb habitual ways of feeling and perceiving can be seen, even if in a negative way, in the violence of the reaction to Schoenberg's music, or indeed that of the Rolling

Stones (it is, after all, only sounds) and in the violence perpetrated in London on the sculptures of Epstein (they are, after all, only pieces of stone or metal). The subversive power of these and other works of art must have been apprehended, however dimly, for them to provoke such responses.

But the real power of art lies, not in listening to or looking at the finished work; it lies in the act of creation itself. In the process of artistic creation the creator engages his whole self; his reason and intuition, together with the most ruthless self-criticism and realistic assessment of a situation all come into play. He sets himself a goal, a short-term, one-at-a-time goal, capable of realization within the framework of the *present* composition (which may, however, like Proust's or Wagner's or a medieval artist-monk's, extend over twenty years or more) and sets out to achieve it, while acknowledging, like any true explorer, that he might not know where he is going until he gets there, and delighting in the features of the new terrain that he is discovering for himself. He is working to the extent of *his* own powers, not those which someone else, however well supported by educational and psychological research, thinks he ought to have, and finally, he is learning to order his own sensory, sensuous and emotional life, making his own models of possible alternative realities and futures.

None of this is, of course, new; I am only restating what was said over thirty years ago by Herbert Read. Observations like these are scattered through his *Education Through Art*: 'The closest parallel to the structure of personality of the child is not the mental structure of the logician but that of the artist .... This is shown by the loving attention to the matter in hand, by that close union of object and subject in children and in artists'.[12] The relevance of the last sentence to the role of art in healing the scientific split between subject and object is clear.

It is Herbert Read, too, who leads us into the wider implications of the artistic approach to education, saying, 'The purpose of a reform of the system of education is not to produce more works of art, but better persons and better societies. But ... such artistic activity in children may be the beginning of a wider reform. Once the creative powers are freed in one direction ... once the shackles of school passivity are broken at one point, a kind of inner liberation, the awakening of a higher activity, generally sets in.'[13] And again: 'The purpose of aesthetic education in children can, therefore, never be the production of a type of art conforming to a canonical or "superior" aesthetic standard, even though such a standard be admitted .... The purpose of art in education, which should be identical with the purpose of education itself, is to develop in the child an integrated mode of experience ... in which "fought" always has its correlate in concrete visualization – in which perception and feeling move in organic rhythm, systole and diastole, towards an even fuller and freer apprehension of reality.'[14]

Once one accepts that such an approach is possible not only in artistic pursuits but throughout the whole field of education, once one abandons the idea of education as preparation for life (I wonder what young people have been doing since birth, if not living) and sees it as a part of life itself, once one allows the idea that there are as many ways into knowledge as there are people, that the logical, straight-line arrangement of syllabuses, with their linear progression from one stage to another, is based on a fantasy about the way humans learn, then many of the arguments concerning 'equality of opportunity' versus 'excellence' reveal their meaninglessness. Examinations designed to separate the 'brighter' from the 'dimmer', or whatever terms we might care to adopt, work only along one axis, which we might call the intellectual-verbal, and test only that arbitrarily chosen variety of excellence (which may in any case boil down largely to a specific skill in sitting examinations); all other kinds of excellence, of which there are as many as there are people, are ignored.

The account given in Chapter 2 of musical, and general, education in other cultures can perhaps be of help to us here. I do not suggest that the answer to all our problems lies in the East or in Africa, but it has been a thesis of this book that other cultures have at least as great a store of experience and wisdom as ours and that, just as the individual can learn from others, so one culture can never maintain that it has nothing to learn from the rest of mankind. It can be asserted with confidence not only that any theory of aesthetics that confines itself solely to the musical experience of post-Renaissance Europe will be incomplete or even seriously misleading, but also that any system of education that neglects the educational experiences of other cultures will distort the lives and the experience of those whom it purports to educate.

It might be asked what happens to Beethoven, Bach, Brahms and Webern and the other great 'classics' in this new approach to education in music which stresses the process of creation more than the finished art object. The answer must be that they will either remain, or they will not, according to the extent to which they are found relevant to the lives of those who hear their music.

But they will be known for what they are, as part of the past, which we may love and revere but need not idolize. They will be seen as men, not as ethereal spirits, their music as more, not less, fully alive and breathing; we shall hear it not less but more clearly. It has, in any case, ever since their own day, been only a minority of people to whom they have spoken and who have shared their values (the history of the music of the majority has never been, and probably cannot be, written – which may be all to the good); that minority will continue to exist as long as the western middle classes exist, and will represent the dominant culture as long as the middle classes are dominant, but we can no longer afford to insist that their values constitute the only musical (or human) values. It may in fact be argued that the great classical composers are no longer of anything more than historical significance in the world into which we are moving at such uncomfortable speed. Certainly to confine our teaching, in this time of profound and turbulent change, solely to the traditional values of western music is to risk limiting the imagination of our charges to those modes of thinking which have brought our culture to its present disastrous condition. One must consider at least the possibility that there might be a conflict between the 'propagation' of Mozart and Beethoven (and their latter-day successors) and the real interests (in both senses of the word) of our pupils.

But of course the imagination of the majority of our pupils will not be limited to anything; we shall find that they have gone away and left us, like John Lennon's Father McKenzie, writing our sermons that no-one will hear. We must admit that this is largely happening today in our schools; in fact, I should venture to suggest that the increasing breakdown of the school system in western countries is due to this very fact: we have nothing to tell children that most of them want to hear. We cannot expect them to put up with giving up more than a sixth of their life expectancy to incarceration in an environment that cannot, by the very definition of its aims, pay any real attention to the quality of their present experience, nor can it give anything to most that they perceive as being of use to them, even assuming that they are prepared to delay gratification of impulses and wants in the approved middle-class manner.

The scientistic, fact-oriented model of education is disastrously failing young people. It is true that a brave and noble attempt to break its stranglehold is taking place, in Britain at least, in many infant and primary schools. But once children reach the age of eleven or twelve, all are pushed willy-nilly on to the escalator which leads the lucky — or are they so lucky? — ones to 'A' levels and a degree, whence they proceed to a higher degree and the trappings of success, while the less fortunate — or sometimes more independent — children must undergo a disillusionment which is all the more cruel because of the expectations aroused by a primary school experience which is more in tune with the way people actually learn. As long as the pathway to success lies through the narrow examination gate, such attempts at humanization are doomed to peter out at the start of secondary schooling.

The rapidly changing situation in our society today, its uncertainty, its economic instability and its challenges demand that the artistic model of education be given its chance to develop those powers which in the present model are so grievously neglected. We do not need Robert Ornstein's findings, interesting as they may be, on the functions of the right and left hemispheres of the brain[14] to tell us this; the communality of artistic, mythopoeic and ritual life of Bali and black Africa, to mention only those we have looked at in this book, tells us clearly in which ways the west remains an underdeveloped area. I have tried to show how the music of our century adumbrates a society which is struggling to emerge from the old; it may be that if teachers could learn the lesson of art, and use the experience of art as a model for their approach to children they teach, we may after all become influential in making the new birth (which will happen anyway with or without our help) a sturdy and worthwhile one. That such a move could begin in school music rooms may sound absurd, but only because we are unaware of the power of the artistic mode of thought; the leverage on education and, through education on society, may be small, but because of the power of art to change human perception, it is real.

It is not my purpose here to detail a blueprint for the reform of the educational system, nor, I believe, is it necessary. In any case, to replace one system with another would be merely to replace one heresy with another; the purpose is to replace the education *system* with an educational *community,* and this can evolve only from the efforts of individuals and small groups to create a rich diversity, and an interlocking network of educational communities, from the exploration of reality by explorers who will often not know where they are going until they arrive. But consider a situation in which all are allowed, or rather encouraged, to work on their own interests under the guidance of older people, in a world no longer bounded by the walls of the classroom, or even of the school. There are powerful arguments in favour of incorporating children from an early age into the economic and political life of the community; much of the discontent which children feel with school as at present organized must arise from their total isolation from such life and the 'as if' nature of all the work that they do. The gradual assumption of responsibilities in the community by children is practised in any village culture – practically everywhere, in fact, where children are not herded into classrooms – and it is a practice from which we could learn.

With each working to the extent of *his* powers towards *his* own goals, we need no formal curriculum, no intelligence or aptitude testing, since each is setting and sitting his own test all the time, no streaming by ability, since there is no criterion on which to base it, perhaps only minimal age segregation, since it is western society only which seems to believe the fiction that older children have nothing to teach younger ones other perhaps than 'bad ways'. We need no research into the stages of maturation and 'learning readiness', since all will make their own decisions on such matters – and who is to tell a child that he is not yet ready to learn something he can learn? Thomas Mann, whose *Doctor Faustus* abounds with insights into the ways of our culture, puts into the mouth of his elderly narrator these words, as he tells of a series of lectures on Beethoven which he heard from an inspired teacher in his early youth:

> ... we listened to it all with the dimly excited fantasy of children hearing a fairy story they do not understand, while their tender minds are none the less, in a strange, dreamy, intuitive way, enriched and advantaged. Fugue, counterpoint, 'Eroica', 'confusion in consequence of too strongly coloured modulations', 'strict style' – all that was just magic spells to us, but we heard it as greedily, as large-eyed, as children always hear what they do not understand or what is even entirely unsuitable – indeed, with far more pleasure than the familiar, fitting and adequate can give them. Is it believable that this is the most intensive, splendid, perhaps the most productive way of learning: the anticipatory way, learning that spans wide stretches of ignorance? As a pedagogue I suppose I should not speak on its behalf; but I know that it profits youth extraordinarily. And I believe that stretches jumped over fill in of themselves in time.[16]

This insight of Mann's reminds us, too, that we need not rule out the formal course of lessons. We can all recall gaining much from such courses in subjects about which we were interested with good teachers. But to be effective they should be attended voluntarily and be open to all. If a ten-year-old wishes to attend a course on atomic physics he should be allowed to do so, even if he has little chance of understanding what is being said; it can become, as Mann says, a magical experience — fairy stories have always been as much a medium of education as have textbooks. I myself recall an experience very like that of Mann's narrator, when I was taken by my mother at the age of nine (under what circumstances I do not now remember) to a lecture at an educational conference on what were then revolutionary ways of teaching art to children. The talk was illustrated with slides of children's painting, of a kind which are now fairly common, but were a revelation to teachers in 1936. I did not understand a word of the educational theory involved, but it was a magical experience for me, and one which I am sure has proved important in my life.

The concept of the educational community that this evokes is that of the resources centre, freely available, and having arrived at such a concept one wonders why its availability should be limited to children; if learning is to continue throughout life, why not make it into a centre that all can use, at whatever age? Dr Harry Judge, Director of the Educational Studies Department of Oxford University, said this in a recent lecture:

> What would schools be like within a social system that was itself educative and in which instruction (to use too sharp and acid a term) was freely available to postulants regardless of age? Or, the other side, again, of the wafer-thin coin, what would schools need to be like in order to ease the birth of such an educative society?
> The answer is so simple as to be embarrassing. It is necessary that schools should first be freed from many of the pressures now imposed upon them — pressures of time (mediated by an undue concentration on the early years of life), of academic status (by undue exaggeration of the value of general or humanistic education), of coercion (reinforced through the extension of an anachronistic concept of obligatory schooling), of social selection (transmitted, for example, through an elaborate examination system) and of narrow functionalism (expressed in a practical theory which requires schools to do things to children) ... I very much doubt whether the concept of a school curriculum, national or international, would or should in these conditions survive. The school in the educative society will no longer need to pretend that it

has a curriculum, in the conventional sense of the term, through which a generally agreed deposit of learning is somehow transmitted from one generation to the next .... Examinations, like the extension of compulsory schooling, are rich in historical explanations but poor in contemporary justifications.[17]

Dr Judge insists that the only way to achieve these ends is through a radical re-education of teachers in the first place. 'Any society', he says, 'which wishes to reform its educational system will first demonstrate the courage of its convictions by making an immediate investment in the recurrent education of its own teachers, then trusting them to do the work which can no longer, if it ever could, be defined for them.' It would seem that the time for such a scheme is now, with the current drastic shrinkage in the teaching force. A small, radically re-educated teaching force, aided by those resources of the community which could be contributed by those very adults who returned for further education throughout life, could provide an educational community which, unlike the present disintegrating system, our society — indeed, any society — could actually afford.

Under such conditions the pupils are no longer objects of our instruction, but active agents whose researches are the curriculum, whose experience is the syllabus; it is they who are doing the research, into themselves, one another and the world around them. The word 'research' returns us abruptly to a consideration of science. The primary purpose of a teacher is to help his pupils learn to live in the world, and the practice of art, in its widest sense, is a major tool in that learning, a learning which should continue throughout life. Learning to live in the world, of course, includes the exploration of nature, but it is an exploration which is drained of the urge to domination which has powered western science since its beginnings in the sixteenth century. The way to a true science, a true knowledge of nature, a knowledge as subtle and as intimate as that which enables the Pygmies of the Ituri basin to live more comfortably and joyfully in their jungle habitat than many a western man in the cities we have built for ourselves, lies in a loving exploration similar to that which an artist makes of his materials. (I trust it is clear by now that I do not suggest that we should all live like Pygmies, even if it were possible — but we do have much to learn from them, as from others of the world's peoples whom we are pleased to label 'primitive'.)

The role of the teacher will under such conditions be

fundamentally changed, becoming more, rather than less, challenging and rewarding. Freed from the necessity to maintain his role as the fount of all knowledge, he can relax and participate in the researches of his pupils. Freed from the artificial constraints of the classroom situation, he can point up the lessons of the genuine constraints of the human situation – constraints which the west often seems to have forgotten, or at least to have ignored in its pursuit of mastery over nature. If a pupil wishes to conduct an orchestra, for example, learn Athabascan or travel to the South Pole, the chances are that it will just not be possible, although investigation of possible ways and means may prove instructive in itself. The role of the professional teacher will, in fact, become much more that of a co-ordinator of learning resources than of a source of knowledge, and one of the most important skills he will have to develop in this situation is that of knowing when to intervene and when to stay out of the way. We do not at present make any allowance for the vital process of sitting still and passive, waiting for the idea to come; we keep pupils constantly on the move, constantly pushed this way and that, from one subject to another, from one activity to another with scarcely a pause for thought, revealing once again our deep distrust for the natural processes of the young minds.

Man remains, indissolubly, part of nature, not only in so far as we are physical beings with bodily needs and an animal inheritance but also, I believe (as Greek and Chinese scientists also believed) in that our intelligence partakes of and relies on the intelligence that pervades the entire natural world. It has been in all cultures the task of art, religion and ritual to maintain the vital contact with this intelligence; only in our own society have we seen fit to break it, to deny the intelligence of nature and contemplate as desirable the possibility of making her the slave of our virtually unlimited desires (the denial of the intelligence of the enslaved seems a necessary step to quiet the slavemasters' conscience, as millions of people of African descent can testify). But, like all masters of all slaves, we have become the slaves of our own mastery, and our slavery shows itself most plainly in the way in which we educate our children, in the way in which we attempt to change, if not negate, her arrangements for the development of the young mind. We try to change the unchangeable, measure the unmeasurable, comprehend the incomprehensible, control the uncontrollable; our treatment of the young mind is as if we were to bind rubber bands around the heart to teach it how to beat. The human mind is a subtle, perfectly adapted and ultimately unknowable process which we treat as if it were a somewhat faulty machine that had to be made fit for action, or a computer awaiting a program, something whose total mode of operation awaits elucidation as object-other by the methods of science. It is impossible, of course, as has already been pointed out; the conscious mind can no more comprehend the total workings of the mind than can a television screen show all the workings of the set of which it is a component. But if realization of this inescapable fact induces in the scientific mind only despair, the artist celebrates it while, paradoxically, carrying out a loving and subtle investigation of himself and of his perceptions of the natural world.

For the methods of modern science to become possible, nature had to die and man to become totally split off from her. This process became complete at around the turn of the seventeenth century, and it is an interesting fact that it was at this time too that the two words *Science* and *Art* acquired the specialist meanings they possess today; as Raymond Williams[18] points out, before that time, and indeed for a long time after in some contexts, the words carried simply the meanings, respectively, of *Knowledge* and *Skill*. Neither word carried the sense of the highly specialized, even esoteric activities that it has today, while the use of the words *Scientist* and *Artist* to denote their practitioners as a profession dates only from the early nineteenth century, when science (in the modern sense) began to pre-empt the whole of knowledge and art (in the modern sense) was finally relegated to the margin of our culture and to the contemplation of our now devalued emotions and intuitions. But art is equally in a deep sense knowledge, while science is in a deep sense skill, and knowledge and skill should ideally be fundamentally complementary and symmetrical. It is a commonplace to remark on the complementarity of science and art; what spoils in practice this complementarity is the fact that art as a means of exploration has been devalued in favour of science and removed from the central springs of action in our culture. This asymmetry arises from the power hunger of the modern west and the apparent ability of science to feed that hunger, to bestow that dominion over nature that was promised in the Old Testament. It is, however, in principle impossible that scientific knowledge as at present conceived should bestow that more precious knowledge which we so grievously lack, of how to live in the world. This is possible only when we recognize that conscious knowledge is at best partial, even misleading, when cut off from its deep sources in that vast hinterland of the mind that we call the subconscious.

Bateson points out that 'mere purposive rationality unaided by such phenomena as art, religion, dream and the like, is necessarily pathogenic and destructive of life ... its virulence springs specifically from the circumstance that life depends upon interlocking *circuits* of contingency, while consciousness can see only such short arcs of such circuits as human purpose may select.'[19]

Art, religion, dreams, ritual — all are means of re-establishing contact with the totality of mental life from which our concentration upon conscious activity has isolated us. To this list one would wish to add science, but it would need to be a science freed from the urge to domination, a science which is that true knowledge which the lover has of the beloved, a knowledge which recognizes and respects the autonomy of the known; this science exists today in embryo among many ecologists and ethologists, and has even gained a little ground among psychologists, sociologists and anthropologists, and especially among those who work on the fringes of all these, students such as Gregory Bateson, Konrad Lorenz, Mary Douglas, Liam Hudson and Colin Turnbull, who have as much of the artist's as the scientist's vision, whose love of those whom they study partakes of the religious, whose sensitivity to rituals and subtleties of meaning enriches our experience beyond the confines of abstract object-knowledge.

It is this richness of experience that is the right of all, but is denied to most in our culture in its pursuit of power and the objects of science and technology, and most of all is denied to those who from the age of five or six to fourteen or even sixteen are obliged to undergo schooling. Such experience can come through the work of artistic creation, in painting, carving, making of all kinds (remembering that 'art' and 'making' were expressed in ancient Greek by the one word, *techne*), writing, dancing and acting, and above all in music, since of all the artistic activities of the human race there is none which more closely puts us in touch with the sources of myth, or magic, of ritual and religion, none which more subtly outlines the forms of that potential society which lies still beyond our grasp.

The creator comes to know that there is a moment at the outset of a project when it is necessary to become utterly naïf, to dissolve all sophistication, all foresight and even all criticism, in the creative intention. He may not know with any precision what it is he wants to do; the outline of the project emerges with any clarity only as he progresses with it. Undertaking an artistic project is thus an act of faith which conscious reason does not fully comprehend, and may even reject. Thus, too, the idea that art may have a part to play in the freeing of our society from its power-sickness is an act of faith (though one which, as we have seen, receives a great deal of support from other cultures), but I dare even suggest that any teacher who does not possess at least a glimmering of such faith has no business to be in charge of anyone's musical education.

We have the chance to contribute to the healing of the fatal split within our culture; call it the split between science and art, between truth and value, between process and product, between matter and mind, it is essentially the same schism. It may be, if we survive the various death-traps that we have set for ourselves and succeeding generations over the next decades, that we may be able to make our own the Balinese maxim: 'We have no art, we just do things as well as possible', and set beside it our own aphorism; 'We have no science, we just know things as well as possible.'

Chapter 9: Bibliography

1. BELL, Daniel: *The Coming of Post-Industrial Society (A Venture in Social Forecasting)*, London, Heinemann Educational (1974), p. 479.
2. STOCKHAUSEN, Karlheinz and HEYWORTH, Peter: 'Spiritual Dimensions — an Interview with the Composer', *Music and Musicians*, May 1971, p. 38.
3. RILEY, Terry: Sleeve note to *A Rainbow in Curved Air*, Columbia Record No. MS7315.
4. BERG, Ivar: *Education and Jobs — The Great Training Robbery*, Harmondsworth, Penguin Books (1973).
5. CAMPBELL, Roy: 'On Some South African Novelists', *Collected Poems*, Vol 1, London, The Bodley Head (1949).
6. POSTMAN, Neil and WEINGARTNER, Charles: *Teaching as a Subversive Activity*, New York, Delacorte Press (1969) and Harmondsworth, Penguin Books (1971), Chapter 5.
7. SCHOOLS COUNCIL: *Enquiry One: The Young School Leavers*, London, Her Majesty's Stationery Office (1968).
8. ILLICH, Ivan: *Energy and Equity*, London, Calder & Boyars (1974).
9. THOREAU, Henry David: *Walden, or Life in the Woods* (1854), Everyman Edition (n.d.), p. 45.
10. VINTON, John (ed.): *Dictionary of 20th Century Music*, London, Thames & Hudson (1974).
11. BEBEY, Francis: *African Music: A People's Art* (transl. Josephine Bennett), London, Harrap (1975), p. 132.

12. READ, Herbert: *Education Through Art,* London, Faber & Faber (1943), 2nd edn. (1958), p. 56.
13. READ, Herbert: Ibid., p. 59.
14. READ, Herbert: Ibid., p. 105.
15. See, for example, ORNSTEIN, Robert: 'The Brain's Other Half ', *New Scientist, June 6 1974, pp. 607-09.*
16. MANN, Thomas: *Doctor Faustus* (transl. H.T. Lowe Porter) (1949), Harmondsworth, Penguin Books (1968), p. 58.
17. 'Plea to Lift "Monopoly" in Schooling', *Times Educational Supplement,* September 6 1974.
18. WILLIAMS, Raymond: *Keywords – A Vocabulary of Culture and Society,* London, Fontana Books (1976), pp. 32, 232.
19. BATESON, Gregory: 'Style, Grace and Information in Primitive Art', in *Steps to an Ecology of Mind,* London, Paladin (1973), p. 115.

INDEX